GLIMPSES OF NOTES MEMORIES OF MGS 1942-51

IAN DAVIDSON

Published by The Development Office of the
Manchester Grammar School in 2016

ISBN: 978-1-911412-05-2
eBook Apple: 978-1-911412-06-9
eBook Kindle: 978-1-911412-07-6

The Development Office of the Manchester Grammar
School is an imprint of

Dolman Scott Ltd

www.dolmanscott.com

Reactions to *Glimpses of Notes* by some other Old Mancunian authors

Ian Davidson is an excellent writer who has an astonishing memory for detail.

He paints a fascinating, vivid portrait both of his days as a schoolboy at MGS in the '40s and early '50s, but also of life amid the rationing and thick fogs of wartime and immediate post-war Manchester.

Although I went to MGS a generation later, his book brought back floods of fond memories.

Michael Crick

It's an achingly familiar world conjured up by Ian Davidson: the seat politics of the school bus, the threat of a Saturday morning punishment, the 'problem of women' occupying the minds of pimply schoolboys. Reading this transports you back to Old Hall Lane - a vivid sensory experience of jostling in corridors, ink wells and raiding other classrooms.

Yet, just as you slip into warm familiarity, the book jolts you into historical reality; that this was taking place not in your own youth, but against the backdrop of World War Two. The blitz damage: the scarred Manchester when the author went to buy his uniform. The blackouts. And, most poignantly, the reaction of the Jewish boys at school once word of the Holocaust began to emerge; some took to wearing yellow stars in solidarity.

Rich in detail, this is a gripping piece of social history that captures a school-life straddling the War. From the momentous, to the fascinatingly mundane - the emergence of the nascent biro supplanting the fountain pen, local lasses inexplicably being drawn to the brash GIs who stayed on in England.

It is also the thoughtful and candid reminiscence of a man looking back at his formative years - without any rose-tinted lenses.

And one is left with a lingering sense of how soft we are these days. As the author notes, when he went back to visit the school, 'Today's generations seem composed and sedate, whereas we were rough and rowdy as we trooped from one classroom to another'.

A thought-provoking, highly-engaging and unique piece of work.

Tim Samuels

A lively, personal memoir of an important decade for the School. Ian Davidson writes with a glint of amusement in his eye and an admirable memory for the little details that make such accounts come alive.

Martin Sixsmith

I am younger than Ian by fifteen years and you might have thought the experience of my generation, in the first half of the sixties - 'between the end of the Lady Chatterley ban and the Beatles' first LP' (when 'Life was never Better'!) as

Philip Larkin put it - was a long way from his: a childhood and schooling in the shadow of war, prep school in the Manchester Blitz. But not at all. Ian's memoir is so poignant, affecting and extraordinarily evocative; but his Manchester was still ours in the early sixties. He has caught the temper of the time spot-on: the bomb-damaged city now in decline, the great age of Manchester over, or so it seemed; the breathless new age of the 'original modern' as the City rebranded itself not long ago, yet to be born.

But this was the moment when, after such a long and distinguished engagement with the community of Manchester, over 400 years after all, MGS rose to become the finest school in Britain, way ahead in academic results, topping Eton, Harrow, Winchester and all the rest; but the best in so many other ways too, it seems to me. It was a perfect conjunction of circumstances with a brilliant generation of teachers; some already in place, some to come under the charismatic Eric James, whose arrival and bedding-down period Ian vividly paints for us. All of my generation too can remember the presence of 'the Chief' by the touchline, or watching in the darkness at the back of the theatre at an after-school rehearsal: it seemed to me, in Middle School, like the proverbial emperor who never slept!

The book is full of fabulous detail: the texture of life in the post-war city, with the Manchester Guardian, the Hallé, and Lancashire Cricket; the texture of life before the age of Twitter and iPhone. We watch in intimate close-up the growth of a person's consciousness; the teachers, the books and ideas that changed his life, from Shakespeare to Baudelaire, Rimbaud and Hesse. As Ian says, our teachers thought 'our heads were bottomless buckets that would take whatever was poured into them.' There are, too, the deftly and humorously sketched markers of growing up: Gitanes in Birchfields Park, the first fumblings of sex, and the hilarious portraits of the more eccentric teachers like the sadistic Billy Hulme; or Simpkins with his great line about learning to make bricks: 'it's a boring business, boys, but soon you'll be able to build something, and that can be fun!" Fun it was, as I remember, too; as Ian says, 'we learned without realising it.'

For me the book will take its place alongside Bryan Magee's Clouds of Glory (the tale of a Hoxton childhood) or James Walvin's recent memoir of his forties upbringing in Manchester, Different Times. Old Mancs will love it - but so will historians, too. It is about the making of a person, as well as the story of a school, and one hopes it might inaugurate a tradition where members of future generations who may also be gifted with Ian's incredible recall might leave their memoirs to posterity too?

The biggest message I get from the book is this. As I get older I value more than anything else the great gift to us from the teachers who shaped us, guided us, and opened our minds, often to worlds we never even dreamed existed. Ian writes: 'whatever I have of intellectual curiosity, benevolence, academic rigour, sociability, and good humour was fostered at MGS'. That is so true. And how important is that word benevolence. From now on, for me, the abiding memory, thanks to Ian, will be benevolence.

Michael Wood

Other books by Ian Davidson

Dynamiting Niagara
or Coming of Age in Broughton Mills
(2005)

A Hatful of Crows
Culture and Anarchy in Broughton Mills
(2007)

More Like London Every Day
or Being and Becoming in Broughton Mills
(2010)

Whisky with Mother
or The Uses of Literacy in Broughton Mills
(2015)

GLIMPSES OF NOTES
MEMORIES OF MGS 1942-51

by
IAN DAVIDSON

Forty years on when afar and asunder
Parted are those who are singing today,
When you look back and forgetfully wonder
What you were like in your work and your play;
Then it may be there will often come o'er you
Glimpses of notes like the catch of a song -
Visions of boyhood shall float them before you,
Echoes of dreamland shall bear them along.

CONTENTS

PART II - GROWING UP 49

PREFACE

We are delighted that Ian Davidson chose 2015, the 500th anniversary of the foundation of MGS, to complete his substantial memoir of his time at the school during World War 2. Remarkably, readers who have known the school since then or who know it today will find that much has not changed. Ian's MGS lived out both the school's motto, Sapere Aude (Dare to be Wise) and the inscription placed on the foundation stone of the buildings in Rusholme when the school moved there from central Manchester after 416 years: 'The place changes, but the spirit remains the same'.

We are grateful to Ian for his excellent memory and his engaging narrative style. Moreover, he has generously donated the proceeds from this book to our Bursary Fund, so vital to preserving future access to MGS for clever boys from poorer backgrounds.

As High Master, I am particularly taken by Ian's account of the circumstances in which my predecessor Eric James arranged for him to leave. I do not expect to have such a conversation with any of my pupils so, in some ways, times have changed.

Martin Boulton

FOREWORD

Most of us remember our schooldays – sometimes vividly - so it is curious how few memoirs of this crucial phase of our lives are written. Most biographies or autobiographies devote no more than a chapter to this period of life and many scamper over those formative years in a page or two. In the case of Old Mancunians there has until now been only one full-length book devoted to their time at school – Ernest Barker's *The Father of The Man (1948)* – a wonderful evocation of the great scholar's years at MGS in the late 1880s and early 1890s. Otherwise we have only a few scraps to reveal what the school was really like in the past.

The first OM to record his (unhappy) time at MGS was Thomas De Quincy but his hostility was balanced by Harrison Ainsworth, almost a contemporary of De Quincy in the early 19th century. In his novel *Mervyn Clitheroe* the school appears much more benign. And so it continued with various writers recording briefly their happy or unhappy memories of the place. The most recent memories come from the scientist and clinician Michael Lee *(Stood On The Shoulders of Giants, 2003)* and the art critic Michael Baxandall *(Episode – A Memory Book, 2010)*. Both are revealing but lacking in detail.

Perhaps the most famous school memoir of all is Alec Waugh's *The Loom of Youth* (1917) –a fictionalised account of his five years at Sherborne School. It caused a scandal at the time but seems rather tame stuff now.

Ian Davidson's *Glimpses of Notes* is quite exceptional in that it combines the best elements of all previous attempts at recalling both the delights and horrors and also the numbing boredom of one's time at school. Having entered the Prep Department of MGS aged nine in 1942 he spent almost a decade at Rusholme – an unusually lengthy stint. As the years passed he grew from a naïve youngster through the pains of adolescence to an independently minded young man. We follow his progress in astounding detail – his description of the school in all its aspects is vivid and revealing – the buildings, the daily routine of lessons and break times, the long journeys to and from home. His teachers and his fellow pupils are all recalled in an amused and unbiased style that is truly unusual. We learn of his friendships and occasional enmities, his growing love of learning, his occasional tussles with authority but above all of his observation of what was going on around him. No account of MGS life has ever matched his extraordinary powers of recall.

But *Glimpses of Notes* is far more than a school story. Whilst his life at MGS occupies centre-stage, it is set against the background of the Second World War and the period of austerity that followed. We see the impact of the war not only on the school but on his family and on Manchester itself. Written from a youngster's point of view there are echoes of John Boorman's brilliantly poignant film *Hope And Glory* (1987) as young Ian takes shelter from bombing raids, plays war games with his friends, samples the delights of a rationed diet or makes his way through the bombed-out suburbs of the great city. Here we have a social history of what growing up during the war was like. The snail pace of post-war improvement in living standards and opportunities is also brought to life as Ian discovers train spotting, cricket and the delights and perils of the opposite sex. And finally it should be noted that although a city dweller for most of his formative years, Ian was a country boy at heart.

Born in Broughton Mills in the south Lakes where he spent his early years and with family still there, he always hankered for that most beautiful of landscapes and after a long career in various academic posts he has retired to the area that he loves the most.

Jeremy Ward

PART I -

THE PREP DEPARTMENT

1942-44

1. PRELUDE

I don't visit Manchester much now, but when I do I make time to go to Rusholme. On the way there, I think not much has changed. The bare bomb sites along Upper Brook Street have been built on, but from Plymouth Grove it is much the same. However, Victoria Park is barely recognisable, the big houses with lawns and tennis courts have been turned into flats and their gardens built on. Dickenson Road and Birchfields are much as I remember them. Coming back to town along Wilmslow Road and Oxford Street things have changed almost beyond recognition, and once past Whitworth Park and the Art Gallery I am lost among new buildings and new roads that form part of the new city. Then, before I realise it I'm on the Mancunian Way and off to wherever I'm really going. But between these fleeting scenes, I contrive to be driven slowly along Old Hall Lane where I can take in a panorama of the school.

The main building is much as it was: solid, imposing, its clock tower rising above Hugh Oldham's hatchment and the great archway leading to the main quad. Wings and annexes have extended the frontage and a fine pavilion faces the first team pitch. From the main gate, still guarded by owls, the drive has been turned into an avenue with a row of trees on either side. But it is still comfortingly much as I remember and the sight takes me back to the days when I was a small boy and wore a dark blue cap with light blue rings and a little metal owl on the front.

Although my antecedents are Scots and Cumbrian, and I was brought up in the South West corner of the Lake District, I have always known that I was part Mancunian. I was born in the city and most of my formative years were spent as a pupil at MGS. There my mind was filled with the knowledge and ideas that shape the developing life, and I guess that whatever I have of intellectual curiosity, benevolence, academic rigour, sociability, good humour was fostered, if not planted, in those early years. Then were laid foundations for an Oxford education and a modest career as a minor academic. On the other hand, that early training must in some way be also responsible for the garrulous, argumentative, bibulous, gregarious, old sod I think I've turned into – which is perhaps not really what the school intended. Whatever it did it couldn't whip the old Adam out.

As I write about my time there, over sixty years ago, I wonder how much of what I remember actually happened. More and more I feel that what is recalled is partly wish-fulfilment and partly justification, and that the recherche du temps perdu is fundamentally a desire to give significance to the random effects of time and accident. I ask myself, 'What did it all signify?' And to hide my uncertainty, I construct a satisfactory story out of what I think I remember about what might have gone on, while accepting that someone else who shared that time and place with me would produce an entirely different tale. As Fichte said, imagination is not memory but a means of communication, the self-expression of the individual, the portrayal of a private world.

I remember my days at MGS with great affection. That's not to say that every day was sunny, for there were black periods and unhappy times, but all in all I was glad to be there. I was barely nine years old when I began, a bewildered, bookish boy with a country upbringing. When I finished I was less bewildered, but also cocksure, strongly aware of my own individuality and not inclined to heed authority. I began in Prep 1 in September 1942, and left in June 1951, having been in Prep 1, Prep 2, iβ, iα, iiα, iiiα, Rα and History Sixth divisions (iii) and (ii). Few pupils, I guess, can have spent so long under the wings of Hugh Oldham and his Owl.

Of the beginnings, my memories are patchy and vague, the mists of time swirl round events and people, part revealing, part obscuring. Like family photographs of dimly remembered places and events, they must be enlivened with stories that give them continuity and a sense of being. Some older actor in the scene must say, 'That was just before your father blew up the primus stove,' or 'You fell out of the boat after that.' The figures need to be given speech and the facts need elaborating. At least that's how it is with me: I need a story.

In the Oxford Schols I sat in 1952 I was asked: 'Is the Historian a Novelist manqué?' Until that time I'd never thought of history as literature, but as I balanced Stendhal and Thackeray against Wedgewood and Woodward, I saw immediately which kind I preferred. The novelists gave me a better idea of Waterloo than Gronow, who'd been there, or Creasy who'd read everything about it and discussed it with survivors. Wedgewood and Woodward were from another era and their dry analyses did nothing to inspire a vital understanding of the action. However, Julien Sorel and George Osborne were figures I could believe in: the account of the one's bewildered wandering over the battlefield and the stark announcement of the other's death provided me with a more satisfactory understanding of what went on than the lists of facts and figures provided by the historians.

I was much intrigued just then with Shakespeare's line in "The Phoenix and the Turtle": 'Truth may seem, but cannot be', which complemented Touchstone's remark in *As You Like It* that 'the greatest truth is the most feigning'. Both – one a solemn pronouncement, the other a throw-away remark – were sharp stabs at pinning down the Proteus I saw as Truth. They persuaded me that I had to make sense of truth from the inside, because it wasn't out there. And so, I present these reminiscences as partial and inside views of the character that is me. They purport to record authentic times and places and actual events, but in the end they are only stories.

2. BEGINNINGS

It was on my father's insistence that I became an Owl. He was a Scot by birth, a Geordie by upbringing and a Mancunian by adoption. Like me, he spent a particularly rich and rewarding period of his life there. He came in 1919 after service in the Flying Corps and spent six years in the Manchester University Medical School, going on to specialise in infectious diseases. Thus he stayed to work in the city's isolation hospitals where his professional interests lay in managing, until he met my mother,

to pass his winters with Hamilton Harty's Hallé at the Free Trade Hall, his springs at the Opera House and his summers at Old Trafford watching Maclaren and Spooner. In between there were the Whitworth and the Mosley Street galleries to see and Miss Horniman's theatre to attend.

After qualifying he was on the staff of Monsall isolation hospital in Collyhurst, where he met and married my Cumbrian mother. This, as she often told the family, ended a promising career in Nursing, where one with her undoubted managerial skills would certainly have succeeded. As I was growing up, I noticed that she was always ready to contradict or at least disagree with any medical opinion my father cared to offer. At length, he would demur when any of the family consulted him. 'You'd better go and see the doctor,' he would say, 'she knows far more about these things than I do.'

I was born in the Manchester Royal Infirmary, over the weekend of the Roses Match in July 1933. My father was in constant attendance, mostly at Old Trafford. This rankled with my mother, and fifty years after the event she still enjoyed mentioning it. My father always felt absolutely justified in his absence. 'Young Cyril Washbrook made his first century,' he said. 'And there was nothing I could have done for your mother even if I'd been there. Far better let them get on with it.'

In the troubled times leading up to the second world war my mother, together with the infant me, moved back north to care for her ailing sister and failing mother. It was what youngest daughters did in those days, whether they'd been trained as nurses or not. The family lived in Millom, a small town with an iron ore mine of prodigious richness and an iron works, just across the Duddon estuary from Barrow in Furness. Already people were fearful of the effects of bombing in cities, and those who could fled to the country. The shipyards at Barrow were sure to be a target, and along with them, the iron works at Millom, and so our family came to settle on the outskirts of Broughton in Furness, nine miles from where my mother was born. Here, in a closely connected community of relations and friends, was the centre of my childhood and it was from here, after a strange year at the beginning of the war at school in Dumfries among my father's relations, that I was transported to MGS.

Moving to a city from the security of the countryside at a time when bombs were still falling might have seemed an act of madness. Manchester was recovering from its Blitz, Trafford Park was still a target for the enemy, and the region was still a dangerous place. Nevertheless, I was glad to leave my Scottish Prep School where the sum of my remembered learning was that the Scots beat the English at Bannockburn in 1314. My Scottish aunt with whom I stayed was rather cheerless, and my cousin John had an infuriatingly supercilious manner. I recognised it as such when I came across the word much later and saw in his behaviour its perfect definition. Despite being called Ian Scott Davidson and wearing a kilt in my clan's tartan, I never felt Scots in any way, nor did my classmates let me forget that I was different. I was rarely happy in Dumfries and felt myself to be in a sort of limbo – another word that I was later able to fit to an experience I was glad to be delivered from.

The first inkling of the new life was when I was brought to MGS during the Easter holidays. I must have been told what was happening, but I was noted, even then, for being able to disassociate myself from what was going on. News of visiting relations or a shopping trip would send me off to the woods with a store of apples and a book. Notice of the Entrance Exam must have been kept from me until the actual event. It was sprung on me on a bright sunny day, when I was summarily brushed up and changed and whisked with my father to Manchester to stay with an old University friend. The following day I was taken to Rusholme and plunged into an echoing cavern of a building, bewildering with noise and people. The staircase was crowded with grown-ups coaxing, chivvying would-be owlets. It was a brave new world that impressed me by its order in confusion. Soon, I was settled in a desk where I did some sums and wrote a composition. I was good at compositions and bad at sums. From time to time I focused my attention on Miss Robins who was firmly in charge. I was also impressed by the manner of a boy I came to know as Rawley who said, cheerfully, 'Blowed if I know,' in answer to a sharp question from her. It appeared to fox her, for a moment.

Weeks afterwards, when I was told that the school would have me, I was alarmed by the thought. From time to time during the summer I was uneasy when people said, 'At your new school…' and I would shut my ears and run away, for it was something I didn't want to think about. Towards the end of the holidays I had a taste of what was to come when we made another trip to Manchester to buy my school outfit. During this visit I was set to learn 'Hugh of the Owl' by one of my mother's friends who had a son at the school. She said that knowing the school song was a necessary part of being a pupil and I ought to learn it before I became one. I was good at memorising poetry and learnt it so quickly she wouldn't believe me until I recited it. 'Tom doesn't know it yet,' she said, 'and he's going into the Main School. You'd better learn "Forty Years On",' which I did, thus earning Tom's lasting enmity.

It was only when I was taken to buy my school uniform that I realised the full significance of what was happening, for in those war-time days buying clothes was a serious matter. It was a hot summer day and we walked from the station, through the canyons of Corporation Street to the rubble strewn wastes that stretched from the cathedral to Cross Street. It was explained to me that this was where the bombs had fallen. It was my first proper view of the horrors of war. Hitherto they had only been pictures in the papers and cinema. A sight of the real thing disturbed me: a house affected by a direct hit which had left the rooms exposed, sitting room, bed room, with all their belongings open to the weather and the world's eyes. 'What about the people?' I imagined how it would be if my bedroom had been blown up and my things, my model aeroplanes, books, clothes, all scattered and spoiled. Nightmare thoughts troubled me in the quiet of St Anne's Square, clashing with the primness and order of Henry Barrie's Gentlemen's Outfitters and Bespoke Tailors. That night I had troubling dreams and the scene of devastation haunted me for a long time. For years it remained a disturbing memory which I shied away from.

3. PREP 1 (a)

The Prep Department occupied the two rooms at the top of the main staircase. I was directed into Mrs Gaskill's. In the other was Miss Robins. These rooms were in a little recess, with a radiator on one side, round which we huddled in winter, and when it wasn't cold we would hang over the banisters, flying paper aeroplanes down the stair-well and cheeking our elders as they came up the stairs. Sometimes our activities would attract the attention of a master on his way into the Staff Room and he would terrify us by coming to the bottom of the stairs and glaring. I once proposed a slide down the bannister, which was spiked at intervals with brass studs. 'Rip yer ballocks off,' Williamson said. I still wasn't quite sure what 'ballocks' were, and wouldn't, then, have considered them as an impediment to a slide. It was the fear of the dizzying drop to the basement that put me off.

In the Prep we were MGS boys with a difference. Our caps had red rings on them rather than blue, and similarly red stripes on our ties. Our caps bore the little metal Owl of Athens – I still have one – which could be used to inflict a nasty scratch if the cap was folded in the right way. We wore grey shorts, with a grey pullover and grey shirt, stockings and black lace-up shoes.

My father took a commemorative photograph of me kitted out on my return from Henry Barrie's – 'I might never see you looking so respectable again, boy,' he said. He always called me 'boy'. A fortnight before he died at eighty-eight he said, 'I've had enough, boy.' – I look hesitant and uncomfortable, poised as if ready to take flight. My teeth show on the corner of my bottom lip and I'm not looking at the camera, but at the door.

Unlike Miss Robins who was red-haired and busy and had a taste for bright clothes, Mrs Gaskill was quiet and sedate. Grey hair and grey dress, with spectacles, I wondered whether our school uniform was modelled on hers or hers chosen to conform with ours. But her manner and teaching were far from grey. She could quell with a glance and control with a whisper, and had no trouble at all with Rawley, whose imperturbability was a model for us all. He was confident and affable with a shock of hair that seemed to burst out round his head like foliage – except it was yellow rather than green. Miss Robins, whom he'd briefly fazed, could put on a spectacular display of fireworks if he provoked her, but Mrs Gaskill was quietly firm. Her strongest expression of disapproval was a quiet sigh, which showed us that we had disappointed her. Her room had windows on two sides and it was often flooded with morning sunshine. At such times she would make us do deep-breathing exercises. 'To keep you brisk,' she said.

I remember little of the actual lessons. We learned without realising it. Knowledge, it seemed, was simply absorbed. Most of the time, I think we educated each other. Mrs Gaskill simply facilitated the process, largely by reading to us at the end of each day. Thus I was introduced to *Ivanhoe* and *Bevis* and *Wind in the Willows* and *Cranford*, which I took to be about her own life, because she'd told us she came from Knutsford and I wondered whether the lace collar she sometimes wore was the one the cat sicked up. She read us a lot of poetry too, from an anthology called *The Poets' Company* which I still have, scuffed and tattered with 'I Davidson. Prep One' blottily written on the inside of the front cover. I loved the bouncing rhythms of *The Pied Piper of Hamelin* and soon had most of it by heart, though the rats biting the babies in their cradles made me squirm. In *Morte d'Arthur*, the 'great water' was one of the Lakes and even now, whenever I fish on misty mornings I expect an arm 'clad in white samite' to reach through the surface and catch a whirling sword. I didn't much care for Wordsworth: no music, and his ballads weren't like *Sir Patrick Spens* or *The Wife of Usher's Well*. At home, under the tutelage of my mother and my aunt, much emphasis had been put on learning tables and spelling and poetry. Before I came into Prep I, I could recite the whole of *The Lady of Shallot*, most of the verses from *Now We are Six* and large chunks of Belloc's *Cautionary Tales*. This gift won me favour with Mrs Gaskill and went some way to mitigate my ineptitude at maths.

My friends in Prep I were Williamson and Lewis, and I learned much from them. Lewis and I swapped things. I was interested in his stamps and he in my dinky toys – a battered collection handed down by my cousins, but very acceptable at a time when they were no longer being made. We traded covertly, often in class, by passing notes and agreeing deals, sometimes in cash, which we settled at break. He taught me how to do percentages and work out averages, passing me his exercise book showing how they were done. In return, I would prompt him when he got stuck with the poem we'd been set to learn. He was numerate and I was literate. After Prep II I'd nothing to do with him until we met in the Sixth – he in Maths and I in History. We had a short embarrassed reunion, then we went our own ways.

Williamson and I were at opposite sides of the room so we only communicated during breaks. At lunchtime, we would race away to Potts' shop on the other side of Birchfields Road and look at things we might buy. Around Potts', on the Meldon Road, there was a small shopping centre, which was somewhere to go out of school. It was always fairly crowded with boys wanting to escape from the atmosphere of order and restraint and get back to the real world. The wide pavements would be crowded with knots of boys, chatting and arguing. It was as if they felt the air was free-er here in the outside world. Behind the shops was a maze of paths and ways through a large housing estate which reached up to Stockport Road. Here would wander those in search of a quiet smoke.

On Birchfields Road itself there was a pie shop which always attracted a crowd at dinner time. Williamson and I both had to buy dinner tickets and seldom had cash to be customers there, but we would always pause to gaze through the window and watch enviously as those coming out of the shop tossed hot pasties from hand to hand to cool them down. A great tail of MGS boys stretched across the pavement waiting to get at the trays of tarts and cakes which vanished almost as soon as they appeared. Once, while the girl was fetching some more, a knave in the queue leaned over the counter and stole a tart. As he popped it into his mouth, there was a murmur of disapproval which grew as we watched his bulging cheeks grow less. When the girl came back the queue fell suddenly silent and she sensed something was amiss. No one peached, but she knew, and we knew, and the culprit knew. Ever after he was marked. In the sixth, I saw him in the library and someone said, 'That's the tart man.'

Williamson and I were close and confidential for a while. We stayed at each other's houses and confessed our ambitions. He wanted to be a pilot and fly to the moon, I wanted to be a civil engineer and build bridges. 'I wonder what it'll be like in 2000?' he mused one night. 'Do you suppose we'll be still around?' 'Doubt it,' I said. 'You'd be sixty-seven then. One of my uncles is sixty-seven and he's as good as dead.' I liked Williamson a lot because he had an inquiring mind and his conversation was full of 'What ifs?' rather than 'I've got...' or 'I can...' and 'You can't...' He was a comforting complement to the friends I had travelling to school on Bowker's bus.

Like Lewis he went into a different side in the Main School and I lost touch with him until we'd both left. Then we met at a dance in the MRI Nurses' Home. It was quite a formal affair and attended, in the early stages at least, by the Matron, to whom the guests were introduced – to see if they were suitable, I presumed. I was at Oxford, and he was a Pilot Officer, so we were all right. By then all thoughts of building bridges and making roads had been dispelled by my developing ambition to write a successful verse drama in the manner of *The Lady's not for Burning*. Williamson was learning to fly faster and faster planes. 'What about the moon?' I asked him. 'Mm,' he said, 'we're getting there. I guess these German rocket men'll teach the Yanks how to do it. They've got the brains and the Yanks have the money. There's some bastard cutting in on my girl. I only sat this one out so's I could have a smoke.'

Despite Mrs Gaskill's deep-breathing exercises, on sunny mornings I often found it difficult to stay awake. When the sleepiness became insuperable, I would ask to be excused and have a stroll down the cool corridor, listening to the teaching voices behind the closed doors. The smooth floor stretched empty into the distance between uniform grey doors on one side and windows on the other. Looking onto the side of the

Memorial Hall and shielded from the morning sunshine by its bulk the vacant corridor reached into as yet unknown regions. Here were dens of ogres, lairs of tyrants whose names were heavy with ill omen – Chang Lund, Harry Plackett, Billy Hulme, Killer Maugham. Sometimes I would stray down the corridor and listen at the doors, trying to fit voices to the names I'd heard. On the way back I'd linger for a while in the toilets, making a perfunctory effort at a pee which I didn't really need.

In the room directly opposite the toilets Johnny Lingard taught 3C, a notoriously difficult class. It included Catterall, famed for insubordination and slovenry. I knew him from Bowker's where he often mentioned Johnny Lingard in an aggrieved and sceptical way. 'He goes to bed at twelve and gets up at four,' he said. 'It's so's he can get the most out of life, he says. He's barmy.' Unlike the droning voices that came from most rooms, Johnny Lingard's rose and fell in waves of impassioned sound. I would pause and listen for a while, in case he gave way to one of his famous dramatic outbursts. I knew him by sight as a wild figure rushing past the Prep Department, spectacles flashing, gown flying, as though he were pursued by the Furies – I'd read about them and heard my father say they were a set my mother belonged to.

Years later when I was in iiiα and a member of the Gramophone Society, I came to know and like him. He was the Society's Staff Member and our weekly meetings were held in his room because that's where the gramophone was. It was there I was introduced to the symphonies of Mahler and Sibelius which were the preferred listening of most members, though mostly I remember we listened to Beethoven. Johnny Lingard was an enthusiastic proselytiser for Baroque music, some of which he insisted on playing at every meeting. It was thus I first gave a serious hearing to Bach, which I never heard at home. Even now, the jingling harpsichord at the beginning of the fifth Brandenburger transports me to those times and in particular, a winter Thursday afternoon when the fading blue of the sky was etched with the darkening shape of the school clock tower. I sat, sprawling over the desk, half on the seat, half off, bemused by the mathematical certainties of the coda before its return to the main theme.

Lingard was a man of strong views, which he strenuously expressed. He had a disdain for Wagner – 'Hunnish belching after sausages,' he declared – and scorn for ballet music which he said was musical syrup, only played so dancing girls could titillate the Czar – a verb whose meaning I understood but whose derivation I mistook. These views perturbed me because I was fond of the Nutcracker Suite, and my father thought highly of Wagner, bits of which thrilled me to the core.

4. BOWKER'S BUS

As with most MGS boys who lived at a distance from the school, getting there was part of our education. Many travelled long distances every day. Charlie Dover came from Southport, and others from Northwich, Macclesfield, New Mills, Oldham, Rochdale, Bolton, Chorley. All the towns round Manchester sent a daily quota. For my first three years I came in from Worsley and travelled on Bowker's bus which went from outside the Court House directly to school. Most other travellers had to make their way from the city stations to Albert Square or Piccadilly and there catch a tram to Rusholme. Being a Bowker's boy put me in touch with many opinions about the school. Gossip about masters passed pretty freely amongst the travellers and in good time I learnt about the madness and the badness of the tyrants I would shortly be subject to. Thus, while they were still only names, I knew about Billy Hulme's spoons, Killer Maugham's run-up with his gymshoe from the other side of the corridor.

The only other Prep boys on the bus were Caddy and McElvie, both in Prep 2. They'd been warned about me as someone it was their duty to look after, but I became a protégé, then a friend, not only while we were creatures enduring a common bondage, but outside school as well. At first they looked after me in a paternal way, sharing their sweets, which were rationed, and 'bringing me on' with what they discovered about sex and football, as their minds were broadened. They referred to me as 'Young un,' which was a comforting change from the formal 'Davidson', used by everyone else. As the term went on we formed a small defensive group on the bus and became prepared to stick up for what we felt were our rights.

Bowker's was an Institution and to go on it was an education in itself. Driven by the eponymous Mr Bowker, it was an ancient charabanc which seemed to have run boys to MGS ever since the Owl flew from the city's heart to fairer, greener Rusholme. Starting from Worsley at half-past eight, Bowker's wound its way through the south-western suburbs of Manchester, picking up boys as it went. It trudged through Monton and Eccles and Pendleton to Salford, by which time it was uncomfortably full, the seats occupied by disgruntled scholars and the aisle packed with small boys. The return journey, which was generally much more cheerful, started from Birch Hall Lane at ten to four.

Before I'd even started school, I was put in the care of my mother's friend's son, Tom. 'Tom will look after you,' the mothers said. But Tom was diffident about the relationship, and I never warmed to him. On my first journey he nodded to me as a distant acquaintance, and thenceforth left me alone. In the third row down, left-hand side sat Mr Tenen, who taught History, and was undoubtedly Master of the bus. Large and solid, behind his Manchester Guardian, he could be marked immediately by his trilby hat in a sea of caps. On my first journey I settled into a window seat thinking it was mine. Two miles down the road a wave of dark blue and light blue caps flooded in and I was washed out of my window seat by a thug, who gestured with his thumb. 'Mine!' he said. 'Out!' I looked in vain for help from my carer, but he was studiously busy and he'd already discouraged me from sitting next to him. I found somewhere else, only to be ejected at the next stop, and so it went, until the aisle between the seats was full of small, disconsolate boys. Apart from some seats, which were the subject of private disputes, every place in the bus might as well have been labelled and the only permanent unclaimed position was next to Authority. This was sooner or later uneasily occupied by one of the dispossessed, pushed into the aisle. Mr Tenen was affable but not inclined to chat, 'What form are you in, boy?' he would say as you edged into the place beside him. When you made your halting reply he would make some remark about your form master – like, 'He's a terror. You'll have to watch yourself,' – then return to his paper.

Memories of those morning journeys remain with me still: the jolting of the bus, the line of dark blue raincoats carefully buttoned up, each with its satchel on the back. Down the middle of the bus the file of small boys swayed and bumped as progress was interrupted by road junctions and traffic lights. With little to hold onto but the handles on the backs of the seats, we all fell over like a row of dominoes when the bus stopped suddenly, and the end of the file landed on the knees of those on the back seat, where the privileged sat. As I write, I feel again the chilling disdain with which our elder fellows treated us, and sense the utter desolation of being a small, helpless entity wholly subject to the will of others. The last stop to collect passengers was at Monton Green. After that, we settled down into readers and chatterers and late-homework-finishers. Some would be hunched over their schoolbags seemingly in a trance, others studiously conning homework, one scribbling lines as though his life depended upon it.

As our journey progressed, I found it a relief to get out of dingy Salford and into Manchester proper. After we crossed the Irwell and went up Quay Street it was clear we were into a different kind of place. The Opera House was a pale baroque wonder amongst the five-storey offices. The posters without proclaimed the wonders within. The Christmas before I'd joined Prep 1, I'd been taken there to see *Peter Pan* which I still remembered vividly. For two hours I was part of a world where horror and humour, dream and reality were mixed up in a story about fairies. Was it right that you only had to believe in something for it to be true? I wasn't prepared to believe I could fly, but Captain Hook and the crocodile were as real as the alarm clock which tick-tocked at my bedside. Smee, the sly, punctilious Smee, who "stabbed without offence", haunted my dreams along with visions of the bombed and the dispossessed.

Along Deansgate, where we dodged the trams, the bustle on the pavements and the tall buildings on either side produced an authentic sense of being in a real city. There was John Rylands library on one side, a different kind of Gothic from Pendleton Hospital, which itself was different from the angular glory of Manchester Town Hall. On the other side, beneath a formidable massif of offices, I was puzzled by a long arcade of ten or a dozen identical windows, each bearing the name HEYWOOD, with, ELECTRICAL WHOLESALER in smaller letters underneath. What, I wondered was a 'wholesaler' and what were 'electrical goods'? Why did he need so many shops to sell them from? Then we were at Knott Lane and up to the Oxford Street traffic lights with the Palace Theatre almost opposite the Tatler Cinema, where, in times to come, I spent many afternoons watching Bugs Bunny and Flash Gordon.

The centre of Manchester was always interesting. The playbills at The Palace advertised comedians we knew from the radio: Rob Wilton, Charlie MacArthy, the ventriloquist's dummy who strangely became famous on the air, and singers like Anne Ziegler and Webster Booth. The Christmas Pantomimes starred Hetty King in *Puss in Boots* or Frank Randle in *Jack and the Beanstalk* with Vera Lynn. They seemed to run until Easter and were seen by everyone. We just had time to glance down the chasm of Whitworth Street before we turned into Oxford Street, then down past All Saints, surrounded by ruins, to turn left at the white-tiled cinema into Grosvenor Street, and so into Upper Brook Street.

Here was the devastation of the blitz and all that remained of rows of terrace houses was a grid of cobbled streets. By Plymouth Grove, some buildings had survived and once smart detached villas were already turning into solicitors' offices and Spare Parts Dealers. By the time we got to Victoria Park we were back in the last century where the big houses with tennis courts still survived as independent dwellings. That ancient cycling figure might almost be the ghost of C.P. Scott pedalling down to Cross Street to oversee the next edition of the Manchester Guardian. Then, at Dickenson Road came a plebeian Manchester council estate opposite the militarised Birchfields Park, and so to Birch Hall Lane, where we disembarked and entered the school by the back way, under the bronze gaze of Hugh Oldham.

Going home on Bowker's, I remember being tired and hungry, standing in the aisle until a seat became free, then collapsing into it in a kind of a trance. As we Prep boys were let out of school ten minutes before the rest, we would usually be standing under the trees in Birch Hall Lane when the bus arrived. Mr Bowker kept the door shut until the Main School was out, and Mr Tenen arrived. Then, after way had been made for him, there would be a surge of big boys, tossing us small ones aside, so though we were always first in the queue we were always last on the bus. It was less crowded on the way home and sometimes it was possible to sit down for the whole of the journey. The atmosphere was lighter, for we were returning to the upper world rather than heading for Cerberus and the Styx. At Worsley, Caddy, McElvie and I would wait in a dreary shelter for the service bus to take us on the last lap home.

Mr Tenen's presence kept us quiet, but the bus was liable to become rowdy in his absence. The homeward journey, especially towards the weekend, was often quite jolly, with lots of singing – 'Harry was a Bolshie' and 'Didger ever see, Didger ever see, Didger every see-ee-ee, Such a funny thing, before,' and, if authority wasn't aboard, 'Three German officers crossed the Rhine'. Always there would be the heartfelt plea, 'Oh hear us when we cry to thee / For those in peril on the bus.' A pooty prefect was supposed to keep order, but he lacked presence and authority. Mr Bowker was fairly patient, but on occasions he would stop the bus to caution those who had become too exuberant. Somebody was once put off for cheeking him, and quite right, too, was the general opinion. On one glorious occasion the boot, which used to hold sports gear and bags, fell open, and above the general cries of dismay, rose the stentorian voice of Mr Tenen, 'Stop the bus, Mr Bowker! The back's fallen off.' He had a strange, echoing voice that sounded as if it came from the back of a cavern. It was much imitated, and the cry, 'Stop the bus, Mr Bowker!' became a sort of rallying call for those of us who were fellow travellers.

5. PREP 1 (b)

I found the Main School an alarming place. As Prep boys, we didn't change rooms at the end of each lesson and our developing knowledge of the geography of the building depended upon explorations at lunch time and what we could pick up on the weekly visits to the gym. The long corridors were full of big boys, with gruff voices and abrupt ways. They rushed about jostling us as they went. Their size and energy frightened me as they pushed through the swirling groups of smaller boys gathered in the quads and the cloisters. The noise and the people, the lack of anywhere warm or comfortable, the unrecognised and unseeing faces that brushed past, heedless, almost paralysed me. Hunched against the lukewarm radiator at the back of the recess in which our classrooms were, I waited almost in suspended animation for the end of the break when Mrs Gaskill would appear. After the maelstrom outside, the classroom was a refuge and I sought my desk almost as a drowning mariner clutches the lifeboat.

The vast building that comprised the school, with its echoing corridors and great halls, was a place we got to know gradually. As Prep boys, distinguished by the red stripe in our ties, if not by our obvious infancy, we had limited freedom to roam. There was a Prep table in the refectory, and we were excused assembly, although we had prayers of a kind in our classrooms. I'm sure we would sing hymns with Miss Robins, but I don't remember it. Our religious education would be non-denominational, if only because some of the class would be Jewish – a distinction I didn't recognise until iβ when I had a Jewish friend whose home I used to visit at weekends where it was like being in another world.

On Games afternoons we were taken down to the Rectory, where we changed into shorts and second hand football boots – no one had 'new' football boots in those days. I didn't like games. Football – and we were encouraged to play both sorts – left me frozen and bewildered. It seemed that I must become part of a pack that chased a ball from one end of the field to another. Rarely did I get a kick at the ball, or even a handle, and on the one occasion when it fell at my feet and I ran with it between the posts, my goal was disallowed for some reason I didn't understand. I couldn't share the partisanship that some boys felt for particular teams, and although in later years I 'supported' Manchester City, and even Bolton Wanderers, it was entirely because my friends did. I never felt that passionate attachment to a team that some of them had. I was a 'supporter' because my particular friends were and not to be was disloyal. I could take my part in a spat with fans of the much-despised Manchester United, but my heart was never in it. The Blues were the team in those days and the Reds were nothing. Cricket was different, and I became passionately attached, but I didn't get into it until the main school.

Once a week we made the trip along the south-east passages to the cold regions of the Gym and the Baths. The baths were 'closed for the duration', the phrase still echoes. It was not yet the time of the appalling Mr Cuggy, who hurried us along with a big gym shoe as we ran naked round the edge of the swimming pool, but the Gym was bad enough. It was run in military fashion by Mr Saunders, who always addressed one as 'Boy', and imposed detentions for the slightest misdemeanour. We were put into lines and squares and set to do drills, like jumping on the spot with arms and legs apart. We did these until I was ready to drop. I would count the jumps by twenties, starting again after each score and thinking, 'if we don't stop before the next twenty I shall die.' Gym was always a bruising experience, both physically and mentally. Mr Saunders seemed to have no compassion for us, no sensitivity to the fact that we were small boys, shorn lambs to whom the wind ought to be tempered. To him we were raw recruits who had to be ground down until we were de-humanised. He was a strutting, fearsome figure who spoke through his nose in a way that invited imitation, which we essayed when reciting, 'I am Mr Saunders, nasty Mr Saunders / Down in the gym I dwell. / You've been naughty. / Come in at three-forty, / Down to my private hell.'

At lunchtime the corridors were patrolled by Prefects wearing mortarboards to emphasise their authority. Ostensibly they were to prevent trouble but their presence often served only to provoke it. With their licence to award lines and compel attendance at the Prefects' room, they had almost as much authority as members of staff, but the lads from Oldham and Rochdale, Scholarship boys from the outlying districts, thought nothing of such 'fancy buggers' and took delight in showing it. The corridors at lunchtimes were full of malcontents who had been locked out of their form rooms, for whether they were open or not was a matter of trust between class and master. In Prep 1 and 2, for reasons I never understood, we were always denied the sanctuary of our rooms. Most other forms in the lower school seemed to be in or out depending upon the phases of the moon or the state of the war or some such condition. 3C's room was always locked and outside it would be gathered a disconsolate and often truculent group, sitting on their schoolbags and leaning against the radiators, ripe for trouble. Hemingway, one of the travellers on Bowker's Bus, had particular trouble with them when he was first made a prefect. I remember him being aped and catcalled until another Bowker's senior quelled the mob. 'Cut it out, chaps,' he said. 'Play the game,' using phrases that might have come from *Tom Brown's Schooldays*, but were only effective because he was the size of a gorilla.

My previous school, small enough for everyone to be known, had been a model of order and propriety – well, most of the time. Mischief makers, actual or potential, were quickly spotted and stopped. But at MGS there were so many of us that it was often possible to act under an alias. 'What's your name, boy?' 'Smith, sir, One C.' 'Right, Smith, I want two hundred lines from you by break tomorrow: "I must remember to perambulate the corridors with decorum and discretion". Got that?' In most cases that would be enough and the culprit could slip gratefully back into the anonymity of the crowd. However, there was always the risk of such encounters developing into a nightmare scenario. 'Who's your form master?' 'Mr Jones, sir.' 'But Mr Jones is form master of 2B…' It was as well to have one's second identity well worked out before assuming it. I often felt I was a nameless figure buffeted by a crowd of super-confident egoists who ignored me apart from occasionally acknowledging that we suffered a common bondage. 'Watch out,' said an anonymous passer-by as we were lurking under the arches throwing sand-balls at each other, 'Sutton's coming.' Sutton was the Porter who stalked the precincts of the school at lunchtime, seeking miscreants who were sent to stand outside the Staff Room to be 'dealt with'.

I found it hard to accept being just one of a group and tried to substantiate my identity by inking DAVIDSON on the label inside my school cap. Davidson wasn't someone I immediately recognised. First names had no significance in this new world: they belonged to home and relations. Even when the two worlds met and a school friend came to stay, he was still known by his school name. Caddy and I were in the garden when my mother called us for tea. 'Ian!' she shouted. Caddy looked up, 'Is that you?' I nodded. 'Come on then, Ian,' he said with a sly grin. 'We'd better go.' I don't think he called me 'Ian' ever again.

Belonging to Caddy and McElvie helped me find out who I really was. My country upbringing had given me a sense of identity. In the small valley where I was brought up everyone knew who I was, and as I grew up I gradually learned to name and locate the people who addressed me as 'Ian' or 'mi lad' and clearly knew all about me and my condition of life. They not only called me by name but asked pertinent questions, like 'Have you picked those plums yet?' or 'Are you all going to the Show on Saturday?' Occasionally they would give me messages, like 'Tell your mum there's a Christmas Party meeting on Wednesday'. This I could only relay be saying, 'A woman in the shop asked me to tell you …' to which my mother would reply 'That's Mrs Atkinson.' So, I would know in future. At home there were always points of reference against which to test the provenance and reliability of these messages. At school, there was only precedent and conformity as a guide to how I should behave. I was recognised, not as x from y, but as one of a set of m functioning in the locus of n.

6. THE CITY

The daily journey through the dreary wastes of Manchester's suburbs was a revelation to me. Hitherto, the horrors of town life had only been glimpsed through the windows of the train, or imagined from the pages of *Picture Post* and my mother's *Daily Mail*. Father took *The Manchester Guardian*, with a front page consisting entirely of adverts. Inside, the pictures were usually of bomb damage, dramatically presented, with shattered buildings outlined against the sky above a tangle of roof timbers and fallen brick, captioned: 'Family of six survive in Anderson Shelter'. I found no solace there, despite the essentially optimistic message. What depressed me most in what I saw from Bowker's as we descended from Irlams Heights towards Salford was the terrible sameness of the scenery. Long rows of houses gave way to untidy parades of shops, interspersed with churches and occasional areas of greenery known as 'parks'. The nearer to the city centre we approached, the more signs there were of bomb damage. Gaps showed in the rows of houses, many of which had their doors and windows boarded up. The intervening areas of flattened rubble often held large tanks with EWS stencilled on the side to show they were Emergency Water Supplies for the Fire Brigades.

There were no bright colours in this landscape even in summer and the winters were characterised by choking, tawny fogs, which took one by the throat, blocked the roads and doubled, trebled the time it took to get home. In a bad fog, school would finish early and we would be dispersed into it, like lost souls in limbo – which Pansy Mason directed me to read about in Dorothy L. Sayers' 1950 translation of Dante. The density and nastiness of those fogs of the forties are scarcely credible now. In still, dank days between November and March, we would sometimes leave Worsley in pale sunshine with the frost glittering on the trees and at about Monton Green run into a yellowy-grey miasma.

Stretching from Irlam o'th'Height to the Cheshire suburbs, it covered the city like a quilt, opaque and suffocating. Penetrable by only the most determined, it brought the city to a standstill. The street lights were scarcely visible, sound was deadened, vehicles trailed nose to tail, barely exceeding the pace of those who tramped along the pavements. The fog put a greasy film over everything, making everything we touched feel sticky. Worst of all, it filled the mouth and the nose with a sulphurous, metallic tang that tainted everything we ate or drank. We wore our handkerchiefs over our faces like bank robbers and exulted because we got out of school early; sometimes we were even prevented from getting there. Nothing could lessen the fog's pervasive nastiness: it was man-made, it was lethal – it was supposed to have killed more people than the Blitz. Miss Robins said it was the product of man's selfishness and greed, and we believed her. When we emerged into the bright blue sunny afternoon at Worsley we felt that the city forefathers should have served us better.

But even on sunny days, the journeys into school became tedious. There was little of interest to catch the eye and a gritty pall lay over everything. An architectural novelty like Burton's new factory, built in the shape of a sewing machine, was something to look out for and essentially cheering, for it seemed to be a building with a sense of humour. But I found something chilling about the black Gothic spires of Pendleton Children's Hospital. Fenced in by a palisade of spiked railings and accessible only by a gated lodge, it seemed more like a place of punishment than a haven for the sick and injured. Above all, I found the rows of featureless houses stretching at right angles to the main road into the city almost unbearably depressing. As one who had been brought up among green fields with the fells always on my horizon, I could not imagine how people might live happily in such places.

In 1942 there was much evidence of bomb damage in Manchester and stark mementos remained of the great blitz of Christmas 1940, when the centre of the city was devastated and over seven hundred people died. On the journey into school, from Pendleton onwards increasing numbers of buildings were damaged. In Manchester itself, there were large stretches of flattened rubble. From Quay Street across to Bridge Street, where now stand the Law Courts and the college of Arts and Technology, an open space reached down to the Irwell. At the bottom of Deansgate, an area the size of a football pitch stretched from the Royal Exchange down to the cathedral, revealing the brick ramparts of Exchange Station like a wall at the northern side of the city. At the very edge of this devastation, as if to mock the Victorian builders in granite and Portland stone, stood the half-timbered edifices of the Old Shambles and Sinclair's Oyster Bar – dormant signifiers of the good life. In times to come I often mounted the worn wooden stairs to what I took to be a garret, where there was a Fishing Tackle shop. Another devastated area stretched along Upper Brook Street from the Grosvenor to Plymouth Grove. As we passed this flattened area, once covered by a network of shops and houses, chapels and pubs, I had to be careful not to let my mind drift back to the horror of the day my school uniform was bought, and wonder what had happened to the people who lived there, and if bits of them were still buried under the rubble.

From where we stayed in Worsley, the bombs dropped on Manchester were clearly audible as deep, flat booms, punctuated by the snap, snap of the anti-aircraft guns. The raiders concentrated on the south-western edge of the city, round Trafford Park and the docks, so we never had trouble getting to school. On moonlit nights when a raid seemed likely, I would be bundled with the girls from next door into a Morrison shelter, which had been erected in a downstairs room and was therefore warm and dry, unlike other people's shelters, which were often where the lawn had been. Sometimes we were allowed to watch the searchlights, stroking the sky with wands of light, but when we heard the sharp reports of the ack-ack guns we were rushed inside for fear of being struck by shrapnel. I longed for the bombers to come nearer for I was an eager collector of the, jagged, razor sharp fragments of exploded shells and bombs. Once or twice, and much to my excitement, a bomb would fall nearby and I would eagerly visit the crater to marvel at the ridge of yellow clay which had been thrown up around the hole. Once there, I would look for the jagged fragments that were tangible evidence of the enemy.

The school itself wasn't much damaged by the blitz, though a bomb falling in the playing fields was supposed to have been an unlucky attempt to get the High Master, whose house was just across the road. The windows in the main building were masked with a wall of sandbags, as were the windows of the library and the gym. Elsewhere, they were covered in a lattice-work of sticky tape designed to stop flying glass. I guess there were other, similar barricades in vulnerable places, but by the time I left the Prep Department, and was free to wander round the school during lunch hours, the threat of air raids had gone. The sandbags themselves had frayed into ragged pillows of compressed sand, which could be quarried into small, throwable lumps. Inspired by the Pathé News Reels of the war in the Western Desert, we would re-enact the battle of

El Alamein, without the tanks, usually round the arches under the Art Room. There, the whole building seemed propped up by crumbling ramparts of decomposing stone round which we skirmished until someone, usually Sutton, the school's resident gauleiter, came to stop the fun.

7. PREP 2

Life was much more serious in Prep 2 as we came under the influence of the red-haired, quick-tempered Miss Robins. I was again impressed by her manner, especially the way she managed Rawley, positively annihilating him when he forgot his games kit for the third week running. She was fond of giving us what she called 'Pep Talks' – I thought they were 'Prep Talks' until someone put me right. In these she set out to instil in us a sense of the privilege we enjoyed as junior members of MGS, and how we must work hard to justify our good fortune in being educated at such an old and famous school. 'Sapere aude,' she said. 'Dare to be wise. Dr Johnson said, "Learning is like old lace. Everyone should strive to get as much of it as he can."' Why old lace, I wondered, reminded again of Mrs Gaskill and the cat in *Cranford*. They clearly though it was valuable.

Miss Robins was famous for her jokes, as she said so herself. A sample: A boy went to Belle Vue Zoo where he was much impressed by the dangeroos. 'Kangaroos, surely,' said his father. 'No,' replied the lad. 'It was written on the cage, "These animals are dangeroos."' We laughed dutifully. She would often tell us about parents who asked what jokes had been told today, then she would get back to teaching. Very severe she was, I remember, about long division and adjectival clauses and the tropics – in which she preceded Toby Cantrell, who was equally severe when he taught us Geography. But she did make things fun, whereas he, a small, rancorous Scotsman, made everything a trial.

In Prep 2, I had to make new friends. Caddy and McElvie had gone into the main school and were inaccessible, except on Bowker's. Even there, they drew apart, not only from me, but from each other, one in the Classical side, the other in the Modern. McElvie was expecting to go to Rugby at the end of his second year, and was only filling in the time before his real education began – at least, that's what he said. We no longer met at weekends. As circumstances changed I formed alliances with my new neighbours in class. My association with Lewis started to fall off when he no longer sat at the desk in front of mine. Williamson, still on the other side of the room, also 'palled up' with the chap who sat next to him. I found a new companion in Sammy Boliver, who had a large set of Minibrix, the rubber building blocks that preceded Lego as the principal construction toy – apart, of course, from Meccano, and everybody had a much-used set of that. These toys were irreplaceable as their makers were directed to producing items that were 'in the national interest', another of the phrases that haunt my memories of that time.

Of my other classmates, I remember little, being almost entirely occupied with finding out what kind of animal I was in this human zoo. I was attracted to Rawley, but he was always getting us into trouble, which he didn't seem to mind but I did. He was a bit like Tigger and 'bounced' people, and was always puzzled when they didn't like being 'bounced'. He was the despair of Miss Robins, who publicly 'looked forward' to the end of the year when he would become someone else's problem, and he became another of those I lost track of. There was another boy called Leeming, who impressed me by being very snappish and decisive. 'I don't know what you call it, but I think it's disgraceful,' he said, when someone threw a snowball at Miss Robins. He had a kind of following which I joined for a while but eventually took against him when he wouldn't lend me a book I wanted to read.

Neither Rawley nor Leeming was the sort of confidant I needed – someone like Rockhart, the imaginary playmate of my childhood with whom I could discuss the things that puzzled me. With Caddy and McElvie, I had accepted my role as the 'Young 'un' and benefited from their superior knowledge of the world, without being encouraged to ask too many questions. Now they had gone into the unreachable regions of the main school, I sorely felt the lack of a mentor. Without someone to talk privately with and depend on for a sympathetic hearing, I felt I was nobody. Who would listen to my independent views about anything? I needed to be able to say, 'Caddy and McElvie and I think so and so...' or 'We don't do that...' I lacked a constituency which would give force and body to my opinions as well as refining them. With some of my birthday money I bought a bottle of purple ink to go with the fountain pen that had been one of my presents. No one else I knew used that colour, so whatever I wrote would be recognised as mine. I think I did it because it made me different and gave me a sense of identity.

The classroom of Prep 2 was large and L-shaped. I found it gloomy after the sunny atmosphere of Mrs Gaskill's room and we needed no deep-breathing exercises, for Miss Robins herself was like a fresh breeze. Her room backed on to the Memorial Hall, and while we held our own daily "Prayers", we could hear behind us the full-throated roar of the whole school going through the morning hymn. It was a mysterious room with large cupboards and a piano in the short leg of the L. The windows overlooked Birchfields Park, which was then an army camp with Nissen huts and interesting military equipment, like barrage balloons and ack-ack guns. We longed to see them in action.

I found it an entertaining life in Prep 2; something was always happening and it seemed fun. As far as I could gather from hearing about lessons at other schools, MGS was special in making learning a game. At cousin John's new Prep School in Kent, it seemed that the only games were those played in shorts and shirt on wet and windy fields – not much fun there. In Broughton the village school was conducted by an Ogre who was famous for his feats with the cane – certainly no fun there. I guess MGS was special in this respect and I generally found lessons to be entertaining if not amusing. In iα, Bozo Hindley would join us as we chanted, 'Hic haec hoc' and other paradigms, always finishing with 'Caesar ad some jam for tea. Pompey ad a rat'. Even in iiα with the sainted Simkins and the Remove with Holy Willie Graham there were comic interludes, although I think in the case of the latter, they were generally by accident.

Miss Robins introduced us to the 'Game of Clause Analysis' – that was how she described it. She presented it as playing trains. There were carriages and stations and each carriage must go to its proper station and the game was to sort out how to do it. The stations were set out at the top of a page in little boxes labelled: Subject, Object, Verb, Conjunction, Definite article, and so on. Really it was a matter of identification. Once the subject and verb were settled, the rest of the sentence could be shunted into its appropriate siding. It was quite fun and only when it involved adverbial clauses of concession or phrases of modification did it get past being a joke.

Besides these entertainments, there must have been a deal of good solid learning, but I don't remember much of it happening. As I said before, we absorbed knowledge through a process of osmosis, whereby it seemed to pass into us effectively but unnoticed. It was only with my removal to the main school that I became conscious of having to learn, and that learning was divided into sections and subjects, which were ultimately tested by exams.

While my main memories of Prep 1 are of poetry, what I most recall from Prep 2 is the singing. In my first year, I enjoyed the poems both for the pictures and the sounds they made. I loved accounts of country life in 'Renard the Fox'. I was thrilled by the image of 'river of death' that 'brimmed its banks' in 'Vitae lampada', and the 'bold Sir Bedivere' haunted my imagination as he waited beside the great water where the 'moon was full' – of what, I sometimes wondered. In recollections of Prep 2 I hear us singing with Miss Robins, for she was a boisterous, vamping pianist, and with an instrument ready to hand she would have us singing our hearts out. From the school Song Book – the one I'd learned "Hugh of the Owl" from – we sang, "Green Grow the Rushes O" and "Woad", a fine parody sung to the tune of "Men of Harlech". It had compulsively memorable lyrics like, 'The Romans came and crossed the Channel/All dressed up in tin and flannel/ Half a pint of woad a man'll/Clothe us more than these'. We also sang regularly: 'Music everywhere, finiculi finicula', 'The Ash Grove' and the 'Skye Boat Song'. The sub-choir – of which I was a member – learned a descant to it.

We held it as a matter of fact that Miss Robins had a sweetheart in the person of Dickie Radford, who taught music throughout the school. Tall and slim with a commanding presence – he was, after all Commandant of the School's Cadet Force – he would sometimes come and join our singing lessons. He had a Bowker's reputation for extreme severity, but he was always gentle with us as he went through the class selecting the sweetest and truest voices for the sub-choir. This performed at Founder's Day, when we assembled in Manchester Cathedral, and again at the end of term concert in the Memorial Hall. We noticed that Miss Robins was much less abrasive with us when Dickie Radford was there. She was more maidenly, if not actually coquettish. She played while he coached the singers, and when he directed her with a wave of his baton, she would positively simper, before she bent over the piano to do his will.

8. THE WAR

The War was never far from our thoughts. As well as the signs of destruction in the city and the regular news bulletins, at every turn we were constantly reminded that we must beware of the enemy. Blazoned on bill boards and the hoardings erected round bomb-sites, in the newspapers and at the cinema we were admonished: 'Careless Talk Costs Lives', ' Is Your Journey Really Necessary', 'Dig for Victory', 'Buy National Savings Stamps'. On the radio and in the scores of Ministry of Information leaflets, in family gossip even, we were told that this was total war and the citizen at home was as much a fighter as the soldier at the front. And yet, for most members of my generation, this was life as we had always known it. But for our elders complaining about shortages and inconveniences, we wouldn't have felt deprived. Privileged middle-class boys living in relatively safe places, it didn't seem to us that we ever went short, for we were only vaguely aware of what life was like before the war.

And yet, most households were upset quite badly in some way as husbands and sons were inexorably borne away to distant lands, sometimes never to return. At home in the Lakes, evacuees, not just children but mothers with babies, were billeted on those with room for them. Here, on the outskirts of Manchester, most families seemed to be putting up relations or friends, directed to war work, or bombed out of their own homes. On Bowker's we heard of boys whose fathers were wounded or taken prisoner, even killed in action. Caddy's father was in the Air Force, part of Ground Control at an aerodrome in the midlands. He got home about once a month for the weekend, when, according to Caddy, it was like Christmas, except there was no turkey. McElvie's father, like mine, was in a 'reserved occupation', which, he explained, meant he stayed where he was until he was ordered to go somewhere else, 'at a moment's notice'. But the moment never came. In one of our rare meetings after he'd gone to Rugby, McElvie told me how father's bag, packed for his instant despatch, was ceremoniously unpacked on VE night, then packed again a week later when he was ordered to a hospital in the south east to look after the wounded returning from the continent.

My being uprooted from the Lakes and sent to MGS seemed part of the general upheaval most families suffered. Apart from missing the countryside, I didn't feel uneasy or deprived. Talk of the war and then the war itself had been part of life for as long as I could remember. I remember in Broughton Mills the grown-ups with grim faces gathered round the wireless set listening to the News. It was positioned on the window sill so the aerial could go outside and up to the roof. Next to it were the big glass jars where the current was stored, for we had no mains electricity. A disembodied voice with a BBC accent told us that the Germans had invaded somewhere, somewhere had been bombed, and Mr Chamberlain said we were at war. The situation was serious; people said so. But outside the autumn sunshine was hot, and there were plenty of conkers and apples and pears. What did it matter that we had to have window blinds to keep the light in, rather than 'keep the dark out' as my grandma used to say when she wanted the curtains drawn.

Even being bundled off to school in Dumfries with my cousin was a sort of adventure. At first it had been like going away on holiday at the end of the summer rather than the beginning. I was staying with my aunt and I got on all right with John, despite his irritating tendency to think he always knew better. I'd tried to kill him once in the sandpit, when he jumped on my tunnels. But that had been ages ago and he said he'd forgiven me, although he still bore the scars. There were no real signs of war in Dumfries and there was always lots of sugar and butter, which I suppose was because Uncle Ned had a grocer's shop.

It was only in Worsley where bombs actually fell that the war became real. But even then, the air raids were almost fun. At the sound of the sirens we were bundled into the shelter in the lounge, myself and the girls from next door, and it was a lark. We played cards and read and chatted ourselves to sleep. I didn't connect these raids with the scene of devastation that upset me when we went for my school uniform. At that time, the war was something in the background, not yet a nuisance or a likely danger, just part of things as they were. Not until much later, at the time of the V2 rockets, did I realise what happened in these moments of destruction, and actually began to be afraid of what might drop from the sky.

Quite often at weekends we went to the cinema – 'the flicks' is what we called it. 'Let's see what's on at the flicks,' the adults would say. Then, we would rush out to the local 'flea pit' in time for the first showing, and see *In Which We Serve*, or *Mrs Miniver* or *The First of the Few*. Our cinema, which was appropriately named The Kinema, showed films every night except Sunday. Then, nothing was open but the churches. The pictures, carefully monitored by the Ministry of Information,

were potent shapers of our opinions. The Pathé News Reels that featured in every show honed our patriotism by turning every Hun into a savage and every Tommy into a hero. Consisting of three or four minutes of intense action – explosions, planes crashing, guns firing – they would show our men charging with bayonets fixed, or dead Germans or heartening clips of the 'Home Front', with housewives 'Digging for Victory' or making nettle soup. These films inspired our war games and although what we went to see was Will Hay or George Formby and another episode of 'The Lone Ranger', there was always a quarter of an hour of News Reels.

At weekends, Caddy, McElvie and I played war games on a large waste behind McElvie's. Known as Mosley Common, it became the enemy occupied land. We stormed its hills and defended its hollows, uttering staccato cries in imitation of sten-guns. We were commandos, recapturing Dieppe, landing again

at St Nazaire. We knew all about these from the Pathé News. Caddy wore a tin helmet, which left him blind or strangled, depending upon whether it slid forward or back. McElvie had a bandolier for the grenades of dried mud we spent so much time making. I had a red and black swastika arm band my father had brought back from a holiday in Germany, but though they admired it, Caddy and McElvie were agreed that I shouldn't wear it. 'Someone might come along and think you were a real

German,' McElvie said. Occasionally we would interrupt our battles to stalk Pickup (another Bowker's man) and his girl as they wandered through the sallow willows in fruitless search for seclusion. War was a game, but sex was serious and we needed to find out as much as we could about it.

I don't know what we thought we were doing in these games, beyond passing the time. We engaged in them with all seriousness, and often discussed them in the mornings on the bus. We were play-acting, no doubt, playing the Cowboys and Indians that our fathers had played, also inspired by the cinema. I'm sure if some trustworthy adult had said to us, 'Don't be silly,' we would have shamefacedly put aside our gear, stopped making those ridiculous sounds and set to building tree-houses or playing chess. But at the moment, sheer exuberance drove us to race up hills and roll down them, crawl through bushes to throw our pretend grenades at imagined enemies and mark their exploding with a kind of guttural grunt that it's impossible to render in print. For a while we would live in a world that was entirely of our own making. Then it would be shattered by someone walking a dog or us stumbling across huddled groups of men playing pitch-and-toss in one of the hollows, or wandering sweethearts like Pickup and his girl

A lot of our indoor games derived from the war, for we each had private armies of toy soldiers. Most of these were relics from peace-time, another much used phrase from the period, heavy with a sense of nostalgia. I had a much admired Camel Corps, inherited from my Barrow cousins, and consisting of six gorgeously uniformed Arabs with lances mounted on their racing camels. Quite inappropriate for our games, they were kept behind the lines as reserves. The designs of our heavy equipment, guns and tanks and transporters were from the

First War, and often out of scale with the Dinky toy Bren-gun carriers and trucks. McElvie had a much prized model of the famous 4.7 naval gun that could shoot small nails across the carpet with sufficient force to knock down the soldiers ranged in fighting formation. A favourite piece of mine, which got me into serious trouble when I was in iβ, was a little cannon with a bore and power sufficient to fire sawn-off bits of pencil across the room.

9. WEEKENDS

Caddy and I visited each other's houses at weekends and, sometimes, stayed overnight. His mother was big and brisk and cheerful and made much of my visits. Caddy's father was away in the Air Force and since, like me, Caddy was an only child, having someone else as part of the family, if only for a night, maybe helped brighten up her weekends. She was a great baker of rock buns and jam tarts and little bread rolls she called 'fadgers', and there was always something special for supper, like scalloped potatoes fried in batter or welsh rarebit. And she made Cremola pudding, which I loved but never got at home. We ate at the kitchen table and it was all very jolly, quite unlike my usual Saturday nights, which tended to be frantic as my cousins, after a day lounging about doing nothing, rushed round getting ready to go out. After supper, if it was dark, Caddy and his mother and I went into the lounge and listened to the radio.

In the long, light nights – made longer by the double-summer time – Caddy and I would play outside. Across the field from Caddy's house was a Tennis Club where they often had Saturday night dances. On fine evenings we would sit on the fence and watch the dancers arriving. About half-past eight the entertainment would start with young swells, arriving early to lean over the pavilion rails with pint pots. Staid couples came later on foot with baskets full of shawls and dancing pumps, groups of girls giggling with their things in little bags. They looked more like people turning up to a jumble sale than a hot night out. There was much squealing and showing off on the veranda, especially by those whose partners were in uniform. They all stood round a big bowl in groups, clinking glasses – which we saw rather than heard. We were enthralled by this real representation of the high life we had seen something of at the cinema. Then someone would start the gramophone and they would all go in.

It was vaguely exciting sitting there in the gloaming, listening to early Frank Sinatra and late Al Bowly while the dancers whirled and flashed around the floor. Then someone would shout, 'Blackouts!' and in a trice, the screens would be up. The first part of the show was over. Then we would sneak across the courts and creep on to the veranda – like Indian scouts, Caddy's phrase. Peering through chinks in the blackout we had glimpses of the dancers as they swirled past. We took turns to spy for we were very interested in anything to do with mating and sex, when it caught our attention. Not the sanitised romance of the cinema, with Nelson Eddy yodelling across the canyon to Jeanette MacDonald that ended in a close-up of the kiss, but the real, hands on, practical way people actually went about it. Even before it became the intense interest of our adolescence, we didn't like to miss any opportunity of watching how it was done. There were kisses and cuddles on the veranda and occasionally a couple would drift into the darkness beyond. Then we would fly into the undergrowth on the far side of the courts, fearful of getting too close to see what actually happened, then creep home in case we disturbed them.

One of the pleasures of winter weekends at Caddy's was listening to the Saturday Night Theatre. I'd been stirred by radio drama a year or so before, when staying with Williamson. We'd listened attentively - one paid attention at Williamson's while the wireless was on, and didn't fiddle about – to a production of Capek's RUR, Rossums Universal Robots, in which the world is taken over by robots – the very word dates from the play. It gave us much to think about and we talked it over in bed for ages. For many months after it would crop up in general conversation, as if seeds sown then had just begun to sprout. 'What if the world were really controlled by robots who treated everyone the same?' 'Do you think she really fell in love with a robot?' Romance was something we knew about only from the cinema, love and affection were not words that we used much, but took for granted as being a normal part of life. But what if...? It was a question that could give rise to dreams of unreason. Mrs Gaskill once disturbed me be asking us generally, 'What if you lived in a world where no one waited for you when you ran after them, or helped you up when you fell?' How would it be in a world that was devoid of – the word rarely a part of my vocabulary, forced itself upon me – love?

Reports were beginning to come out of Europe in Pathé News reels, pictures of ordinary people – folk you might almost know – turned into destitute wanderers, passed like packages from one unfeeling authority to another. One picture in particular haunted me. It was of a small boy with big eyes, standing by himself in a crowd with a little bundle beside him and a label fastened to his coat. No one owned him and he belonged to nobody. Might not the same thing happen to me? For a moment, I was possessed again by the horror of the afternoon we went to Henry Barrie's. Where would I go when everything

I had was blown away? Who would look after me? How could I get back to the safety of Broughton Mills where everybody knew me?

10. MEMORIES

Some things I remember clearly, others I imagine, and as I write I wonder about the stages in my developing awareness. When did I start to reckon time; how long after Prep school days was it before I started to see myself as an actor in someone else's play rather than the principal figure in the one that was all about me? When I was told to bear in mind something planned for next week, I would immediately shelve it as being irrelevant to now. Then, my mother would say, 'Don't forget, John and your Aunt Peggy are coming tomorrow,' and I would be thrown into confusion, remembering now the things I'd promised to get ready for their visit. 'But I thought it was ages away,' 'No, I told you last week.' 'That's what I mean…'

At the age of eleven, I think I was entirely engrossed in the present. What was happening now was enough. I was like Polixenes imagining 'there was no more behind / But such a day tomorrow as today / And to be boy eternal.' Time was a mystery. Christmas was an unimaginable distance away, and the period between Monday and Friday, a lifetime. And yet my life was measured out precisely. I was up by eight o'clock to catch the eight forty-five to be at school by nine-thirty. The school timetable divided the day into discrete packages until three-forty when I had to hurry into town to catch the four-sixteen. Only when I was at home could I feel confident that I had fulfilled all my obligations to the clock and therefore able to drop into my own timeless world. But then, there were programmes on the wireless I wanted to listen to at six forty-five and eight o'clock – if I was allowed to stay up.

I've always wanted to be what I was and where I was for as long as I liked. Ever since I can remember I have relished days with no obligations, when I am free to do nothing but follow my own bent. I never possessed the urge to dominate or organise, or indeed be fully a part of any institution. In Prep 1 I was an observer, a half-hearted participant, an attendant lord, never an actor. I guess what fascinated me about significant figures like Rawley was their being prepared to meet life head on, almost to challenge events and make things happen by provoking and posturing and asserting. My preference was always for ducking out and heading for the woods with a book and an apple. Years later when I chanced upon Logan Pearsall Smith's aphorism, 'Some people say life is the thing, but I prefer books,' I knew exactly what he meant.

As an only child, I was cocooned in my own perceptions. For a long time I had no peer to discuss things with. At home, in the Lakes, I was a part-time member of a group of children who were cruelly direct in pointing out what they saw as my failings. But these were different from what mattered in my parents' world and what they censured, the group was generally indifferent to. I was by far the youngest of my cousins who sometimes acted as intermediaries between me and the grown-up world, but then their advice was nearly always prescriptive. 'I should do that…' they would say, or 'Next time, remember to say this'. They were rarely speculative and avoided answering questions, like: 'Why did she say that…?' Or, 'Why doesn't Mary come any more…?' When my grandmother was dying, I was hurried away to stay with friends in Broughton, and largely left to work out for myself what was happening. It was only when I saw the passing hearse, followed by cars containing my parents and relations that I realised what was going on. On my return home, all signs of grandma had gone. In place of her big bed were two divans, the room had been redecorated and new curtains hung in the window. When I asked my mother why, she would only say, 'Because…'

Some past events I can almost re-live, like the time I agitated to be put higher up the batting order because those at the tail-end seldom got an innings. 'All right,' said the captain irritated by my whining, 'you can go in next.' I took my guard, asking for an adventurous middle and off because I fancied I was good on the leg side. 'You can have midland hotel, if you like,' he said, 'but it won't do you any good.' Nor did it, for I was out first ball. Other occasions, which I ought to remember, like the time somebody set off the fire extinguisher in the Woodwork room, I have to imagine. With my mind's eye I can see the horror on his face as the foam spurts out, the group's rush away from the widening jet, the decisive removal of the cylinder by the little, gnarled woodwork master, and his return to conduct the inquisition. All this happened, I know, but I cannot remember it actually taking place.

Another significant event I ought to remember clearly but don't is the great upheaval of our moving to Bolton at the end of my Prep school days. I recall the oddness of seeing all our things packed in the removal van. Then I have a picture of a bare, sunny room which was to be my bedroom, with patterned lino and a musty wall cupboard. Our things from Broughton Mills seemed magically to appear in our new home, and Cragg House was henceforth to be 'our holiday cottage'. These disturbances which I thought would have pierced me to the heart, seemed to pass by as part of a normal week. I woke up one morning to a new life in another house, with a different way of getting to school. And yet I recall clearly my first day in iβ, in a desk in the third row along, second from the front, right under Mr Morton's eye.

There are from this time no involuntary memories – no tisane-soaked madeleine calls them forth – those are of an earlier period and evoke my childhood in the Lakes. The smell of woodsmoke, the sound of wild geese, the taste of the dandelion wine all take me back to my grandmother and a pre-lapsarian time when the sun always shone, even when it was raining. The memories of schooldays are quarried from a not so distant past and like materials from crumbling buildings reconstructed into the façades of buildings and streets. They are like theatre sets, they don't have to keep out the rain or withstand the wind and, peopled by my actors for the brief duration of the play, it is enough that they are credible and last out the performance.

From my days in Prep 1 I most clearly remember events which now seem trivial. They are mental snapshots, short films almost, often to do with the time of the year and the weather. One afternoon I was part of a group sitting on the bank by the playing fields. I can smell the new cut grass, feel the heat of the sun, see the green plain, shimmering in the heat, where white figures moved. Past the rectory the school grounds seemed to stretch to the end of the world. Whiling away the time, we lolled on a giant heap of grass cuttings hurling handfuls at each other, stuffing them down each other's shirts and trousers. We were like puppies in a basket, rolling over each other in a warm writhing heap, happy that we were what we were, no more, only faintly conscious of being rather silly, but not caring. The grass would stain my shirt, I knew, and it would be damp and uncomfortable in my trousers. But none of this mattered, it was enough that we were here and it was now.

Another reel is of being bundled out of the warm fug of Bowker's one morning into a large white world of fresh snow and hurrying through a barrage of snowballs to the shelter of the door by the Memorial Hall. The snow, gathering on Hugh Oldham's outstretched arm, was cold enough to sting my cheeks and lips. A greying vista, flecked with white, reached down the vast side of the Memorial Hall, filling me with an unutterable sense of despair. Perhaps this was really what life had in store: a sudden ejection from warm and familiar surroundings into a cold, friendless passage leading through hordes of whirling demons into a harsh and indeterminate future.

PART II -

GROWING UP

1. THE MAIN SCHOOL

In the autumn of 1944 I went into the main school. I found it a very stimulating place, though I had a bewildering sense of dislocation, for it involved more than just moving up a year. The sheltered, cohesive group I had been part of in Prep 2 was broken up and its members, enemies and friends, were distributed amongst the six forms that constituted the main school's first year. The three who moved with me into iβ were almost strangers. I was thrown into a whirlpool of new people, new places and new subjects. Gone was my sense of place and belonging for at the end of every lesson I moved to another classroom. Also I no longer travelled on Bowker's.

The shock of being uprooted from the Prep Department was compounded by an upheaval at home. As the end of the war seemed in sight and the likelihood of air raids receded, we went to live in Bolton. Furthermore, the family was extended as Betty and Joan, my Cumbrian cousins, came to live with us. They were just old enough to be directed to jobs connected with the War Effort and were sent to work in Manchester. The immediate family remained intact as my father was too old to serve. 'Did my bit in the first fiasco,' he would say. Nevertheless, like everyone between the ages of eighteen and sixty he was liable to be sent wherever it was felt he would be most useful. As a specialist in infectious diseases, trained to deal with smallpox or the plague, he was put in charge of a hospital for venereal diseases. I fancy he enjoyed the work for he had a little research laboratory with two assistants and they produced papers on the treatment of gonorrhoea. 'Never thought I would end up as a Pox Doctor,' he said. 'But then it's repairing weapons, so it's vital war work.'

When he was released from what he called his 'venereal servitude', he got what my mother called 'a proper job working for the Council.' From being Hospital Superintendent, he became Medical Officer of Health, running baby-clinics and doing school inspections and generally supervising the well-being of the borough. 'I've given up medicine, boy,' he said. 'Penicillin and other antibiotics have made me redundant. It used to need weeks of nursing in special hospitals to cure diphtheria and scarlet fever. Now it's all done by tablets.' But despite his grousing, I think he enjoyed his new job even more than being at the Pox Hospital – as we knew it. The work put him in touch with lots of ordinary people and as the war drew to a close and the Victory Tests were played he found he had plenty of time to go to Old Trafford. 'There's this chap, Denis Compton,' he said to me confidentially. 'He's worth keeping an eye on.'

Ironically, we moved when the Flying Bombs and V2 rockets were falling in the south-east. I'd had an excited postcard about them from cousin John, now at prep school in Beckenham. He was afraid we in the north would miss out on the fun, because the places they were launched from would be 'liberated' before they were able to reach us. I was more afraid that they wouldn't, for it was just as we settled in Bolton that I had my last experience of an air raid. Wakened by the eerie wailing, and bundled out of my bed by my mother, I found myself shivering with apprehension as I sat with the family in the kitchen. At Worsley, air raids had been something of an adventure, crammed into the Morrison Shelter with next door's girls, where we fell asleep in a jumbled heap – like puppies in a basket. But now, scarcely two years later, I was terrified. It wasn't the lack of a shelter that worried me so much as thoughts of the devastation and dislocation that might ensue.

Exposure to the effects of war via newsreels and newspapers had sharpened my understanding of what might happen, even on what was militaristically known as the 'Home Front'. Recent pictures showing the effects of Flying Bombs had made frighteningly clear what high explosives could do to houses and people. During that last air raid, while my father fiddled with the radio and four of us sat round the table, hardly daring to look at each other, I was terrified by the thought of what might happen. 'Just enough for a game of whist,' said my mother. 'Someone get the cards.' But no one moved. We were all subdued by the imminence of something that we had come to believe was no longer a threat. 'It's the Flying Bombs,' said Betty. 'They're able to reach us now. They said they would.' She voiced our worst fears, and for a moment we were horrified by the possibility of boundless destruction. Just then the all clear sounded a reprieve, and chattering with relief we fled back to our beds. The following day we learned that it had been a false alarm, but the horror of what it might have been lingered with me for a long time.

At Bolton I found myself for the first time living in the sort of streets which Bowker's Bus had driven along. Lines of almost identical houses with small gardens and no views seemed to stretch interminably across the north-western edge of Manchester. We were number 679 in a row that went almost without interruption from Bolton to Salford. I sometimes travelled along it by bus and strove then to work out where one town started and another began. Farnworth, Kearsley, Clifton, Pendlebury, Salford each merged into the other. It was a foreign country where I knew no one and had no connections. The weekends also stretched interminably with nothing to do outside and no one to play with inside.

Now, my journey to school was by train and tram, and for the most part, alone. At first I saw it as a journey full of potential hazards. What should I do if I lost my purse, got on the wrong tram, went the wrong way, missed my station and got carried on to Preston? The list of possible calamities continued. At first I caught the train with Joan who was secretary to a 'Ministry' man – Betty worked shifts, and sometimes left disturbingly early, and sometimes returned disturbingly late, always managing to wake the whole house. Joan worked in Manchester so she walked with me to Albert Square and saw me on to the tram to Rusholme – at least until the second morning, when I caught the scornful glances of other Owls. I intimated to her that I would prefer to be on my own for the last few yards of the journey. Coming home, I was entirely on my own and for the first few days made my cautious way down Cross Street and Corporation Street, fearful of traffic, clutching my contract and terrified by the thought of missing my train. By the namby-pamby standards of the twenty-first century it would seem an unwarrantable responsibility for an uncertain eleven-year old, but my case was by no means unusual. MGS attracted pupils from a wide area and boys travelled to school from all the surrounding towns and I soon realised that I was merely one of a large group hurrying to the stations at the end of the afternoon.

The radio played a big part in our lives. It provided us with a common experience, gave us catch phrases, new jokes and new songs to sing. It didn't, though, have the force and effect of later radio like the Third Programme, which had an enormous influence on my intellectual life, giving me much food to store and think about. Popular programmes on the Home Service were 'Bandwagon' and 'Happidrome', but apart from a passing weakness for the latter, I came to enjoy 'ITMA' much more.

It was quicker and wittier and I listened to it at home with my father. Set in the corridors of the Ministry of Aggravation and Mysteries and particularly in the Office of Twerps it featured Tommy Handley, as himself, trying to 'do his bit' – another phrase from the time. Hindered by the office cleaner, Mrs Mop, always wanting to dust his dado – 'Can I do you now, sir?' she would croak, at a critical moment – and fending off the thirsty

military attaché, Colonel Chinstrap, 'I don't mind if I do,' pop, gurgle, gurgle – Mr Handley dealt with a weekly crisis, the climax of which was a phone call from Fünf Vodkin, the German Spy whose sepulchral voice – 'Dis iss Fünf spikking...' – struck them all with consternation.

2. MR MORETON

Our form Master in iβ was Mr Moreton, who was in most ways the antithesis to Miss Robins. Where she was brisk and decisive, he was considerate and non-committal; where she was provocative, he was conciliatory. In situations that provoked her to outbursts of fury – which Rawley managed at least once a month – he tut-tutted and looked solemn. He was avuncular, another of those words like 'limbo' and 'supercilious' which I came to define by finding exemplars of them. At that time I seemed to do a lot of fitting the words I read to the things I thought they represented. "Avuncular" had me in a quandary for a while, because those who had what I took to be its proper qualities weren't relations at all, but friends of my father's.

Mr Moreton was a figure from the past. Old beyond the age of retirement, he must have been brought back to fill the place of those called up to fight in the war. He had white hair and jowls and his expression rarely altered. He was always perfectly in control, and seated at his desk, wrapped in a voluminous gown, he looked immovable. Gowns were as new to us as were our masters. Mrs Gaskill and Miss Robins had worn ordinary clothes. Mr Moreton, as he moved down the corridor with his gown billowing, seemed like a big black barge, an argosy freighted with learning's treasures, bound for the isles of the blessed, which in this case was his form room, and we were the blessed. 'You are very fortunate little boys,' he would tell us. 'Don't ever forget who you are.' My father used to say much the same thing. There we were taught English and Latin by precept, and tolerance and good humour by example. And he read to us. When we were with him at the end of the day, he would sit hunched at his desk and in a voice that was something between a growl and a grumble take us into other worlds. Thus I wandered London with Sam Weller, hurried across the Highlands with Alan Breck, and most enthralling of all, fought across Spain with Etienne Gerard, which thrilled me to the marrow. These readings always ended at a moment of crisis – 'and I felt the cold steel of his blade on the nape of my neck' – His voice would fall, 'To be resolved in the next instalment', he would growl. Then the bell would ring.

I was not alone, I guess, in feeling that these end-of-day readings were the most important part of the day. Both Mrs Gaskill and Mr Moreton read to us, and we sat as though spellbound. We were transported to the worlds of stories, the characters insinuated themselves into our lives. Old Sam Weller gave us a new way of talking and we called each other 'Samivel'. Towards the end of the year, listening to bits of F.W. Anstey's *Vice Versa*, that curious tale of the father and the schoolboy son swapping roles, I first began to wonder whether what we read might reflect on the way we lived.

As I went through school, it seemed to me that each teacher had a special way of winding up the day, of filling in those odd minutes between the end of the lesson and the bell at three-forty. Miss Robins liked to finish the day with a song – 'to get your lungs working', Simkins was apt to end with a spot-test of irregular verbs, Tommy Stott who taught us History would try our general knowledge – 'Which monarch reigned the longest?' But as we got older, there didn't seem to be the time for such simple, worthwhile, relaxing practices as reading aloud. As the School Certificate loomed, Artie Moore was more likely to finish the day with Greek vocabulary than *Tanglewood Tales*. But by then, it didn't matter, for those of us who were susceptible to the infection had already got literature so badly that nothing could stop it raging through our blood.

We were taught French by Mr Hyslop, known as Sloppy F if only to distinguish him from his brother, Sloppy H, who taught on the Modern side. I recall Sloppy F as being small and grey, and slightly irritable. He was quick to hand out a PS – Punishment School – an extra lesson at the end of the day. To me, afraid of missing my train home, it was a terrifying incentive to keep quiet and be good. Alive as I was then to local variations in accent, I recognised that Sloppy F spoke with a Manchester intonation. He flattened his vowels so that he said Mannchister and spoke of buks. As far as I knew, his French accent was excellent. Like most of the staff, he was past the age of military service but had fought in what he called 'my war', meaning the one my father had fought in. When there was a linguistic point to be made, he would sometimes illustrate it with a story from his experiences as an infantry officer. Thus I became aware that what my father called plonk, which we had with Sunday lunch, ought to have been white.

3. THE WAR AGAIN

By the time I went into the main school there was a guarded feeling that the defeat of Hitler was in sight. In the fall the war was always there, but we did not go to it any more. The D-Day landings had been successful and the allied armies were advancing through France. The Americans forces were 'doing their bit' but everyone knew that it was really our lads who were winning. The Eighth Army had captured Rome and the Russians were advancing invincibly, so on three sides the Third Reich was diminishing, and the Yanks had only just begun to help on one of them.

At Easter I had been to stay with cousin John. His parents, like mine, reckoned that the end of the war was in sight, and had moved from the safety of Dumfries to Bromley in Kent. When I visited them, they were just beginning to waken up to the horrid possibilities of the new threat. They lived in the corridor the Flying Bombs passed through on their way to London. One day, cousin John and I cycled out beyond Maidstone to the North Downs with the undisclosed intent of watching out for what he called 'Doodlebugs'. We reclined as we ate our sandwiches and scanned the distant horizon. 'Look,' he said. 'There's one.' And an ungainly, top heavy kind of aircraft came into view. It seemed to puff its way across the sky, going neither too high nor too fast. 'There'll be another in a minute,' he said. 'They usually come in threes.' There was the whine of another aircraft which appeared in pursuit, then an orange flash and a distant boom. Then a man came out and shouted at us to come under cover. 'Idiots,' he said. 'All them bits blown up comes down. An' one might land on yer bonce.' Nevertheless, I was entranced, there was never such excitement at home. It was like a shooting gallery, and from under shelter we watched as other Flying Bombs came over the horizon and more planes attacked them. Sitting there admiring the spectacle did much to mitigate my cousin's tedious tales of what went on at his Prep School. It was quite different from mine, with beatings and exeats and Common Entrance and an altogether more brutal and exacting regime than the one I was under – Mr Saunders notwithstanding. 'Of course you won't have these things at a Grammar School,' he said in a lordly way. 'You'll probably have to leave when you're fourteen and go out to work.'

Other events that summer reminded us that the war was far from over. The failed attempts to capture the Rhine bridges at Arnhem and Nijmegen, and in the early winter, the German offensive in the forests of Ardennes, not only held up the Allied advance, but actually pushed their line back. This registered with me because it coincided with our reading *As You Like It* – a fact of remembrance which establishes the relative importance of literature and war in my scale of values just then. But far more disturbing – even to us in the north – were Flying Bombs and the V2 rockets that had started to fall in increasing numbers on London. The Flying Bombs were frightening enough but the rockets were truly appalling. According to cousin John, more terrifying than the tremendous destruction they caused was the suddenness of their arrival, such being their speed that the explosions they made preceded the sound of their approach. 'First there's the bang,' he said, 'then you hear it coming. Odd, really. I expect they'll be landing in Manchester shortly.'

Away from such actual theatres of war, and only experiencing its horrors at second hand, I was disturbed again by the pictures I saw in the Pathé newsreels and the newspapers. Both my mother's *Daily Mail* and my father's *Manchester Guardian* showed maps of France and Holland with big arrows on them marking the progress of the Allies. But these encouraging messages were undercut by photographs of ruined churches, burnt-out tanks and lines of prisoners, who were scarcely distinguishable from our own men. Around this time, along with photographs of paratroopers and the bridge at Nijmegen, were much more disturbing pictures of wrecked English houses in rubble-strewn English streets. One, hanging in a back gallery of my mind which I tried not to visit, was of a devastated High Street, strewn with scraps of clothes and scattered shopping and imagined bits of people, where a rocket had landed on a Saturday morning market. This image, along with the ruined houses in Manchester and the labelled boy with his bundle, led to endless unsettling speculations: 'What if it were our house, what if the boy with the bundle were me?'

I find it difficult to assess the kind of life that we led in those days. The bombs, the rationing, the constant sense of alarm and urgency most adults showed, the continual Government urgings to fight, to be on our guard, to mind the War Effort, were what we'd always known. It was plain that the adult world was rank with dissatisfaction, nothing was as it should be, but what that was I couldn't recall. The war had become so much a part of my consciousness as to be one of the conditions of existence – part of the unvarying state of things as they are. Much, much later when I read Hemingway's *In Our Time* I was haunted by its opening sentence. It had a resonance that was in key with my own memories of that time. Living on the outskirts of the blitz-damaged city, I daily passed through areas that had been subject to sudden and terrible violence which was still at large, but not imminent. At school there were often reports of old boys in the forces. At the end of morning prayers, casualties would be announced. In the Prep when we weren't part of morning assembly, rumours reached us via elder brothers or other connections. On Bowker's we got to hear the news as it was passed round and discussed by those who had heard it at first hand. We would hear about Smith in 4A, whose father had been killed in action, or Jones in Science 3F whose had been taken prisoner, or Robinson whose had been 'mentioned in despatches'. For a while these boys would have a kind of notoriety, a sad moment of fame as they were pointed out.

Nevertheless, it seemed clear that the War, which had dominated our lives for the past four years, was drawing to a close and plans could be made for a fairly certain future. An end was in sight which had been so long in doubt that we had stopped thinking about it. It was like scanning the horizon for signs of an expected ship. First what might be the masts appeared, then the funnel, but only with the coming into view of the superstructure and the hull could we be certain that it was our ship and it was heading our way. With the Normandy landings came a subdued optimism that buoyed up people who had nearly sunk. I felt it in my parents and relations, especially when I visited my aunt in Barrow who had been bombed out. 'It won't be long before we're back to normal,' she would say cheerfully, adding, 'Whatever that is,' as if she felt such an expression of optimism needed qualifying. However, she was sure that the regime of petty restrictions was coming to an end and with it the sense of living an unreal life, the putting off of expectation explicit in the tattered 'Closed for the Duration' notices pasted on swimming baths and other places of entertainment. The era of 'Make do and Mend' was drawing to a close and soon there would really be Blue Birds over the White Cliffs of Dover, and Johnny might sleep in his own little bed again – except he'd grown out of it.

While I was busy adjusting to the main school and my new address, a great source of comfort was in my books. Double summer time meant I could read in bed till almost midnight, and with my windows open, for in the summer of 1944 the Blackout ended. Domestically, it was the most irksome of the petty restrictions we were burdened with. In the Lakes it had never bothered us much as there were no air raids and nothing to bomb, but in Worsley it had been a matter of serious concern. A chink of light from a carelessly drawn blind could result in prosecution and a fine. On her return to Barrow, my aunt had had frequent dealings with the officious Air Raid Warden in her street. 'We've been bombed out once, Mr Glover,' I heard her say. 'Lightning doesn't strike the same place twice.' 'I don't care about you, Mrs Fulton,' he replied. 'The devil looks after his own. But it's the rest of the blinkin' street I'm worried about.' No one grown-up, and at all proper, would have said 'bloody' then, even in such extreme circumstances.

The high spot of the summer had been the battle at Arnhem. The operation had all the ingredients of the stories we read in *The Rover*. 'Our lads' dropping from the sky to the astonishment of the Boche. Individual acts of bravery, casual heroes outside the control of HQ, and the cowardly orders of the pusillanimous generals shown up for what they were by the young lieutenant taking over from the dying major – 'You're in charge, now, Mackintosh. I'm a gonner. Give those Gerries hell.' It was the kind of thing Caddy and McElvie and I used to enact triumphantly among the spoil heaps on Mosley Common. Except Arnhem turned into a defeat, and at a time when we only expected victories. There were lots of pictures of skies full of parachutists, our soldiers in action, the bridge itself framing the smoke of fires and bursting shells. The horror was trumped by the scenic, and gave rise to the disturbing thought that the enemy wasn't beaten yet. After it was over, there seemed to be an unstated but widely held opinion that someone had blundered. 'Colonel Blimp still in charge, boy,' said my father. 'Left to themselves those chaps would have captured it and held on till they were reinforced. Someone…' he dropped his voice and paused for emphasis, 'someone told them to pull back. American high command, I shouldn't doubt.'

4. DISGRACE

One day while I was in iβ, during school dinner I shot the head of the table. There was no animosity for I only knew him as one of those anonymous representatives of authority. Black gowned and stern faced, he kept order and called everybody "boy". I remember he had sandy hair and his spectacles seemed to flash fire as he seized hold of me. He was beside himself with rage, indeed, he was so agitated that I thought there were two of him. I'd no idea why he was so angry because I didn't know I'd shot him and I certainly didn't mean to. He came down on me like a thunderclap, yanking me to my feet and plunging me immediately into the most serious trouble.

I had long cherished as part of my army of toy soldiers the small howitzer that fired bits of sawn off pencil. As I ran out of pencils and sought other kinds of ammunition, I began to use gramophone needles – the short, pointed metal pins from the pick-up of the radiogram. With my father's passion for opera and my cousins' fondness for Bing Crosby, the house was alive with music and the used needle tray was usually overflowing. My cannon would hold a bunch of three or four, and I considered them to be a kind of grape-shot, which I knew about from stories of Gerard and Hornblower. These wouldn't carry as far as bits of pencil, nor would they knock tin soldiers over, but there was something gratifying about the glitter of the shower of needles as it sped across the room. In trying to demonstrate this aesthetic effect at the dinner table, I crammed my cannon full and fired it at random down the table. One needle bounced off the cheek of my nemesis and fell into his mashed potato. That stirred him into action and as I stood before him quivering with apprehension, he assailed me with the furious words I remember yet.

'Wretch. Imbecile. What are you playing at?'

'Me, sir. Why, sir. I don't know, sir.'

'Don't know! What do you think you're doing? Did it never occur to you what might happen – if one of these,' he held up the needle, 'had gone in someone's eye… What if one has fallen in someone's food and been swallowed…'

All eating at our end of the table ceased. Plates were pushed away. Dinner ladies quickly appeared and removed the dishes amidst angry murmurs, quieted only by the promise of fresh helpings.

'I didn't think…' I faltered.

'You didn't think!!!' he thundered.

He was right. I hadn't thought. I was an artillery man and only interested in the capability of my ordnance. I was like the rocket scientist in Tom Lehrer's song - "Once it goes up, who cares where it comes down?" A simple demonstration for a group of friends had turned into a disaster. It was as if a trap door had opened beneath me and I had fallen into another existence. The sun ceased to shine, friends became enemies and the horror of having unwittingly done something utterly unforgivable was thrust into my mind. I was immediately set apart at the end of the table where I became the focus of accusing eyes.

Mr Moreton, summoned from the staff dining table, came hurrying down the refectory like one of the horsemen of the Apocalypse without his horse. He tut-tutted at me and made me realise, more than my furious victim-captor, that what I had done was very serious indeed. His voice dropped to a hoarse whisper as he told me so.

'Very foolish, my boy. Quite stupid of you. Why! You might have been the cause of someone's death. Just think of what might have happened if Mr Ormerod, or anyone, had swallowed one of those needles'

'Someone's death'! The phrase struck me with the force of a blow. Death was final; death was the end; no more of anything. Grandma's empty room. My mother giving Aunt Dora's shoes to the Red Cross – 'She doesn't need them anymore.' I looked cautiously at my fellow diners to see which one of them I might be guilty of killing, but they were all avidly interested in the spectacle of me being killed.

They hadn't much time for gloating for I was swiftly taken from there to another place, my form room, and thence I was led to the place of execution: the High Master's study. Waiting to be sent for, I slowly realised the potential enormity of what I had done. I imagined what it might be like biting into something as soft and yielding as mashed potato and feeling the spike of a needle spearing my gums, sticking in my tongue, scratching my throat. Would I have felt it as it made its way through my stomach? Would it stick there and go rusty, or would it find its way out, or stay to form an obstruction, and eventually block everything up?

And what about me, fortunately as yet uninjured, but already doomed to punishment? Would I be handed over to some latter-day Smee and fed to the crocodile? The direst images from the darkest stories of masterly atrocities, retailed by the knowing lads on Bowker's, especially for the benefit of tiros like me, flashed on and off in my mind like a Belisha beacon. I thought of the Chateau d'If and the Count of Monte Cristo, images from *A Tale of Two Cities* floated through my mind. Was there a Bastille for boys? Would I be bundled off to Strangeways and put in the charge of Sammy Boliver's father? I wondered if I would be allowed to speak to them at home before sentence was carried out. In mitigation of what I'd done I might argue that I hadn't actually hurt anyone. I'd just been playing, showing my friends how well my cannon would shoot. I had no evil intent, I hadn't actually shot at anyone. Surely they must see that. As counsel for my own defence, I reasoned that what I'd done seemed trivial, I'd just fired my cannon across the refectory, and it hadn't actually hurt anybody. Surely they must see that. And I certainly wouldn't do it again. And the boys sitting next to me didn't see anything wrong in what I was doing....

However, the High Master thought differently, and when I appeared before him, he made me realise clearly what might have happened. Douglas Miller was a tall man with a lined face, surmounted by a thatch of silver hair and he seemed to tower above me. He spoke quietly and firmly and logically. Much of what he said was repeated by Mr Moreton, my father, my mother, and in the letter to my parents.

'When you throw a stone,' he said, 'you must first consider where it is likely to land. You say you 'didn't think'. One of the things you are here for is to learn how to think. You must bear it in mind that even the simplest of actions may have the direst of consequences. In this case, I expect you have already had spelled out to you what those consequences might have been.

Only one of those missiles which you so thoughtlessly loosed into an unsuspecting crowd has been found. We must hope that the others fell harmlessly. Time will tell. And till it does you might reflect on the harm you may have caused. If such comes to light, further penalties may be exacted. For the moment I am sending you to two Saturday morning schools. This afternoon I shall write to your father.'

This sentence, my punishment, was pronounced in mild tones that somehow did more to convince me of the gravity of my offence and the seriousness of what it might have led to, than anything else connected with the affair. And so, for the next two Saturdays, instead of lying in bed and reading, I rose and donned my school uniform and, without the comfort of my familiar travelling companions, made a strange, solitary journey to an empty school. There I sat with a couple of other malefactors and copied out the first chapter of Macaulay's *History of England*. It was a grievous time and for two whole weeks, the punishment hung heavily on me. It was small solace to reflect that I was relieved of queuing at the grocer's, or any of the other Saturday chores my mother had for me. But most of all, I bitterly regretted the loss of the confiscated cannon.

5. CLOTHES

It was in iβ that I got my first long trousers. New things to wear then were often only hand-me-downs which I got from my mother's friend's son, the hated Tom – now said to be 'doing quite well' in Upper 3c. He was two years ahead of me and in the growing time between ten and fourteen I came in for a lot of his cast-offs. I got his blazer, his school shirts and, what seemed to me the final indignity, his trousers. 'I've washed them twice,' said my mother, coaxing me into them, 'they're all right.' All right for her, I thought, but she didn't have to suffer his sneer when he saw what I was wearing. He didn't say anything, but just looked, knowingly. To prevent that, I would willingly have endured a month of Saturday shopping with my mother. After weeks of pestering, it was with unspeakable relief that I persuaded her that I needed some pants which hadn't been worn by someone else. Ignoring the expense of clothing coupons, themselves a high value currency, and avoiding Henry Barrie's – 'Too far and too expensive,' said my mother – we went to Burton's in Bolton on what turned out to be a quick and un-embarrassing operation. We left home at ten and were in Collinson's for coffee and cakes by eleven, after which it became a normal weekend.

My new trousers were too long and too baggy, but they were indisputably mine. They felt a bit odd after the tight, short shorts I had been wearing and I no longer needed to wear the knee stockings that always needed pulling up. I was proud of them for they were a definite step away from being just a "boy". Acquired with my development in mind, they now had to be turned up so they could be let down, and bunched in so they could be let out. They were a bit uncomfortable at first, but I was delighted by how quickly my body expanded and it seemed no time at all before there was a space between my turn-ups and my shoes. The green and white elastic belt with the snake clasp was to be abandoned for a proper leather belt with a proper buckle - one of Tom's - but since it was covered by my pullover, he couldn't see it. At first my new gear made me feel self-conscious and I expected the change to cause some comment at school, but it seemed that I was the only one aware of it. The class was divided about equally into longs and shorts, and the only person to remark on my new trousers was Logan who told me to pull them up a bit as I sat down. 'That stops them getting baggy at the knees,' he said.

Few people at school paid much attention to clothes. At home my mother and my cousins seemed to spend most of their spare time agonising over how to make do with what they had to wear. They were all talented seamstresses, altering old clothes, adapting what they could buy to suit their taste, making and mending. Frayed cuffs were turned on my father's jackets, leather patches were put on mine. Sheets were split and sewn sides to middle so the worn parts were at the edge. The one that was on my bed every other week had an uncomfortable seam running down the middle from pillow to foot. Despite the war ending, there were few signs of life getting 'back to normal', which was how grown-ups thought it ought to be. I marked the improvements in daily life, like the lifting of the Blackout, the end of Flying Bombs and Rockets, the end of casualty lists or bereavements. As far as clothes were concerned, I didn't miss what I never remembered having.

During the week I wore school uniform, school blazer, grey shirt, pullover, black lace-up shoes with the pattern of holes on the toe. Weekend and holiday wear was just as uniform, khaki shorts and aertex shirts with a pullover and sandals. There were no such things as leisure clothes for messing about in. During the Worsley days, when I was engaged in war-games with Caddy and McElvie, we purposely wore our oldest clothes which had already suffered much hard wear. We played on slag heaps and the spoil of the coal mines that had once been there. Crawling up such mounds to surprise the enemy machine gun posts made us so seriously dirty that from time to time we were forbidden to play there. Moving to Bolton, more than the allied victories, put an end to my war games and I had nothing to do in the evenings and at weekends but ride my bike and explore the long reach of the Irwell valley as it wound down to Radcliffe. As I grew out of shorts and aertex shirts, my trousers were let down and became baggy at the knees. They were worn at weekends and were replaced, as were the grey school shirts, when it became easier to get clothes and the era of austerity – another word redolent with the spirit of the times – receded and coupons dropped out of use.

In iα I was kitted out with cricket whites, complete with cable-knit pullover and socks. Boots were second hand, being still hard to come by. I was passionately fond of cricket and absolutely useless at it, but having the right gear somehow made up for my utter ineptitude. I oiled my bat, but it only ever seemed to be used in knockabouts at the nets. I spent hours bowling against a wall to get my length right, but when I managed to get an over in a proper game, I was quickly taken off. Albert Booth, the school coach, slow, left hand over the wicket, once top of the county cricket bowling averages, tried to help me, but in vain. There was something radically wrong with my action, and my co-ordination was all wrong. My father, a keen and expert cricketer, was saddened I guess by my inability to either bowl a length or keep a straight bat, but divining my love of the game, made me a junior member of Lancashire Cricket Club to which he had belonged since his student days. It was just in time for the Victory Tests, when I was entranced by the flashing bats of Hutton and Washbrook and Compton. Watching them was the provenance of my love for Old Trafford and the many afternoons I spent there. These increased in number and length as I went up the school and became bolder about ducking out, and eventually led to my being excluded from the club I felt MGS had become.

6. THE END OF THE WAR

Gradually hostilities lessened and the war drew to a close. The Allied armies raced for Berlin, over-running the bases from which the rockets were fired, and occupying those parts of the continent from which the mobile launchers could operate. The full horrors of the concentration camps were revealed, and also the pitiable state of life for those who lived in the bombed cities. A distasteful sense of vengeance permeated the national attitude. When there were newsreel pictures of bombs falling and cities devastated, like Cologne and Hamburg, there was almost a buzz of satisfaction in the cinema.

In the Spring of 1945 the Allied armies reached the concentration camps and disclosed the horrors of what had taken place there. First Auschwitz, then Belsen, then Dachau. I found it hard to comprehend what had gone on. I did not think such things could happen in real life but there they were, revealed by the pictures in the papers and the newsreels. I could barely tolerate the idea of such extreme suffering in fiction, let alone relate it to classmates and other known figures at school who had relations in the camps. David Cohen's elder brother, very clever, strongly eccentric, started to wear a skull cap and had a Star of David sewn on his shirt. For a while, every week seemed to reveal fresh atrocities, which together with the increasing horrors of Flying Bombs at home had the curious effect of devaluing religion. God, it seemed, was dead, so why continue to pray? The Crusaders, a proselytising group of what would now be called, 'committed Christians', were sorely beset and I remember someone asking what God was doing to let such things happen.

Our form's hard-pressed member said, 'Perhaps he thought we ought to suffer. After all, he did.'

'You mean he let it happen because he thought it would do us good?'

'Well, sort of.'

'So much for your God of mercy and forgiveness.'

This kind of thing did the cause of religion no good at all and seemed to many of us justification of the Allies' determination to reduce Germany's major cities to rubble.

The end of the war, when it came, seemed to be a giant anti-climax. People had become accustomed to believe that all their efforts must build up to the accomplishment of victory. When the moment came, it was registered with fireworks and bonfires, shouting and drinking and weeping but then life went on pretty much as it had before. But when the great day came, which was to bring floods of sweets and trees of bananas, butter and bacon, sugar and steaks, and all the goods we'd missed or been short of, what happened was that things got worse. The new government imposed more restrictions, shorter rations, more directives until my father said it was like living in an occupied country. At that time, I remember people being more crabby and discontented than at any time before, but then it may be that I was becoming more sensitive to what was going on around me.

A couple of incidents at this time served to bring me out of the cocoon of childhood and make me more aware of the world as it related to other people. The first was overhearing a row between my parents, not as an eavesdropper, but as someone who happened to be there when it happened. It was about money and my father's extravagance, and took place in the kitchen just after New Year's Day 1945, not long after he'd started his new job. It was the first time I ever saw him dumbfounded.

He had come down from the comfort of the sitting room to see how dinner was going on. My mother, in an apron, busy with the cooking, asked him curtly about their bank account. It is the tone of her voice that I remember, not what she said, for she was bitter and scornful in a way that I'd never heard before. It made me cringe. It seemed there were bills to be paid and not enough in hand to pay them, and she held him to blame. As I ran away to the sitting room I heard her say, 'If only you weren't so pig-headed, and left me to manage things…' He followed me shortly and slumped into his chair by the fire and said nothing. I avoided looking directly at him. He took up his book, but I could tell he wasn't reading.

The meal, which should have been special, was eaten almost in silence and shortly afterwards I went up to bed filled with a terrible foreboding. Poverty was something I'd only read about in Charles Reade and Dickens. I didn't want to be like David Copperfield. I wondered if I was I going to be sent out to work? Would Aunt Nan in Barrow be another Betsy Trotwood? I knew we were not rich and had been led to believe that money, though not to be sought above anything else, was too precious to be frittered away. But I had never imagined that we could be poor. More than our apparent lack of money, I feared the effects of my mother's anger and the apparent helplessness of my father in the face of it. Black thoughts of our imminent destitution haunted me for days. Hesitantly, I confided these worries to my cousin one morning as we travelled in to Manchester. 'Pooh,' she said, 'I shouldn't worry about it. It's just after Christmas. Everybody's hard up now.' And it was like the clouds breaking up after a rainy morning.

The second window that opened on the adult world came some months later. The war was drawing to a close yet no one seemed glad. The joyousness I expected to break out when the end was announced seemed as far away as ever. One Saturday morning my other cousin specially asked me to go with her to Manchester. 'It's to see Bill,' she said. 'You remember him? He came to stay one weekend and you liked him. He can't get out this weekend so I'm going to see him at his camp. Come and keep me company. On the way back we can go to the Kardomah for coffee and ice cream.' At first I demurred. I did remember Bill's visit. He was tall and gangling and impractical. He'd missed the train he should have caught and came by bus, so Betty, waiting at the station, found that he was not on the next one, either. It was only by great good luck that she found him in time to stop him going back to Manchester. He was only a corporal, so everyone pushed him around, but he was what we called 'nice', which meant he was pleasant and friendly and thought about other people. Betty was right. I had liked him, but not enough to sacrifice a Saturday morning for, so I demurred again, but she was persuasive and persisted and eventually we went.

I found it odd to be travelling in the train in my weekend clothes and not be going to school. From Piccadilly we took a bus through streets and streets of drab houses until we reached its terminus in the middle of a large housing estate. From here we walked to a park much like Birch Fields and similarly surrounded by a high wire fence. Standing behind it was Bill, looking as if he'd been there since dawn. 'Wait here,' said my cousin, 'I'm just going to talk to him.' I watched her cross the road fumbling in her bag as she went and standing close up against the wire. They only talked for a moment then she walked briskly away, not looking back, not breaking her stride when she reached me. 'Come along,' she said.' It's ice-cream time.' I stumbled after her, glancing over my shoulder at Bill, who had slumped down against the wire with his head between his knees. 'Bill's fallen down,' I said. But she strode on, bright eyed, gazing steadily ahead, almost leaving me behind. 'But Bill…' I said. 'Perhaps he's hurt…' She was quite well ahead of me now and I'd to run a few steps to catch up. 'But Bill…' I began again. 'Oh shut up,' she said. 'Shut up, do.' I could see tears on her cheeks as she stepped fiercely out as though forcing her way into a new life and determined to stamp out a memory.

Later in the Albert Square Kardomah over coffee and cake – the promised ice-cream was 'off' – she said, looking straight at me. 'It had to be. That's all. It just had to be. And if you tell anyone about it I'll kill you. I really will. But thanks for coming. You're a brick.' I could tell how upset she was for her eyes were still bright and the tip of her nose looked red and raw as though she'd been squeezing the drops from the end of it.

The memory of her artificial brightness as she hurried away from that slumped khaki figure daunted me and, like the row between my parents, it made too great an impression on me to remain quiet about it. Despite the threat of what would happen, I again sought comfort with my other cousin as we travelled on the morning train. After Clifton Junction when the Exide workers got out, we had the compartment to ourselves and my story lasted the rest of the journey. Walking up Bridge Street she gave her view with a long sigh. 'Betty's always getting herself into scrapes like this. It's her romantic nature. She never knows when to say "no".' I wasn't much worried about Betty but 'What about Bill?' I thought. And for weeks, off and on, I wondered about him and what he'd done after we left, and whether Betty, now with a Yankee pilot, ever thought about him again.

7. Iα

My birthday is towards the end of the academic year and in iβ I was the youngest in the form. In view of this it was deemed good that I repeat and so I began my second year in the main school in iα. Bozo Hindley was my new form master and I remember little of him compared with what I recall of Simkins or Artie Moore, which is hardly surprising because he disappeared to another job at the end of my first term. He was dark and handsome in a boyish-manly way, much like the principal characters of stories in *The Wizard* and *The Rover.* These were very much Biggles figures, capable of succeeding in any circumstances, and without being flashy. It was rumoured that Bozo was, or had been, a considerable sportsman, and I could well imagine him striding out to the crease to prop up a collapsing innings, or coming on to bowl the last and crucial over of the match. Now, I see that he must have been something of an oddity, as a young member of a staff of oldies, for comparatively, he was a teenager amongst grown-ups. At that time, most men below the age of forty were in uniform of one colour or another, and Bozo should have been a dashing pilot or a gay lieutenant, but he seemed just a slightly untidy, tweed-jacketed, newly-graduated junior master. He could have been another Paul Pennyfeather, escaped from Llanabba Castle, or someone captured by Gabbitas and Thring to fill one of their vacancies.

Lessons with him were fun, loud and boisterous, with much chanting of paradigms – hic haec hoc being performed as though it were a nonsense poem of two verses with five lines each. It didn't mean much to us at the time, but he assured us it would constitute an essential store of knowledge without which we 'wouldn't get anywhere'.

It was around this time that I was much concerned with the upheaval of the move to Bolton and ceasing to belong to the fellowship of Bowker's as I adjusted to new ways of getting to school. Furthermore, although it hardly affected us lowly first formers, High Master Miller – at the mention of whose name I still trembled – was replaced by Dr Eric James, whom I heard described as 'a whizz-kid from Winchester', which I only knew of then as the site of the Round Table. Furthermore, my move from iβ to iα had put me in a new form which was composed entirely of strangers who were mainly hostile.

In the midst of these preoccupations Bozo had ceased to figure in the affairs of my school life. As far as I was concerned he just disappeared. He was there just long enough to make a deep impression and then he was suddenly gone. A new form master took over and it was Easter before I realised that a definite change had taken place. Unthinking, un-inquisitive, used to being disposed of by powers beyond my ability to influence, I took the change to be just another aspect of the new life I was becoming accustomed to. Like a slave in the galleys, I suppose, I didn't bother much about who strode the gangways wielding the whip, or where we were going, my only function being to keep rowing.

So sudden had been his departure that there were rumours Bozo had done away with himself and I was at a loss to comprehend what had happened. Until recently, sudden and violent death had not been an unusual occurrence, and for Bozo to die after the end of the war seemed some kind of anomaly. However he'd just gone to work in Glasgow, which might, just then, have been an improvement on Manchester. We lived in an atmosphere of violence. Bombs and bullets had made life a chancy business, and scarcely a week would pass but news would come of the death of some known figure. None of our family had been affected, but in the days when I travelled on Bowker's and was party to what was going on in a much wider spectrum of school life, whispered reports that 'something had happened' to so and so's father, brother, neighbour, were commonplace. With the previous summer's celebrations of VE and VJ days, I thought we had said goodbye to all that, but now, in Peace Time – a phrase that had encapsulated all that we were looking forward to – the old Antic was still here, and once more the youths of Arcadia were brought face to face with the tomb. However, Bozo's case was not as drastic as we had supposed, for he had merely gone to another job. But as somebody remarked at the time, as far as we were concerned he might just as well have been dead.

In iα we had science lessons with Mrs Grindley, whom we regarded with schoolboy disdain. Those of us with memories of the Prep Department were most affronted, perhaps because we thought we'd got beyond being taught by women. Our status then, as junior juniors, was made clear on Bowker's by a majestic sixth former who used to sweep us aside as he made his way to the front of the queue, saying, 'These little chaps from the Dame School must come out of a man's way.' Mrs Gaskill and Miss Robins were a proper schoolmistressy age, which was something between eighty and a hundred and twenty. But Mrs Grindley was young and pretty, as some of us allowed, and she didn't seem to be much older than my cousin Sylvia who had just gone to University. She spoke in that clear, decisive way that I associated with bossy big girls from boarding schools. Two of such used to summer near us in the Lakes, when I played with their brothers whom they routinely persecuted. Me, they treated as Estella treated Pip at Miss Havisham's.

Mrs Grindley didn't persecute us, but she made clear her disappointment that we were missing great opportunities by not giving her our full attention. She desperately wanted us to be enthusiastic about amoebas and the parts of plants, which we had to draw and label, and photosynthesis, which we couldn't. What we did in her once-a-week lessons was deal with actual objects, which was quite different from what we did with other teachers, except in Art or Woodwork. In a perverse sort of a way we were prepared to memorise vocabulary and lists of irregular verbs and recite their principal parts, but not to learn about the calyx or stamens or pistils, though the names made us snigger. It was as though we sensed a difference between the mental and the physical and felt that our business was with the affairs of the mind rather than the raw material of the real world, which we paradoxically believed in.

The Science Department was at the Birchfields Road end of the school and did not seem to be an integral part of the main building. It was almost as though it had been tacked on to the kitchens and Refectory to fill in a little area of land that was left over from the main plan. Once a week we left the familiar corridor where most of our lives were spent, and trekked along the cloisters and past the Refectory to this strange region of laboratories and demonstration rooms. Here in the unfamiliar surroundings of a science lab we sat on stools at benches, which had sinks at the end and gas taps at intervals along the outside edge. The rooms were cold and echoed and always smelled strange. Instead of a gown, Mrs Grindley wore a white lab coat which someone christened her dressing gown, adding, 'I'll bet she's got nothing on underneath.' Creatures of our time, the thought of nudity excited us to laughter rather than lust.

What we did know, even then, was that science had nothing to do with the main business of our lives. That, we knew, was with Latin and French, English History and Maths. Geography we had learned for one lesson a week from Toby Cantrell, a peppery Scotsman with a ginger moustache who was subject to sudden fits of rage which paralysed my mind so I couldn't learn anything. Science, Woodwork, Art were peripheral, too. In iiiα we would start to learn Greek and that would take up all the time now spent on these subjects. Mrs Grindley knew this, too, but nevertheless she persevered, though, I fancy, at times we almost drove her to tears. We had, no doubt, been represented to her as a bright lot, capable of great things, for after all, we were the seed corn from which the school's fine academic reputation was grown. We were generally well behaved, despite the opportunities for mischief in a Science Lab, always polite and submissive to a degree that might be taken for torpor. I can visualise now, a row of propped heads along the bench, half listening, scrawling on the edges of our books, glancing at the time and strangling yawns into the merest of grimaces as she pleaded with us to be interested in frogs' legs.

Like Woodwork and Art, of which we also had a lesson a week, Science was a sort of game. In Woodwork, we struggled to make a joint with tools we never became familiar with, and all I remember is the untimely discharge of the Fire Extinguisher. Of Art, in the light, airy Art Room over the archway leading into the Main Quad, I remember the light coming from above, an interesting clutter of pots and busts and paintings on easels, and an easy affable air that encouraged you to be inventive. I was no good at drawing, writing was my trade, and I struggled to show shapes by shadows. Despite my utter inadequacy, our mentor, Mr Tunnicliffe – C.F., no less – had become a friend. We talked about the country and fishing, goldcrests and why I called marigolds gollans. He would watch me working, shake his head and sigh at my efforts. 'I don't know, Davidson, why you can't do it. Perhaps if you tried with the other hand...'

It was about this time that the school was favoured with a visit from Field Marshal Montgomery. We all knew of him as the general with two badges in his hat, the hero of El Alamein, vanquisher of Rommel and commander of the Desert Rats. We understood that his principal enemies had been the Americans and that left to him the war would have been over months earlier. To mark this special occasion, the whole school was paraded in the Memorial Hall for his inspection.

As one of the first formers seated on the first row of the steps I had a close view of the slight figure of the great man as he followed the Chief – as we had come to call the new High Master – onto the platform. I thought such an august figure ought to have been a much bigger man. Generals, in those days, were like footballers. Their names and battles were reported week by week. We followed their progress as their armies fought up Italy and then went across France. There was much patriotic antagonism against the Americans. Eisenhower, Bradley and Patton were seen as so many bunglers who got in the way of our men, who could have won the war much quicker. Monty, in particular, seemed to have been done down for the top job after D-day, when it was popularly supposed that he would have driven straight to Berlin. This, at least was the view of my father's friend, Jack Bamford, who was a farmer and took his news from the *News Chronicle*.

As a boy brought up in wartime, I felt that something of military glory should emanate from so notable a figure. Here was the man who had stemmed the advance of the German army and won a battle that, according to Mr Churchill – another of our household gods – proved the turning point of the war. I had seen pictures of him with other allied generals accepting the German surrender. And here he was on the platform of the Memorial Hall, a slim figure in a loose fitting uniform with nothing about him to suggest that he was already a part of History.

I can't remember much of what he said – something about his school days at St Paul's where they also had a High Master, something about working hard and playing hard and making sure that we were right with God, at least I think that's what he said. I couldn't be sure because we were behind him. But I did hear him say that it was his right as a visitor to ask for the school to be given a half holiday to commemorate his visit. At which we dutifully cheered and the Chief smiled, a reluctant half-hearted smile that suggested he had known what was coming. As he left the platform Monty looked round at the small boys who had been behind him on the steps. I was almost at the end of the first row and he caught my eye, piercingly. It was a keen, knowing look and I quailed before it – at least I think I did.

8. MORNING BREAK

At morning break there was milk in the Refectory. In the winter of 1947, which seemed to go on for ever, I would hurry down there, through the open cloisters, past the Lecture Theatre and the Late Boys entry to the shuttered counters where the still dormant Tuck Shop was. Off the empty Dining Hall in part of the kitchen, crates of milk in third-of-a-pint bottles were there for the taking. On sunny mornings a cheerful yellow light flooded the open spaces between the tables. There was a heartening smell of cooking and the warmth from the ovens made it a pleasant place to be. The milk was icy-cold but I found it comforting. I felt it did me good, and the bottles in their crates reminded me of the dairy at home in the Lakes. We were encouraged to use straws, boxes of which stood on the tables but straws were cissie so we picked out the cardboard stoppers, using the hole provided for the straw, and drank straight from the bottle.

It was now the only place where I might expect to meet Caddy or McElvie. They were strange meetings, for we never had anything to say to each other. Too young to know how to make small talk and still in the cocoon of our private worlds, we would share a companionable silence. Usually I was on my own by the wall, leaning against a radiator, always a prized station, watching what was going on for the five minutes or so it took to drink my milk. It was an odd time, characteristic of many such at school when I felt I was just filling in, preparing for the real living which would come when I had finished being prepared. Only just now, I was just hanging about, waiting for more preparation.

Morning milk in the refectory attracted a regular and recognisable clientèle and I mixed there with boys I didn't meet at any other time. We shared a sort of camaraderie, a bit like the travellers on Bowker's, united by an experience not shared with the rest of the school. When we passed in the corridors, a raised eyebrow or a wink acknowledged our connection. The kitchen ladies made jokes with us – 'Spotted Dick, terday, lads. That'll stick te yer ribs.' – 'Oh no! Not that again! After the last lot I couldn't go for a week.' – 'Ah well, thes movin juice in this, so ye'll be all right.' Mrs Bedford, large and imposing in a white overall, would come down from the kitchen and urge us to put our empty bottles back in the crates. 'Tidy up, boys!

Tidy up! Save my girls a job.' She would encourage us to have another bottle, for there was always plenty to spare. 'Do you good. And it's a pity to send this lot back.'

In the spring, as the snow receded and the sun was warm enough to wipe the rime off the playing fields, a craze spread for competitive milk drinking. I was generally satisfied with one bottle, especially in the cold weather, but some boys regularly drank two or three, or four even, as an act of bravado. It was not time yet for proper drinking contests, like 'Boat Races' and 'Cardinal Puff', which we would encounter in our first year at college. Drink in its alcoholic sense figured little, I guess, in the lives of most of us. For a start, it was in 'short supply' – our Yankee weekend visitors, figures from a Welfare Scheme my mother belonged to, were welcomed especially because they brought lots with them – furthermore, the licensing laws not only restricted drinking times but absolutely banned under-eighteens from pubs. As a child, I daren't so much as set a foot over the threshold of the Blacksmith's Arms in search of Dot, but had to go round the back, or shout her name through the doorway.

The drinking competitions aroused much interest and were approved, if not encouraged, by Mrs Bedford who noticed the increasing number of empties. Quite suddenly rumours spread about super drinkers, chaps who could sink six or seven bottles and still stay upright. I knew one of these champions as a boy with bright red hair and an aggressive manner. He was a head taller than most of us, cocksure and loud, with the nick-name of Coppernob. His rival, part friend, part antagonist, was known as Caz and was always egging him on to a match.

'Wessy did five, yesterday - without drawing breath,' he would say. 'You should have been here, Copper.'

Copper would bluster, 'Wessy's nothing. Five's nothing. Do that standing on me head.'

'Drinkin' upside down, then?'

'While riding mi bike.'

'Wessy says he can drink five, easy.'

'Huh! I'll bet. Drink more'n 'im anytime. Drink more'n you, anyway.'

'Ses you.'

'Try me.'

'Drop dead, Cop. You aven't a chance.'

'It'll be hard cheese for you, Caz, if I tek you on.'

And so on, and so on, and so on. Coppernob and Caz were adepts at the game. There was no comfortable end to such exchanges. The contestants carried on a kind of verbal potlatch, expending their sharpest and most elaborate insults until one stepped down or a challenge was made or in extreme cases a blow was struck. Barbarians that we were, we had no notion of negotiating, side-stepping or simply walking away from a situation that didn't really allow for a winner.

There was always a group of boys round this pair, almost as if they were recognised as contending champions. They stood together, stolidly, like rocks at the edge of the tide, while other boys flowed into the kitchen, round them and past them. Parties of three or four blue-blazered figures would push through to the tables and then recede with bottles of milk held against their chests, only to be met by fresh waves taking back their empties. I was usually alone, thankful for the peace and the freedom it offered to be just me, with my milk against my radiator, which was not only warm, but a good place to see what was going on.

Standing there one day I watched Coppernob goading Caz into a contest. Above the hum of general conversation, their voices were loud and indistinct but at a pitch to make people look up. They were standing opposite each other, between them a crate of milk, and it was clear that something was up. Spectators, more than usual, were offering advice and encouragement. Caz was standing four-square and challenging; Copper, yapping loudly but clearly on the defensive, held a half-empty bottle in front of him, almost as if it offered some protection. CA's bottle was empty.

'Seven,' he said.

There was a lull as Copper swallowed, then excited chatter as they each took another bottle. Then another lull, followed by more advice, more bickering, more cries of encouragement. Caz took a swig.

'Go on!' he said, 'you've hardly started yours.'

Mrs Bedford, cruising down from the far end of the kitchen, broke through the circle just as Caz, staring triumphantly at Coppernob, downed his eighth. There were shouts of amazement. Copper, ginger hair drooping, bent over the half-full bottle in his hands. He was pale and panting, gulping air. Caz held out his bottle, upside down.

'Eight!' he said. 'Beat that!'

9. THE CHIEF

Dr Eric James, the new High Master, was a slight but impressive figure. Billed as a hot-shot scientist from Winchester College, he was thought to be young for the job and there was much speculation about how a smooth, southern scientist would go on amongst a crowd of rough northern classicists. The Chief – I never heard him called anything else in school – presented himself to the whole school at his first morning assembly. Unlike his predecessor who had customarily led a stately procession to the dais, he appeared as a slim vigorous figure with aquiline features and billowing gown marching briskly into the hall, with the staff running and stumbling after him. Mounting the platform he turned to face the whole school, his school, for the first time, and there was a moment's silence when both sides looked each other in the eye. It was a significant moment. Immediately after prayers he made his mark by rising from his seat to quell the hubbub which customarily broke out as the masters left the hall. From then on, the school dispersed from assembly in a decorous hush, if not an absolute silence.

Under the Chief, Morning Assembly from 9.30 to 9.45 became more of a secular gathering than a religious service. We sang a hymn, one of the prefects read a lesson, then there were five minutes of school notices. During this time, the Chief sat back in his chair in the middle of the platform, and watched his school. From time to time he would address us about the present political situation as it affected education, or the distasteful amount of litter round the newly opened tuck-shop, or something he'd read recently and enjoyed. Under his direction, the school flourished, and became the cynosure of academic excellence. Frequent articles in the serious press and appearances on radio and television made him a public figure who laid down the way education should develop. We were proud of him, and as he entered the Hall after some public honour – it wasn't his knighthood, for that was in 1956 – the whole school rose and applauded him to his seat.

Occasionally he would harangue us about bad behaviour, both in and out of school. With many of us making considerable journeys into school there was much opportunity for malfeasance. From time to time, those who travelled from Victoria Station on the such and such to somewhere would be commanded to stay behind for a special investigation, travellers to Rochdale and Littleborough being especially prone to such inquisitions. I was once interrogated about a snowball fight when the Rochdale lads – always a rough bunch who departed from the platform next to mine – pelted the Station Master as he made a run for his office.

The Chief quickly established himself as a familiar figure, striding about the school and the playing fields, gown flapping, talking to people as he met them. Usually on these walkabouts, he was affable in an authoritarian way, ending his chats with some advice or instruction. I was one of a group he came across kicking a ball against a newly painted door. It was what we did when there wasn't enough of us for a proper kick-about. 'Yes, I know, you've been doing it for weeks,' he said, as we offered the excuse of custom and use, 'but you ought to have seen that it was newly painted. You'll all go to PS for two nights next week. What form are you in? Two alpha! Goodness gracious! I'd have expected more sense. I've a good mind to make it three nights.' And he went his way without bothering to take our names confident that we would turn up for our punishment.

We first met, as man to man, so to speak, the Chief and I, when I was in iiiα. The autumn edition of *Ulula* had printed a nostalgic essay I'd written about the Lake District, yearning for the fells and the becks, the sights and sounds of home. The piece was a simple description of a summer evening, the sights and sounds of my valley as it settled down for the night. I'd written it to cheer myself up in the middle of the autumn term, fed up with town and feeling marooned. Writing, almost as much as reading, was a frequent resort at such times. Later, it had served as a homework essay, and my English master had passed it on, without my knowledge, to the editor of *Ulula*. I remember the shock when I saw my name in print at the foot of column of words which I had actually written. I had scarcely recovered when the Chief sent for me.

My piece had taken his fancy and in mid-morning he sent his secretary to fetch me out of class. Her arrival in the middle of a maths lesson was a heart-stopping moment in a passage of high drama, for I was already being grilled by Ernie Cropper about a late homework and some unproduced lines. She spoke to him quietly and in a way that made him start. He shot me a sharp look. 'I gather I've been superseded by a higher authority,' he said, in a way that suggested I'd really got my come-uppance. 'The Chief would like to speak to Davidson.' And with a courtly wave he ushered the pair of us out of the room. Relieved to be rescued from the lions' den, but terrified by the prospect of the fiery furnace, I trailed her, white-faced, along the corridor past the cloakrooms. With memories of my last visit to the High Master's study, I could only fear the worst. 'It's all right,' she said, sensing my unease. 'You're not on the mat. It's something nice. He's pleased with you.' I couldn't for the life of me think why.

In the presence, I was overwhelmed with relief and flattered to be congratulated. It was always a pleasure to talk about the place I regarded as home and find a fellow lover of it. He too had strong and affectionate feelings about the region, having spent much time in Ambleside while he was courting his wife who then had something to do with Charlotte Mason College. He had walked up most of the fells, knew the lakes and had spent much time in the Duddon valley which was right next to ours. 'It's a magical place' he said. 'You must keep on writing about it. You never know what it might lead to.' He sent me back to class, glowing. The piece won me the *Ulula* prize, but more important discovered for me the Chief's love of Lakeland. After that, whenever we met about the school, he would stop and chat about the Lakes.

10. IIα **AND SIMKINS**

I found Simkins formidable but friendly. Whatever it was, he knew about it and could explain it in a quiet, logical way. He was strict but scrupulously fair and severe without being frightening – unlike Tommy Stott whom I found frightening without being severe – being able to punish you in a friendly sort of way. I thought he was a bit like Gentleman Starkey in *Peter Pan* who was 'once an usher in a public school and still dainty in his ways of killing'. Simkins was known to be 'all right', from the way he behaved when he was out of school at Camp and on Trek. Too old to have been 'called up' – another phrase redolent of the times – he nevertheless seemed quite youthful, an impression strengthened by my seeing him cycling into school. There was something scoutmaster-ish about him and I could well imagine him to be most himself when striding about camp in khaki shorts and a bush hat – which was, in fact, how I found him one summer when there was a camp in the Duddon valley and I cycled over the fell to visit it.

One term he set us to collect Bun pennies for him. These were the big bronze coins first issued in 1860 to replace the old copper currency, and they showed Queen Victoria with her hair in a bun. They were also known as Honolulu pennies, because the reverse side showed Britannia with her trident apparently resting 'on her lulu'- a joke that even the staidest of my Scottish aunts laughed at. Simkins aimed to have a good specimen from each year until 1894, when the image became that of a veiled Dowager. He set a tariff for coins of different years and varying conditions, so a penny from an unexceptional year in an ordinary condition was worth tuppence; those from special years or in a good state could be worth twice or three times as much. There were still lots of these pennies in circulation and since nearly all of us came to school by bus, there were ample opportunities to acquire lots of small change. There were special prices for those in fine condition and from rare years which were, I think, 1869, '70 and '71. There was the equivalent of a golden fleece for the rarest of all, which was 1882. Every morning for a term, five minutes or so was given over to money changing.

After haggling we turned to Latin grammar and vocabulary, irregular verbs and the fourth declension, Kennedy's mnemonics: Ante, apud, ad, adversus, circum, circa, citra, cis ... These, added to the paradigms we chanted with Bozo Hindley, enabled us to work though the exercises in Hillard and Botting and eventually struggle through Latin proses. Simkins was the school's foremost classical scholar, in charge of the Classical Sixth where, we were led to believe, the School's real scholars were to be found. In teaching iiα he was spying out and bringing on those who would later do him credit by winning the open scholarships. We were all thoroughbreds, I guess, or we wouldn't have been in his stable, but it was his training that brought on the winners. As a teacher he didn't have the verve of Bozo, but rather a steely determination to see that we all did our best. The second rate was not allowed. He once had a drive to improve our punctuation which was expressed in the formula: -2 FS = 1 PS. Its application resulted in three quarters of the form ending up in Punishment School one night. After which the rule was applied no more.

Our form room was our base, to which we returned at break and lunchtime; generally left open for us, it was a valued refuge. Possession of it was a privilege, granted and withdrawn according to relations with the form master. To be excluded was to be cast into a cold and windy desert. A circuit of the upper corridor any lunchtime would show which happy forms enjoyed the luxury of somewhere warm and comfortable to sit, and which were evicted into a malebolge of restless brooding, discontented figures, like Johnny Lingard's U3c, hunched over their bags under the windows or leaning against radiators that were only ever lukewarm. Like damned souls they wandered about during the breaks, clutching their belongings and hunching down in the bays that were half-way along the corridors. There was one such outside iiα's form room, and on wet days in winter it made me think of newsreels showing displaced persons huddling in discomfort over the remains of their belongings.

Our desks were our only private and personalised spaces. A few cautious, mistrustful, derided bodies fitted them with locks, and sometimes lost the key. I remember the general glee when Logan was punished for failure to hand in homework which was locked in his desk, or so he said. At the right hand corner of each desk was an inkwell though, even at that time, few boys used pens with nibs that might be dipped into it. The days of the ink monitor – such as we heard about in *Vice Versa* – had ended, I guess, with the move from Long Millgate, but the inkwells remained, unused, perhaps simply as evidence of progress, signs of better things. Nevertheless, the inkwells often contained ink, which was used to consolidate blotting paper into ink pellets that could be flipped across the room. Once, after a rain-storm flooded the basement, we dyed the water blue by dropping all the inkwells into it – a minor act of vandalism for which Simkins gymshoed everyone who had been in the room at the time. It took him twenty minutes.

As was proper to our standing as nicely behaved middle-class boys, with fathers who were members of a profession, we had fountain pens, Parkers, Watermans, Swans, items now that are collectors' pieces. These were often rewards for having passed the entrance exam. Our pens were filled at home, or at least from our own personal supply. Mine was purple now, almost magenta – the green ink having run out in iβ – and this made the corrections less obvious.

But even then, the days of fountain pens were drawing to a close. Already the smart guys, the ones with connections in America, or relatives bringing booty home from the war, were using new, 'inkless' pens called Biros. The same sort of progress that slowly replaced the portable Remington with the stationary Amstrad and the Amstrad with the portable laptop, made fountain pens redundant in the years after the war. Along with nylon shirts, whose dazzling whiteness they indelibly stained, Biros were the latest products of the New World and were seen as further benefits of our American alliance, although they came from the Argentine. Used in the war by fliers, because they didn't leak at high altitudes, they wrote for weeks rather than days. My father had been very enthusiastic about one our Yankee visitors brought. 'Start of a new era, boy,' he said. 'The end of ink.' Certainly it seemed so for they were pencils that wrote like pens. But like pencils, they were not amenable to fine penmanship. Thus, an art in itself, generally taken as a mark of scholarship, was passed over and forgotten in less than a generation. No longer was writing used as a guide to character, a medium capable of expressing more than the message itself. It came to be seen simply as an instrument of communication that was as characterless as typeface.

It was a decade or more before Bics became the universal writing tool. The Biro my father had, and which I was sometimes allowed to borrow, was as thick as the cheroots he smoked and almost as long. Writing with it was quite different from using a pen, where the angle of the nib was important. You held the first Biros upright and they glided across the paper, leaving a featureless scrawl interrupted by blotches. At least, it was so with me. 'Fads of the moment,' Simkins said, holding one up in disgust. 'In five years' time, they'll be forgotten.' But they were much easier to keep and use than pens, whose nibs were sharp and liable to bend, or fountain pens that could break quite easily in the grabbing, free-holding, wrestling hurly-burly of twelve-year old schoolboy life. At first there was much opposition to them at school where rules were framed to hamper their use. They were not to be used for homework. Tests and exams were always to be written out in pen and ink.

When Simkins was upbraiding the form for some collective misdemeanour, like bringing our coats into the form room instead of using the cages outside the Memorial Hall or packing our things up before the bell went, I often used to wonder whether he was really annoyed or just amused. His eyes seemed to be sparkling behind his rimless spectacles and a grin to be hovering at the corners of his mouth. I felt this was born of a kind of affection for us and that even at that stage, we were his boys, and he was preparing us for the Oxbridge Schols, even if we didn't become classicists. We knew, from him – if we didn't know it before – that our founder, Hugh Oldham, was a considerable benefactor of Oxford's Corpus Christi College, founded two years after MGS by his friend Bishop Fox, the former Bishop of Exeter. He told us of closed scholarships there for MGS boys – 'Plums for the picking,' I remember him saying. The reputation of the school derived from its Classical scholarship, and we must realise, that as well as providing us with a liberal education in the Humanities, our studies were also designed to equip us for Oxford and Cambridge, where honour and glory were to be won. Under the Chief the school became noted for the number of its Oxbridge Scholars, vying with Eton for the most and the best in English academia.

11. REPORTS

A regular cause of tension was the presentation of the Fortnightly List, which ranked us all in order of achievement if not merit. Thus we knew who was top and who was bottom and where the rest of us stood in between. Although it was called the Fortnightly List, in effect it was compiled about once a month, so together with the end of term report we had three separate statements each term of how we were doing. A couple of poor homework marks could cause a drop of six or seven places and a bout of serious work a corresponding rise. The marks were collected in class as our names were called so we all had a running notion of how we were doing. There was a little grid at the bottom of our Timetable cards where our position in the

List was entered and a space for a parental signature to show that it had been seen at home.

I assumed this system encouraged competition, by showing how you were doing compared with your peers. It chiefly showed who was working and who was not. As one whose application to the work in hand varied considerably from day to day I worried about the way the lists were interpreted at home. I was average bright and usually managed to stay about the middle without much effort, coasting along at fourteenth or fifteenth out of twenty-eight. Once after a short period of idleness I dropped into the twenties and got into so much trouble that I buckled to and got into the top ten. The three or four swots who hogged the top places took it very badly if they slipped. I remember one breaking into tears because he he'd gone from second to fourth. As I became more aware of the way these systems worked I realised that the really clever chaps, the ones who later got Open Scholarships and took Firsts, only worked as much as was necessary and were content to fill the places between eighth and the early teens.

The End of Term Reports were issued separately on special forms and included the form master's comments – 'I don't mind him wasting his own time, but I object to him wasting mine,' that sort of thing. They were fearsome documents, which in those outspoken days gave our masters opportunity to indulge their fancy in potted biographies of those who had troubled them during the past term. I was nearly always surprised by the revelation in these Reports of how much my masters knew about me. 'Tends to live in a world of his own,' Simkins wrote, implying that this was a fault. 'How does he know?' I wondered. 'I do my best in the world he inhabits. How does he know that I go back to my own when I've finished in his?' 'Established contact with him once, this term, I think,' was another remark that took some explaining. 'What do they mean?' said my mother. 'When you leave here in the morning do you go on to another planet?' And in many ways I did. Life, I felt, was compartmentalised into different existences. There was the journey to school for a start, that sent me into another world. Lunchtimes were in another compartment, and quite separate from schooltimes. The weekends were makeshift holidays, rehearsals for the real ones when I would go home to the Lakes, where the real living took place.

Nevertheless, I felt I fared well in the atmosphere of school where I thought I was being smoothed without being in any way made into a smoothie, which was a type to be despised. It was a kind of academic smoothness, which took pride in being right and winning, in a way that didn't make the losers feel at a loss. It wasn't a triumphant, 'There, I'm better than you,' so much as, 'This is the way to do it.' MGS didn't allow much sloppy thinking or loose talking - 'I don't doubt your ability to sharpen your pencil, Davidson. The question is whether I will allow you to do so.' At Fortnightly List times, when Simkins read out the marks and the rank he would accompany them with ad hoc homilies, which could be flattering or scarifying. Eyes sparkling behind his spectacles, a grin sketched in the creases of his chin, he would allow himself a little out-of-school familiarity. 'In this month's race, the leaders have changed places. Todd and Robinson have slipped and Scaife, spying a gap in the ruck, has come through to take first place. Burkhardt has dropped a few notches and Bedson has crept up. Not much change amongst the laggards – all the usual suspects there, taking it easy.'

It was always an uncomfortable time when the lists were read out. Even those of us who didn't take them seriously were forced to consider that they might be important. My parents clearly did. But since there was rarely thirty marks difference between the top and the bottom, it seemed that we had all done rather well. The ethos of the school permitted and even encouraged a great deal of individualism in those who worked hard and enthusiastically at almost anything. We were expected to make our best efforts and it was assumed that we would learn, and consequently know, and thence be able to think for ourselves.

I first became aware that going to Oxford was something to be aimed at while I was in iiα. Returning from a visit to our relations in Kent we drove through Oxford and I remember the broad sweep of the High Street with colleges on both sides. At Carfax tower we turned right, then there were more colleges along St Giles. 'One day you may go to college here,' said my father. We stopped outside the *Eagle and Child* to buy some sweets and a newspaper, then we drove north up the Banbury Road. His casually dropped remark – was it casual? – stuck in my mind. (Much, much later, when I told this story to my adolescent sons, they said it was just what I'd told them as we were driving past Strangeways Gaol.) I'd already noted in my reading that virtually anyone who was anyone was an 'Oxford man', but it hadn't occurred to me that I might become one too. Leaving Oxford, we drove on up the A5 to Stone where we had brown Windsor soup that tasted of fish.

Impressed as I was by my father's words, at the time I was more interested in the colleges themselves. I liked the look of the high walls of honey-coloured stone, fretted with lancet windows and interrupted by huge oak doors. The domes and towers and half-glimpsed courts seemed to exude a sense of leisured ease. I had just read Lamb's essay on "Oxford in the

Vacation" and fallen for his evocation of a drowsy atmosphere of intellectual luxury engendered by the quiet streets, old buildings, cavernous bookshops and an immense sense of privilege. I decided shortly after that it was the place for me.

My father, himself a graduate of the Manchester University Medical School, would talk about Glasgow University, the oldest in the realm, where his brother and their father had been students. With justifiable Scottish pride he would mention John Balliol who left there in about 1260 with a chest of his wife's money, and travelled to Oxford to found the college that still bears his name. We'd looked for it as we drove through, half expecting the colleges to have signs saying which was which. But then as now, they proudly preserved their anonymity, and we slid past Balliol, not knowing that most of it was rebuilt in the 1860s in the style of Victorian Railway Gothic, causing one observer to remark, 'C'est magnifique, mais ce n'est pas la gare.'

In the sixth form we used to argue about the merits of the different colleges in the two Universities we were aiming for. Some clever fortunates who were offered places in both would balance Merton against King's, Magdalen against Clare. These blasé dismissals and confident recommendations bemused me, made as they were by aspiring scholars with the scantiest knowledge of these places.

'Downing!' said Hardy, his voice rising scornfully, 'Downing! No one goes to Downing. They say it's the first college you come to, but the last one you go to.'

'But what about Leavis?' said Johnson, a rabid fan of its most contentious don.

'You don't have to go to his college to hear his lectures.'

We were insufferably precious in these matters. One chap winning an Open Scholarship to Durham was regarded as being inveterately second-rate.

12. LUNCHTIMES

The Refectory seems much the same now, as it was then: long and low with fanlights on one side through which the morning sun streamed when we went for our milk. Opposite were large lattice windows looking onto the open quad – now occupied by the staff common room – so we could watch sets of lunchtime footballers kicking tennis balls around. Sometimes two or three different games would be in progress, each played in an area defined by piles of coats marking the goals. The ball from one game would frequently roll into another, and for a moment there would be an intersection of players, each group doggedly playing its own game, ignoring and avoiding others. They were like dancers, whirling, weaving, pirouetting round the tiny ball, rarely losing their footing on the smooth surface. I would watch them until their comings and goings made me dizzy.

I disliked school dinners but not for the food, which I generally found eatable and adequate. In the comics we read, food was often the prize or the reward. Aunt Aggie's Cow Pies were what inspired Desperate Dan, and Billy Bunter was not the only member of the Remove to see the Tuckshop or the Hamper from home as the fitting end to this week's episode. Final frames often pictured food-laden tables surrounded by gleeful faces. Brought up to be omnivorous and at an age when hunger was my most compelling drive, I would avidly consume whatever was placed in front of me. So, although I knew the dire reputation of school dinners in general, it was not the food that put me off, but a notion that somehow school dinners were an extension of school. Anyway I'd had a bad experience there. We were under the supervision of the master at the head of the table, we had to sit in orderly rows, and as I remember, wait until everyone else on the table had finished before we could rise. For me, the bell at five to one signalled a release. I wanted to be out and away at my own devices, free as I was ever able to be within that special kind of bondage. So, by the time I reached iiα, I was pressing my mother to let me have packed lunches.

Boys who brought sandwiches were allowed to eat them on the tables at the bottom of the Refectory. The High table, where the Archons sat, was at the far end and we, the metics, were ranked according to seniority the length of the room. At the bottom, by the tuckshop entrance, was a Low table, and it was here, lunching off broken meats and orts and delicious home-made snacks with fizzy drinks, sat those who refused the pleasures of the set meal. I tried this table for a while but found it almost as disagreeable as eating what I was given in a row with other people. Furthermore, I missed the company of my form mates, whose salty remarks often provided the only savour for the meal. On the sandwich tables were gathered the vegetarians and dietary freaks; boys whose stomachs were too delicate for the rough fare served for the general; grouchy, hairy-old, eccentric seniors inured to isolation by years of staunch individualism and not prepared to talk to anyone. One day I sat next to a boy whose lunch was in little numbered parcels marking the order in which they had to be eaten. This was the company amongst whom the sandwichers had lunch, for we were not permitted to eat anywhere else in the school. Nevertheless, it was possible to get out, and in fine weather boys went out to the benches outside the shops in Meldon Road, just across from the bakeshop. Some free spirits took their sandwiches into Platt

Fields or Birchfields Park, now empty of the anti-aircraft guns, search-lights and barrage balloons that used to fascinate us in Prep 2 when we leant out of the windows of Miss Robins' room.

School dinners provided a theatre for public performances of ribaldry and discontent. A glimpse into the kitchen gave rise to many a quip that set the table at a roar. Like a scene from a pantomime, brawny dinner ladies, sleeves rolled up, stood in the kitchen, doling out the food as the plates came by – slosh, slosh, slosh, then a gout of gravy. It didn't look appetising, but it was hot and it was filling and most of it was eaten. Some coarse characters would contrive by making indelicate remarks to put sensitive souls off their food so that it could then be appropriated. We seemed often to have omelettes or scrambled eggs – a general ways of using the dried egg powder that came from America. These always stimulated the hungry and unscrupulous. 'Just what I like,' cried Hardy. 'Babies' yellows! Pass me a nappy.'

We sat at long refectory tables with a member of staff at the end, passing the plates down the row to be eaten, and passing them back to be taken away. Sausages featured pretty often – 'Sweet mysteries of life' we called them, after the popular song – served with a mash of reconstituted dried potatoes. I knew it was reconstituted because some of it wasn't, turning up as hard grey flakes like nail clippings that floated on the top of the gravy. We were frequently given fish, sometimes fried, sometimes even fried in batter. We were once given a whole flatfish each, which I took to be a fluke, like the ones we caught in the estuary at home. How to tackle it was a feat which seemed to defeat most diners. 'Davidson's managed to eat most of his,' said my neighbour. 'But then, he's prepared to eat anything. You can have mine.' And before I knew it, my plate was piled with leavings. It was one moment when the cunning of the country boy triumphed over the nous of the sophisticated urbs. The sweet flesh had to be scraped from the bony frame of the fish and each mouthful was mostly skin. The dish was a keen disappointment to most because the promise of so much eating was dashed by the difficulty of getting at it.

For a while, I alternated between School Dinners and a packed lunch, which I ate outside. In iiα during the summer term I used to go with two others to Birchfields Park. Here, in a dell surrounded by rhododendron bushes, was a small playground with a banana slide and swings and various pieces of play equipment, all rusted from neglect during the years of war. There was a large swing that would accommodate four or five of us, and a heavy roundabout that needed group effort to set spinning, but once in motion would turn languidly for ages. Our elders who were in charge of this sylvan retreat ran penny sweepstakes on how long it would run. Here during the spring we joined an exciting band of dissidents, some of whom had been there since 'copping out' of School at break. Half a dozen leery characters, wreathed in the smoke of shared Woodbines, grudgingly accepted our right to be there too. Occupying the benches that surrounded the play equipment, they discussed school in a disparaging way and talked about beer and the girls they met at weekends and what they did with them. They all seemed to come from Gatley, which thereby acquired for me a kind of glamour which it has never entirely lost. Mixing with these lawless resolutes was a heady experience for quiet second formers. We were treated with the condescension due to acolytes and made to eat our sandwiches on a bench away from them.

From the first, I was attracted by the swing. It was little more than two gantries with a plank slung between them which we sat on, while two of the adepts, standing at each end, set it in motion by working it backwards and forwards. It was quite a strenuous business getting the apparatus under way, but slowly the pace increased until it was swinging at its limit and the whole structure rocked in its fixings. I loved the sensation of being wafted up into the air only to swoop down again, and found it quite exhilarating to be one of the crew. I felt I was living for the moment, bound on a dangerous journey of discovery and reckless of my destination. The gantries banged and clattered on their foundations, the bearings groaned and shrieked alternately and I had a glorious, irresponsible feeling that the whole apparatus might suddenly take off and we would reel over the park, like the Grand Panjandrum, till the gunpowder ran out at the heels of our boots. And so it might well have done but for its summary removal. One day we arrived to find it had been wholly dismantled, our roundabout disabled and warning notices placed on the rest of the equipment warning us to keep off. "This Equipment is Dangerous" read a large notice. That marked the end. Without the machines the place had lost its magic and we went there no more.

The tuckshop remained closed throughout the war years. The shelf in front of it was used as a place to leave school bags and other belongings before going into the dining hall. For a long time, I didn't think of it as anything more than part of the passage between the cloisters and the Science block. Then one day, the shutters were opened and trays of cakes appeared for sale. This information ran round the school quicker than the news of a half-holiday, but it was of little use to me, for money was always tight, and I had no more than would pay my bus fare back to town. 'Lend me a tanner,' I said to Hargreaves. 'Drop dead,' he said 'Ask Taylor.' But he'd no spare cash either, so we had to stand and watch the plutocrats gorge till the jam ran down their chins – at least that was how I put it to the folks at home as part of my plea for some tuckshop money. In reality purchasers were limited to one cake each. Rationing was in our blood and Mrs Bedford, presiding at the till, saw that no one got more than his share. And as for going up twice, the queue was long enough to deter all but the most determined glutton.

At first, the tuckshop opened intermittently, I suppose it was only when the kitchen could muster materials and time to bake that the shutters were drawn back. For a while the only goods were big, jammy buns, then one day there were choc-ices on sale, at fourpence apiece. I hadn't seen anything like them before: oblong blocks encased in dark chocolate that flaked off as you bit into it. The ice cream inside was hard and had to be bitten, too – unlike the soft stuff you could lick from a brittle biscuit cone. But still they were a sensation. Even before it was generally known that the tuckshop was open, they were all sold, and the following day at Prayers, the Chief commanded us to pick up all the discarded wrappers and 'dispose of them properly'. Litter was then not much of a problem, for individual wrappings were largely unknown as goods came pretty much as they were made or grown.

For many ice cream, like bananas, was only a memory that had been kept alive by the likes of Desperate Dan and Lord Snooty who behaved as though the war had never happened. They still laid bananas skins for the pompous to slip on, and expected enormous ice cream cones for coming out on top. The choc-ice cream was chewy and white with a sticky sweetness, scrumptiously offset by the slight bitterness of the dark chocolate that cased it. I was not alone in finding that it gave me the runs, which I put down to its being an unaccustomed delicacy. Before long a rumour spread that the ice cream was a by-product of the sausage factory, which produced hitherto unusable quantities of lard. But what did we care, they were delicious, and the era of food-faddism was thirty years away, and the choc-ices were a sign that things were getting better.

13. TRAVELLING

I didn't realise until I stopped travelling on Bowker's how much it bound us together. I missed the fellowship of the bus. Rarely acknowledged overtly, there was a bond between us travellers, fixed by the shared experience of stirring events. We could joyously recall incidents like Catterall being put off in the middle of Salford – 'But I've no money, sir.' 'Then you'll have to walk, boy.' The newly empowered Hemingway, trying to exert his authority – 'Look here, I'm a prefect now'. The same Hemingway walking in front of the bus to guide us through the winter smog. And best of all, the golden moment when the back of the bus fell open to strew bags, bats, games kit along fifty yards of Eccles New Road, giving us the rallying cry, 'Stop the bus, Mr Bowker.' In the corridors of school, Bowker's boys made eye contact, perhaps even nodded. I gratefully remember one intervening when I was being picked on in the cloisters. 'Leave him alone,' he said and jabbed my persecutor in the chest with a long, bony finger, before carrying on with his own business.

Now, I travelled to Manchester by train – except I got off at Salford – and I was on my own – as much as I could be in the company of a protective cousin and a host of daily commuters. It was an uncomfortable, uncongenial journey, shoved into a crowded compartment with no one to talk to and often without a seat. At the end of it there was the march at double-time up Bridge Street and John Dalton Street to Albert Square. Here I waited for a tram to sway in from Mount Street and draw up at the traffic island opposite the main door of the Town Hall. The trams were rackety and cold and rough to ride in, with swing seat backs that could be reversed so you could always face the way you were going. They screeched and groaned as they went round bends. Upstairs the ends were open – toast racks we called them on account of their being fenced in with metal hoops to stop you falling out. On summer mornings, though, they were very pleasant places to be in as we rattled through Victoria Park to Birchfields. All in all, my journey from home took just over an hour, getting me to school in good time for Morning Prayers.

Trams gave way to buses when I was in iiα, and it then took less time to get to school. I caught a later train and instead of going with the office staff, I went with the middle management. It was not as crowded and the conversation was better. My friend little George, the porter at Moses Gate, divided the morning passengers into 'Works, Clurks and Shirks'. The Works caught the earliest trains, and I had just moved from the Clerks to the Shirks. The Shirks had a much pleasanter journey and were much more interesting than the Clerks. They were ready to chat to a polite and tidy boy, on his way to school and, not for the last time, I realised the social significance of the owl on my cap.

Mr Worthington, manager at the Prudential, encouraged me to make a career in Banking. 'These Labour johnnies won't be in for ever…' he said, confidentially. Mr Unsworth, manager at the Labour Exchange, talked about Beveridge and the Welfare State. 'The elimination of poverty and idleness is what we are about…' There was also Miss Rigby, small and intense, who worked for the tee-you-see, which I eventually understood to be the Trades Union Council. I thought this meant she would get on with Mr Unsworth, but she always referred to him as a 'Champagne Socialist', and despite his talking loudly about benefits and allowances, kept him at a distance. We all stood in the same part of the platform while waiting for the train, and thus, disparate though our interests and standings were, we constituted a small community, usually occupying the same compartment. Mr Worthington would hold the carriage door open for Miss Rigby, then bow Mr Unsworth and me in before ascending himself. The following day it might be Mr Unsworth's turn to do the honours. They didn't talk much to each other, and I tried to divide my time fairly between them. In this way travelling to school was almost as much an education as sitting in class, and to cap it there was another kind of learning as I walked through half a mile of the city as I went from the train to the bus.

I always found trains exciting. I saw the big snorting, clanking engines as more like animals than machines. The biggest had names and all had numbers, which I collected by ticking them off in a note-book. On the journey home I would lean out of the window as we steamed slowly past Exchange station, where there was sometimes a 'double-header' waiting to set off on the Glasgow run. A consolation for missing a train was the opportunity it provided to walk to the end of the platform and look at the engines. Engine-drivers were still romantic figures, men to be envied, even beyond our adolescence. Cousin John would boast that at his Prep School – which he was still attending when I was in iiα – he was much envied because he'd once been allowed on the footplate of the Royal Scot.

Although I was interested in trains and railways I was never as enthusiastic as he was who had a library of books about them. He could, and would without prompting, tell you how much coal the Royal Scot used on the Edinburgh run, or the length of the platform joining Exchange and Victoria stations, or what were the liveries of the GWR and the LMS. He kept note of all the journeys he made, and his idea of a good day out was to go by rail right round London without using the Underground. I went with him; it took all day. Starting from Croydon, we went via Reading and Hertford and finished at Basildon. Then, I think we went home by Tube.

In iiiα the routine relaxed and instead of getting off at Salford, I sometimes went on to Victoria and walked to Cannon Street to catch the School Bus. Specially laid on for MGS, it was never more than half full and allowed us twice a week to form little self-help groups devoted to completing homework and thrashing out the problems we'd been given to solve ourselves. I found these sessions immensely useful. They taught me the value of co-operation and the superiority of group-think to the individual effort. While sorting out the weekend homework on Monday mornings I learned more about Greek grammar than ever was taught me in the classroom.

The school bus was not altogether given over to academic endeavour for there was also one for the girls at Manchester High, in the next bay. Flirtations were conducted and liaisons arranged. There was much pointing and waving between the passengers and sometimes a girl, usually a small girl, would deliver a note for "The boy on the third seat from the front". Then a group of anxious observers would crowd the windows to see what happened. Usually the message was appropriated and read aloud before being delivered. Sometime the bus would move off before they could be sure that connection had been made. 'Normal service will be resumed tomorrow,' said Hargreaves.

On my way to Cannon Street I would sometimes go by Long Millgate to look at the ruins of the old school. A gaunt façade remained with MANCHESTER GRAMMAR SCHOOL in stone letters above the remnants of an impressive entrance. I would pause and consider who had graced these portals in the old days. De Quincey and Harrison Ainsworth, writers I was beginning to admire; the turn of the century playwrights, Harold Brighouse and Stanley Houghton, gestating *Hobson's Choice* and *Hindle Wakes* and Louis Golding whose stories of the Silver sisters had recently caught my fancy. Closer than these were contemporary figures like Lord Woolton, the war-time Minister of Food, and Harold Lever, stirring things up in the present government. I was surprised by how little space the school had occupied, between Chetham's Hospital School and the cathedral, an area scarcely the size of a football pitch. Now it was merely a shell, the empty window embrasures seemed etched on the sky and the high brick façade hanging over the street was a silent reminder of the imposing building it must once have been.

About this time I nefariously acquired a Late Pass which allowed me to miss Prayers. I used the extra quarter of an hour to saunter up to Albert Square, taking my time in Willshaws or Sherratt and Hughes, or just rubber-necking through the canyons of the city. I studied the buildings which had taken my fancy when I was on Bowker's: the Opera House, John Rylands, the railway viaduct at Knott Mill and the long abyss of Whitworth Street, down which the sun would scarcely penetrate. Now, I could see these buildings at my leisure, instead of being whisked past in a bouncy bus. I wandered round the blackened sandstone of Rylands Library, little imagining how changed it would look after it was cleaned. I longed to go inside. Years later, I loved the afternoons I spent there in the little alcoves with their counterweighted, green-shaded reading lamps, it was temps perdu à la recherche. When I became bored, or sleepy, I would order editions of Aldus, printed and bound in Venice in the 1480s, or Shakespeare's Folios, just for the pleasure of handling them. One afternoon, so choice was my selection that the deputy librarian came to see if I was to be trusted. He turned out to be David Riley, whom I'd known since iiiα. 'Oh,' he said. 'It's only Davidson. He's all right, I think.'

I liked Albert Square with its statues and pigeons perched on them and the Kardomah Café on the corner of Corporation Street, where in my high and palmy days as a sixth former I loitered at length. The rotunda of the new Central Library, just visible over the Town Hall's extension, had not yet been grimed as had the Town Hall itself, soot-black and imposing with pinnacles and balconies. Most of all, I was impressed by the tower with its spire and booming clock. It made me think of Glasgow as it was described in *Rob Roy* or Salamanca as the Hussars of Conflans rode through it, so much was I, even at that age, in thrall to the printed word.

Sometimes, when I missed the school bus I would walk from Victoria Station to Albert Square, through the back alleys round St Ann's Square, and the little yard by the church, even if it meant missing Stanley Gibbon's stamp shop on the corner. At that hour of day the dray horses would be stamping at the kerb as the brewery men re-stocked Mr Sam's Chop House, lowering barrels down the trap that opened on to the cellars and hauling away the empties. I would imagine the sacred meeting the profane as the odour of sanctity rolled down from St Ann's to mingle with great wafts of stale ale and horse-piss.

On the other side of Cross Street by the soot-blackened Manchester Guardian building, I would pause to look at the fishing tackle in Hardy's window and yearn for a new a split-cane rod. Going behind the bomb-site of Cross Street Chapel, where I imagined Mrs Gaskill's grandfather-in-law had been minister, I would come out at the top end of King Street and admire the grandeur of the big buildings around the Cotton Exchange, then go through the little maze of back streets to catch the bus by the Town Hall in Princess Street. Specially, I loved to walk through the Town Hall itself, from Albert Square to Mosley Street, just for the pleasure of following the tessellated floors of the corridors. From Albert Square the bus went along Upper Brook Street past Plymouth Grove to Birchfields – a dismal journey through bombed out Ardwick and Brunswick and tatty Chorlton. There was still little but rubble and dingy streets until we got to the greenery of Victoria Park with mature trees and glimpses of spacious gardens. Why, I wondered, had the Germans only blown up the houses of the poor?

In the afternoons I went the other way back to town, along Old Hall Lane to Wilmslow Road and the bus to Piccadilly. I was always in a hurry then – no loitering on the way home. Ready to leave school at 3.40 and hoping to catch the 4.16 from Victoria, I would covertly arrange my gear in order to spring from my desk the moment the bell rang. Then I would slide through the gossiping, weaving throng by the door and be running down the drive to Old Hall Lane before most of them had got their books together. It's a good five hundred yards' jog from the school gates to Wilmslow Road, nevertheless, even with a quick getaway I was rarely the first at the bus stop. Some of us, it seemed, could hardly wait to shake the dust of school off our feet. Like me, they had trains to catch, and the journey into town was only the first part of the way home. On the bus we sat on the edge of the seat, nervously checking our watches until we got to Piccadilly.

Once there, we sprang off the bus and ran in a pack through the back-streets and passages that led down to Victoria and through the heart of old Manchester. Knowledge of these paths was part of our schoolboy lore. I imagined it being handed down as the city grew and its factories spread up from the river, filling the open spaces with ever more-densely packed buildings. Long before the school moved to Rusholme, generations of MGS boys from the rich southern suburbs must have picked their way through it. Needing to get to Long Millgate in a hurry, they would have learned the way, as I did, by following the leader, at first lagging behind, breathless and struggling to keep up then eventually becoming leaders themselves.

From Piccadilly down to Victoria, we threaded a built-up area miraculously untouched by the blitz. A maze of alleyways and ginnels intersected the centre of Old King Cotton's town. Our footsteps rang and echoed as we raced along dripping passageways, past many-windowed mills, ablaze with light in the winter afternoons. Huge warehouses seemed to block the way until an arch revealed an opening like a giant rat-hole. Engels might have walked through them with Marx, as they went from Ancoats to the Lit and Phil in Mosley Street. Most of the factories were still working and we would pass through yards where horse wagons waited to be unloaded of bales as big as taxi-cabs. At others, high-sided vans of pre-war design were packed with bobbins and reels to be taken out to the weaving towns. Wisps of cotton fluff flew everywhere and from yard to yard the air was heavy with curious smells of resins and acids, oils and steam, and soot everywhere. In one place there was the thud-thud of an engine, in another it was quiet and empty as a country churchyard, a little close with grass growing between the cobbles. At another, groups of women and girls in overalls would be sitting out, smoking and chatting, much as they must have done in the days of *Mary Barton*.

The end was a seeming blank wall, pierced by an opening, no bigger than a doorway. We emerged from this into the modern Manchester of Withy Grove, just above Stensby Pickford's Gun Shop with the big white Daily Express building directly opposite. The street was busy with cars and people who didn't realise that we had just come from another century. It was usually ten past four: no time to look in the window of Stensby's. We darted across Corporation Street and into Cheese Alley which debouched at the south entrance of Victoria Station. There the runners would disperse, each to his own platform, and with the Rochdale boys I would have time to traverse the station hall, flash my contract at the ticket inspector and race down the subway to Platform Four where I hoped the four-sixteen was still waiting for me.

14. LANGUAGE

In the Prep Department we were, mostly, nicely spoken middle-class boys who said 'please' and 'thank you'. Apart from Leeming who spoke loudly and authoritatively in a BBC voice, we were mostly Lancashire lads, although I was teased more than once about the Cumbrian and Scottish notes in my voice. In iα a boy from Glossop sat next to one from Rochdale and in front of one from Stockport behind whom was one from Oldham. Each had his own accent, not pronounced but noticeable. Flab Harrap came from Glossop, and it showed. Bill Kaye came from Northwich and might have come from the Home Counties. There was even one who lived just round the corner in Wilbraham Road and sometimes walked home for lunch, but he spoke BBC English. The Main School was a polyglot community, some of whom were thugs and hooligans, but they were clever as well. These were boys from a wide area of South Lancashire and Cheshire, many of whom had been brought up under much rougher regimes. Mixing was good for us all and formed part of the special experience of the school.

I had become a sort of linguistic chameleon ready to assume the language of whatever folk I moved amongst. After my year at Dumfries Academy, I was much teased on account of the Scots accent I'd picked up. In the Lakes most of us, children as well as adults, had two or three different ways of speaking. They might be classed as: Proper, Rough and Private. Not everyone was prepared to adjust. My cousin John, for instance, kept his prep school, public school accent wherever he went. Even in Dumfries, where I wanted to merge with the mob, he still stuck to his plummy vowels and careful enunciation. This must have been from choice, because his father used the soft tones of Lowland Scots and his mother, like mine, had wiped out all traces of the regional accent she would have had as a girl.

I guessed early on that while I wanted to merge with my surroundings, John was at pains to assert his individuality. I reckoned he did this so he might be quickly recognised by his own kind, who were unquestionably the 'right sort'. He was never in any doubt about their being the 'right sort', because he'd been told so. They were moulded at Prep School and cast at whatever institution they went to afterwards. However, by the time we were both at Oxford, the effects of the 1944 Education Acts were becoming apparent, and no one was quite sure who was what. For, although the chaps from Public Schools – John had been at Epsom – tried hard to maintain an ascendancy, there were lots of uncouth, clever lads from the

Grammar Schools who were adept at cutting them down. In those days, over sixty per cent of Oxbridge places were filled by candidates from State Schools, and you were more likely to hear Barnsley in the Broad than Harrow in the High.

Even at school I was interested in the way people spoke and realised early that most people used some sort of a dialect. In the Lakes the Vicar and the townsfolk who formed the main part of his congregation spoke what almost amounted to different languages and there were clear variations in accent and manners of speaking from valley to valley. My mother had eliminated all traces of her Cumbrian origins from her speech. Her sisters, who had gone to Training College, spoke correctly but with a northern intonation. Her brother, who'd trained as an electrical engineer at Vickers Armstrong in Barrow, spoke Standard Received English as well as they did, while still retaining his native Cumbrian, almost as a second language. He would switch from one to the other in mid-sentence to make a special point or for comic effect. 'It's a bit chilly, this morning,' he would say, striding up to the fire. 'Ah's ganna waarm mi neeuvs.' And he would rub his cold hands together in front of the blaze. In the shipyard, he said, they had a language all of their own. He helped build submarines and, supposedly, he was one of the many who should have been aboard the Thetis when it sank off Liverpool during its sea-trials. An old shipyard man from Broughton once told me, 'If aw them as sed they shud a bin aboard, ad bin aboard, it wud a sunk at t' dock side.'

As a small wondering child I recognised that the differences between our ways of speaking and the rest of the valley's were not simply matters of vocabulary and accent, but of how facts were marshalled and arguments presented. My family was much better at explaining how things were done, how things worked, what words meant. When I asked 'Why?' they would give me a reasoned answer. When I asked Fred Tyson from the farm at the top of the lane, he would wink at me and say 'Becos...' If I persevered in wanting to know, he would say, 'Nay, tha'd best ax thi Dad'. In his world, you learned by watching and doing rather than talking and listening. Talking was telling stories or gossiping or saying what wanted doing. There was no analysis or explanation or speculation. The conversational opening, 'What if?' had no place in their dialogues, which I thought was a pity because it often led to flights of fancy and stories that were vastly entertaining in themselves.

The language we spoke at school was spiced with what we'd learned from radio and cinema or picked up from returning servicemen. Catch-words and vogue phrases changed from month to month, and nothing was as fatal to the success of an exchange as an out-of-date insult. Our freeze-out phrases were: 'Drop dead,' or 'Hard cheese', 'He's had it'. When Bowker's came to a halt in Birch Hall Lane, we all 'baled out' and after boarding it again in the afternoon we 'took off' for the journey home. The clever chaps in the Sixth were 'Boffins', the idle ones were 'Spivs' or 'Dead legs'. We lowly Preps and first formers were known as 'Irks'. One of the changes I felt in the transition from Prep 2 to iβ was that the sacred truce-words, such as 'Bagsy me' or 'Pax', had lost their force. Their ineffectuality in the main school was one of the defining effects of a move into another world, already peopled by those for whom these charms had no power.

I don't remember much of swearing or obscenities, but I guess society as a whole was much more prudish about its language usage than it is now, seventy years later. That great arbiter of public taste, the BBC, wouldn't even allow the occasional 'ruddy', let alone a reference to 'knickers'. In our schoolboy society 'bloody' was considered strong, except in song, as in 'When this bloody war is over'. Amongst us the usual derogatory adjective was 'sodding', as in the answer, 'I don't sodding know', uttered in exasperated tones as if it had been an impertinence to ask, 'How do you do this sodding homework?' 'Sod off, then,' was the common reply. Obscene language was uncommon and tended to be descriptive rather than expletive.

The word 'fuck' – now in common usage, due in no small measure to the proselytising efforts of *The Guardian*, which seemed for a while to stint of no occasion to use it – was a specialist word, a technical term implicit with mysteries we didn't understand. It was what Pickup did, or was intending to do, with his girl on Mosley Common, when we didn't frustrate him. A much recited limerick, evoking both the industrial unrest of the time and the iron discipline the Unions exerted over their members, provided a good example of this usage:-

> When the Bermondsey Union Struck,
> Bert Bloggins was having a fuck.
> But the Union rules
> Said he had to down tools.
> Now wasn't that ruddy hard luck?

To have used 'bloody' in the last line would have been swearing, and 'Tool' was then a common euphemism. McElvie maintained that he once came across Pickup 'on the job', and Pickup chased him away 'with his tool hanging out'. But Caddy reckoned that was one of McElvie's fantasies, like wrapping the cat in a pillow-case and making it drunk with his father's whisky. We were enough aware of things to know it was the 'hanging out' that gave him away.

15. BILLY HULME

Billy Hulme taught us French, and I guess he wouldn't be tolerated in any school nowadays. He was a fetishist, a sadist, a bully, a flogger, a fondler and general pusher around. Famed for his instruments of punishment – his collection of wooden spoons – he clearly enjoyed beating boys. His eyes gleamed as he selected an appropriate spoon, and he licked his lips as he bent his victims over the desks at the front, half a dozen at a time, giving them two apiece on the way down and two apiece on the way up and two apiece more for luck.

All this was, of course, talk, a tale told by our elders who may or may not have read Krafft-Ebing. Nevertheless, it created an easily recognised caricature for there was enough substance in the stories to make them stick. On Bowker's, when the new boys were being warned of the horrors that awaited them, there was always a full session on Billy Hulme, the demon French teacher. His spoons were described and how each was reserved for a particular misdemeanour, how he would reduce boys to weeping wrecks, and regularly manage to beat a whole form in the course of a single lesson. But, as is often the case, the facts didn't match the fame. I entered his classroom expecting to meet an ogre but found instead a jolly goblin. He was funny and engaging, not unsympathetic, and above all interesting. I'd had trouble with French and needed to work hard at it and with his encouragement and drive I improved enough to be put among the best in the class. In this position of minor competence, I flourished, and even managed to avoid being flogged more than once a lesson.

Billy Hulme was a small, round man with a round, shiny face and round, rimless spectacles. He was a peripatetic teacher, never still, and during the course of a lesson he would work himself into a frenzy, jigging up and down the room, roaming between the desks, firing questions, correcting work, handing out punishments. He chanted verbs and declared nouns, recited verses, shouted slogans, so we were made as much aware of the sound of French as we were of the need to get it grammatically right. His lessons were composed of noisy action, and I would go out of his room wound up to a pitch of nervous excitement, as much by sheer exhilaration at what was going on, as fear of making some slip. As a class we saw nothing odd in his performances, for that's how we saw them. They were low dramas: comedies, farces, burlesques, part of what was considered to be a good education in the best establishments, attended by the likes of Stalky and Tom Cherry. This was how it was; masters were larger than life and almost duty-bound to be eccentric.

It was noted, satirically by those who loved impersonations, that Billy Hulme spoke with a northern accent. This was something of a rarity amongst the staff, whose accents varied from the plummy growl of Mr Moreton, through the standard received of Artie Moore and Simkins, to the genuine Public School bay of the Chief. Like Mr Hyslop, another teacher of French, Billy Hulme spoke with the flat "a" and short "i" of the north, saying 'bath' to rhyme with 'lath', and ask us to wait 'jist a minnit'. As a linguist he must have been aware of the way he spoke and he was always at pains to make us know how real French sounded, long before the days of Language Labs and Audio Assistants. He snarled and squeaked at us, exaggerating his nasal endings and his 'e' acutes, grunting and baying, till we imitated his voice and his grimaces. In this way he made us speak something like real French, which actually worked when we went on the Easter trip to Paris. In between spells of French, he would lapse into what Satters called, 'standard received Manchester'. At School Camps he was noted for his authentic Stanley Holloway impersonations, reciting 'Albert and the Lion' and 'Sam, Sam, pick up thi musket' in their Saturday evening concerts. But that was in the holidays, and at school, it was acknowledged, he was different.

But he was chiefly noted for his collection of spoons. He wielded them vigorously and with panache and it was common for classes to present him with another one at the end of the year. They were displayed on the walls of his room in special cases. There were baking spoons, salad spoons, carved spoons, black African spoons, ornate Orkney spoons, love spoons, hate spoons, ranging from three foot monsters to two inch midgets. Each had a name and those on one row were reserved for daily use, where the size of the spoon was related to the seriousness of the offence. For instance, missing two accents deserved a flick from Little Dot, and failing to hand in homework, two cuts from Big Daddy.

These spoons, along with Harry Plant's giant gym shoe, and Killer Maugham's run up, and Chang Lund's special way of 'laying it on' were part of our school lore. There were lots of words about these practices but, apart from Billy's performances, little evidence of actual deeds. The fearsome floggings that caused De Quincey to run away had long gone from the syllabus; might almost have ceased with his departure or just been part of an early opium dream, although Harrison Ainsworth mentions the strict discipline in his day, which was a generation later. The master – I never knew his name – who so justly beat me for slugging Freedman had taken so long to find a suitable implement it was obviously not in regular use. For a while I had thought of him as the fabled Harry Plackett, and took a sort of pride in having experienced the gym-shoe of this legendary hitter, but on having him pointed out to me one day, I saw that my man was someone else, and I never came into contact with him again.

At some time during each lesson Billy Hulme would have a parade of offenders. It was a form of entertainment with a purpose, and in the main accepted as such by both those who watched and those who winced. Those penalised for making small mistakes knew why and tended to remember, I had no doubt that I erred much less after being tickled by Little Dot. Those waiting for Little Daddy and his big partner didn't seem quite so enthusiastic. I suppose the whole show didn't last five minutes and seemed an integral part of our learning French, which we did. Certainly our homeworks were done with care – mine certainly were, but more for the sake of being right than the fear of the spoons.

In those days, corporal punishment seemed to be considered as much a part of education as exams. It was judged to be a painful but necessary part of the process. At home in Broughton, my contemporaries had fearsome tales of the ferocity with which their headmaster set about them. Even now voices are lowered when his name is mentioned, as if the evocation would raise his wrathful spirit and cause old wounds to ache. As far as I was concerned at MGS, it was less practised than preached and as I went up the school I can't remember any accounts of beatings. Punishments were usually in the form of lines or extra work or detentions. Apart from the activities of the Black Hand Gang who used to fuse the lights and nearly killed Sutton, I can't recall any incident that might warrant a beating, although I'm sure that my exploit as a junior artilleryman deserved one.

Billy Hulme was a performer, his lessons were part of a calculated act and his spoons were his props. The punishment parade interrupted the drudgery of the lesson. After five minutes of being moved about and pushed into place and spanked we were all content to resume the hard and careful work of learning a language. The fear of the correctives was more effective than the actual correction, involving as it did a kind of public humiliation. It was being made to look daft rather than being hurt, ridicule rather than pain, having our shortcomings made public and being involved in a kind of abasement that made us sit up and pay attention. Falling off was punished on the spot, and not by a mere flick from Little Dot, but an intermediate spoon and administered with intermediate vim. Between the flick of Little Dot and the stinging swing of Big Daddy there were considerable gradations of force. One lunchtime in the Baths there was a chap with two red circles on his bottom, one each side. A class mate explained simply, 'He fell out with Billy.' They had clearly been laid on with serious intent and from a distance they looked like a pair of spectacles. As with the ejectment of Catterall from Bowker's, the general view was that he must have deserved it.

In the baths all secrets were revealed, for we all bathed naked, and tyros who turned up with costumes were laughed to scorn. During the War, the baths were closed. Once while we were in Prep 1, Williamson and I ventured up the dark corridor beyond the Gym to where our way seemed blocked by a bar of sunlight. Peering through the crack it came through we saw the vast white tank of the empty pool.

'Can you swim?' he said.

'Well, almost.'

'Me too. We'd better hurry up and learn before this is open again.'

I suppose there was not enough fuel then for the Baths. School was often cold in winter and Simkins made us run round the quad to warm up. It was only in summer that Mrs Gaskill opened the windows to keep us brisk.

By iiα I'd learnt to swim and lost touch with Williamson. By then the Baths were full of water again and open at lunch time for all who cared to use them. It was here that I encountered beating of another kind. I already knew that discipline in the Gym was different from discipline in class. The very physicality of the lessons, the release of animal energy coupled with opportunities for larking about, created an entirely different atmosphere, in which we were encouraged to see ourselves as doing rather than thinking beings. Nasty Mr Saunders and his much nastier side-kick Mr Cuggy were both brutal and unfeeling in the way they hurried us up ropes, pushed us over horses, exercised us until we were ready to drop – which I suppose is what they were supposed to do. Cuggy in particular relished his role as drill-master and persecutor of the weak. He had a flair for picking out the 'weeds' in the class and harrying them, to the point of tears.

For a while Cuggy was in charge of the Baths at lunch time and when the session ended he would have us run round the edge of the Bath to get dry. He was clearly excited by this parade of naked lads and used to make us get a move on by lashing the laggards with a large gymshoe. He caught me once with a blow that stung for a circuit of the bath and ached all afternoon, and all for nothing but to give him a kick. His eyes flashed and he laughed out loud when a particularly lusty swipe struck home. Compared with this, Billy Hulme's punishment parades were mere charades, for not only did Cuggy strike with such obvious enjoyment at the bare buttocks flashing past, he put his strength behind the blow. He would pick out two or three for special attention and laugh as they squealed. He only caught me once, but Hargreaves suffered, and named him Commandant Cuggy, after the Concentration Camp guards whose behaviour had shown us the meaning of sadism. In the end, it was Cuggy who stopped us using the Baths at lunchtime, rather than the fine spring weather that came with the start of May.

We were far from being alone in hating Cuggy. His name tainted the whole Gym and Mr Saunders with it, who was fair, if severe, and had kudos as a good athletics trainer. Towards the end of the term he took over the lunchtime Baths and shortly afterwards Cuggy disappeared. This is all I remember from the time, but sixty years later the mention of his name in The Old Mancunian newsletter provoked such a flood of bitter reminiscences that the editor summarily closed the correspondence.

Evacuation day, 1939

Bombed out school 1941

*MGS boys joining the war effort by hoeing peas at Lathom Hall in
Ormskirk, 1941*

Main quadrangle

Milk

Physical education

Rugby 1950

Classroom

Tuckshop

Lunchtime in the Refectory

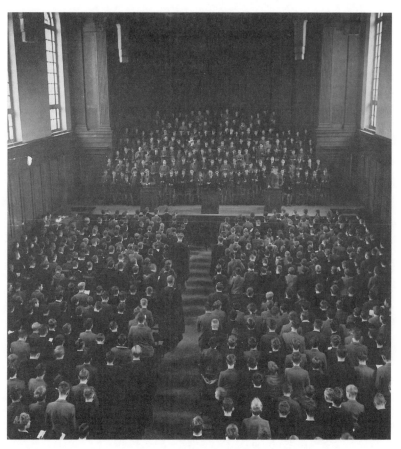

Assembly

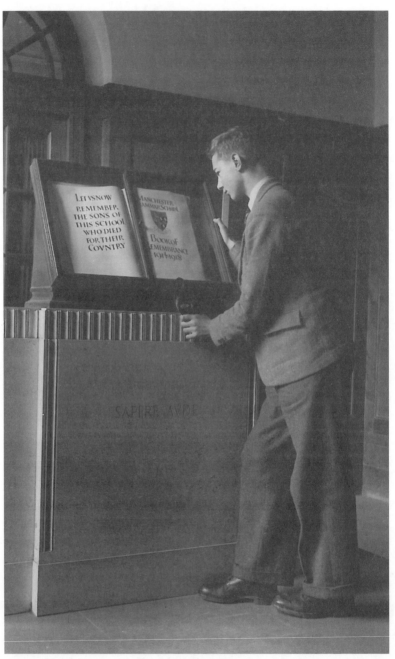

Book of Remembrance

PART III -

THE MIDDLE SCHOOL

1. PREAMBLE

In 1947 as I moved into iiiα the country was slowly recovering from the war, but in the two years since peace was declared, conditions on what was still called 'the Home Front' had deteriorated. Our weekly ration of butter would scarcely do for two pieces of toast, and there was barely a mouthful of bacon. Even bread was rationed, which it hadn't been during the War. My idea of a slap-up feast was bread dipped in a mixture of dried egg and milk and fried in a scraping of our allowance of lard. Properly done it was delicious. As a gourmet's delight, it could be served with Spam fritters. But these were rare items of luxury in an era of austerity. 'Austerity' was a word still much in vogue even in the early years of peace. I knew from my newly learned Greek that austere meant severe. It was one of a dozen or so words of Greek derivation, like 'orchestra' and 'poetry', that Artie Moore paraded for our entertainment at the beginning of the term. In doing so he had the air of a conjuror producing rabbits out of a hat, gesturing like a showman and leering over his half spectacles. I thought it was a good word for the winters we were having, although I never heard anyone talk about 'austere weather', even though the winter of 1947 was exceptionally hard.

At home the Christmas snow was still on the fells at Easter. At school, still in iiα, we huddled round the lukewarm radiators. Simkins sent us on compulsory trots round the quad. Sometimes lessons were cancelled and we were sent home early and often there was the fog, choking, blinding, so strongly pervasive that it seemed to follow us inside, dimming the lights. There was a shortage of fuel, power cuts were frequent and awkward as the electricity went off without any warning. It was altogether an uncomfortable time and the only place to be properly warm was in bed. Despite my father's repeated cry that it was like living in an occupied country, I was sure we were better off than people in Dresden or Cologne. In the spring family life became less hectic as my cousins, released from their war work, hurried away to 'do some living'. One went to Greece with UNRRA, the United Nations Relief and Rehabilitation Administration, devoted to relocating displaced persons, and the other to Rhodesia, 'where it's sunny all the time'. The house fell strangely silent as the records of the Ink Spots and Bing and Hoagy and Frankie gathered dust. At the weekends the radiogram was given over entirely to my father's beloved operas.

In the summer, when there was no one to look after me at Broughton Mills, I stayed in Barrow with my Aunt Nan. On fine afternoons we would ramble through the lanes of Low Furness where the terrain was so different from that at home it might have been a hundred miles away. Instead of long thin valleys gouged out between high fells, miles of open country rolled gently down to the sea; and unlike our pocket handkerchiefs of stony ground, hemmed by stone walls, dotted with rock ends, it was rich and arable, laid out in big fields. On the dissolution of Furness Abbey it had been adopted by the King and remained part of the Crown estates ever since. It looked prosperous and well settled, with large farms, big barns and ample outbuildings. The roads were different, too. Instead of winding up and down between rough stone walls, they were deep, leafy lanes which ran along the sides of fields like grooves worn in the ground.

One we often followed went, hot and dusty, straight and low between high hedgerows, right into the eye of the afternoon sun. It was called Long Lane. As we trudged along its dry and boring length my aunt would say, to pluck up our failing spirits,

'It's a long lane that has no turning.' It was a cry born of near despair, but with a hint of optimism in it – times were bad, but they were bound to get better, and I felt that somehow it applied not only to what we were doing and where we were, but also to life in general. Usually when she spoke, the dark shadow of the bend was already in sight, and I knew that when we reached it, we were almost at our destination. So, although her slightly peevish cry was against the discomforts of the present, it was also the herald of better times.

Looking forward to the next term I thought that my journey along the corridor from Prep 1 to iiiα had been like the long lane with a turning at the end. I had at times found it such a slog that I was almost in despair. For five years, most of my school life had been spent, inching up and down its length, to History with Tommy Stott, at one end, and French with Sloppy F at the other, and in between at yearly intervals, to Mr Moreton, Bozo Hindley and Simkins. There, apart from daily Maths lessons on the other side of the main quad, and weekly outings for swimming and gym, I had spent nearly half of my school days, a good part of it, it seemed, leaning against the radiators, gazing through the windows into the main quad, waiting for life to begin. These rooms where I had grown and learned had been a central part of my experience. They contained the desks and lockers that were the furniture of my existence. They were a kind of home. Hot and stuffy in the mornings, hence Mrs Gaskell's deep breathing exercises, in the afternoons they were often cold and dark. Now I was about to turn the corner, and at the end of my year in iiα, a conviction grew that life was going to improve. I had a premonition one day at the end of the summer term, when Artie Moore's door suddenly opened and sunlight flooded the corridor. 'Dominus illuminatio mea,' it seemed to say.

I think it was in iiiα that I first began to take stock of myself and realise that I was no longer part of a herd known as 'boys', but an individual with some idea of the life I wanted to lead. If growing up is a slow business of coming to terms with other people and realising that their worlds are as important as one's own, then this was the time when I began to recognise what I was in relation to others. When I was small I knew I was the centre of my family and home, here lived the me I thought I was, with the world arranged for my convenience. To a lessening degree this solipsism persisted through Prep 1 and Prep 2, when Caddy and McElvie reflected in 'Young Ian' a picture of the 'me' that I was familiar with.

But now I started to notice a difference between that 'Ian' and the 'me' that I felt I was becoming. I began to realise that I was more the person that other people saw than the 'me' I felt I was. It was just what the Duchess said to Alice, "Be what you would seem to be, or … Never imagine yourself not to be otherwise than what it might appear to others that what you were or might have been was not otherwise than what you had been would have appeared to them to be otherwise." It took me a long time to work out exactly what she meant, and then I realised that she had said so right at the beginning, but doing so helped solve my problem of establishing the satisfactory identity that enabled me to abandon the comfort blanket keeping me cosy in my own little world. The final decisive step towards this goal of realising my true worth and position in the world came one afternoon of thick fog when we had been let out of school early. The trains had stopped running and a stony-eyed conductor stopped me boarding his crowded bus which was bound for Bolton.

'Full up!' he said.

'Can't you squeeze me on?'

'No,' he said, decisively.

'But this might be the last bus,' I cried.

'Couldn't give a bugger,' he said, and clearly meant it.

It was the moment when I realised I was no longer like the small boy with big eyes and little bundle waiting for someone to come and read his label.

It is hard to write authentically about what happened so long ago. So strong is the urge to make sense of what I guess went on, that memory becomes the handmaid of invention. The involuntary recall provoking a genuine response needs a stimulus I can't provide. In the early summer of 2010 I visited the school, and as I went round I waited in vain for some sound, some smell or view, which would revive a long-forgotten scene. The sight of old form rooms, now so lavishly equipped with educational gadgetry, did nothing to stir the memory. I had half expected to be like the Mole when he was brought to a halt by the poignant scent of home when he and Ratty were going back to River Bank one wintry evening, and that I would suddenly be pierced by the recollection of the being I was. But nothing came.

My guide, a Bevis-like sixth-former, in his determination to show me the best of the school, managed only to show me his school, which wasn't my school. Eager to explain, he let his story interfere with the one I was trying to remember and as I struggled to imagine the crowded corridors, frantic with dark figures burdened with books and bags hurrying from one classroom to another in the cold light of a northern morning, I was kept in the present by the sight of his slight, summery figure, pausing on the landing to wait for me, creaking and panting up stairs he had just taken two at a time. He showed me empty sunlit passages, vacant rooms, new accommodation built in places that used to be spaces, chatting all the while of video-links and interactivity in a way that kept me firmly in the present. It was almost as if he wanted to deny me an opportunity of remembering. As I entered what used to be my form room, I looked in vain for the shade of Simkins, spectacles gleaming, ghost of a smile emerging from the wrinkles on his chin. In the corridor I tried to recall Bozo Hindley intoning "Hic, Haec, Hoc"; Sloppy F's snarling, 'Geardan, boy, only don't linger on the en'; to visualise the whisk of Artie Moore's gown as he swung from the top of the stairs into his room; the stately progress of Mr Moreton down the busy corridor, brushing away the boys in front of him as a boat parts flotsam. There was nothing there but the corridor, bare and silent in the slanting rays of the westering sun and my guide saying, 'This is the Classics corridor...' as if I didn't know.

In my days, the form room of iiiα was at the south end of this corridor, but not a part of it. It was a corner room at the head of the stairs coming up from the library so it, too, was a turning point, hinting at better times. It had windows on two sides, one looking towards the gym where the tyrannical Mr Saunders still held sway, but no longer assisted by the egregious Mr Cuggy. The others looked across the playing fields to Old Hall Lane and freedom of a kind. Artie Moore would lean on the sill as he gave us tests.

Next to this room, and at the end of the short passage leading up to the Art Department was the one where Willie Graham presided over Rα. Here we would be next year, from where we would get our remove to the Sixth and the realms of glory.

2. EDUCATION: iiiα

In iiiα I began to grow up and make sense of my world. I still have friends who have lasted from this time. It was then that I think I learned to act independently and stop believing everything I was told. So far I had been merely a foot-soldier following instructions; now I felt I had moved up a rank. Nevertheless, being an ordinary member of a large group was not without its advantages. I had learned as early as Prep 2 that pseudonymity was a good way of avoiding trouble and it was politic always to have a spare identity. 'Johnson, U3c, sir,' I would say when called upon to give an account of myself, cruelly aware that there was a Johnson in U3c. In times of crisis I'd been him since he was in 1c and I never heard of him being unjustly punished, anyway I didn't get into trouble very often. However, with my new-found maturity I felt it was wrong not to be myself.

We were just beyond the age when we formed 'gangs' – those collections of unrealised individuals coalescing round some temporarily charismatic figure. These could be cruelly exclusive: 'You're not in our gang. Sod off', was crushingly dismissive. On the other hand: 'You can be in our gang, if you like. We're just going to raid 2c', was a heartening sign of acceptance. We were just about the same age as Stalky and Co, and entering that time when life-long bonds were formed and like them, we knew we had been raised from a lower level of school society. We had glimpses of a future that wasn't bounded by next weekend, or the Christmas holidays. The world had suddenly opened for us – we were no longer metics, bowed down by custom and inferiority, but full citizens of Athens, individuals with our own rights. The seemingly aimless existence of lower school, drifting from one weekend to another, gave way to an ordered and optimistic progress. We stopped being rude to each other and hived off into small groups capable of self-defence and acquiring a store of common sense which stopped us going beyond the pale.

Under the generally benevolent guidance of Artie Moore, life in iiiα became easier and pleasanter with a better sense of purpose. Simkins was paternalistic, authoritarian at times and kept us in our place. Artie was democratic, prepared to negotiate, and even give way. We were almost grown-up now, learning Greek gave us a sense of exclusiveness and a feeling that we were already marked out for academic success. Some clever-clogs already had ideas about which Oxbridge colleges they would apply to. We swanked with our newly acquired learning and as soon as we learned the alphabet, we used it in notes to each other. Piper, intrigued by the name of his sister's favourite singer wrote to me as ʽωγή, and in the same vein I replied as βινγ, too much of a tyro to realise that it ought to have been βιγγ.

Artie Moore had thin sandy hair that frolicked over his balding head. He wore half-rim spectacles over which he shot enquiring glances at you as you spoke. He was snappish without being disconcerting; you half expected him to blow up but he rarely did. He was a mediator who once rounded on the class and berated them on my behalf. Called to the question, I had risen uncertainly to my feet, fumbling with my newly acquired spectacles, the better to see what I was supposed to be paying attention to. A snigger ran round the class. Artie Moore exploded. 'It is not a matter of jest,' he said, 'Spectacles are not an affliction, they're a blessing – as some of you know already – and all of you will find out some day. Wretches!'

One drowsy summer day he was trying to whip up enthusiasm for Greek irregular verbs, and a soft wind blowing through the open windows made it hard to concentrate. It brought the sound of a mowing machine and the scent of cut grass. Then, the peace was shattered by the sound of derisive laughter rising above the shuffle and chat of passers-by. The U15 XI was off to an away match. Peal after peal of cackling glee invaded the class room, until Artie Moore left his desk and went to the window. Outside in the drive was the capering figure of Hargreaves off with the cricket team. Freed from Greek and afternoon school, his figure was grotesquely contorted as he shrieked and crowed, pointing at the open window. Like the villain in a pantomime, Artie Moore revealed himself, and the cackling ceased. The cavorting figure became one of a trudging line, laden with bags and bats. Artie Moore watched vengefully as it filed past, his hands clasped behind him, his irritation marked by the way his gown rose and fell as he tapped his hands one upon the other. Before he turned round, the class had resumed its place and all was orderly. 'Τυπτω, I smite,' he said. 'Τέτυφά, I have smitten. 'Τυψώ, I will smite.'

We always had to learn a great deal by heart, in the way we had all got our tables in Infant School. Mrs Gaskell had us memorising poetry – Keats, Tennyson, Hardy, Kipling – 'It'll fill the odd corners of your mind,' she said. Mr Moreton had a poetry speaking competition, once a month, with a bar of chocolate as a prize – in the days when it was rationed. The contest was open to all, there was no compulsion but we were goaded to enter by the thought of the chocolate. Learning Greek took me back to when I started Latin and French as I remembered the apparently meaningless lists to be assimilated – conjugations, declensions, vocabulary, rules of grammar. They were like seemingly indigestible food that had to be eaten 'because it's good for you.' They said, 'Just swallow it down. One day you'll see the benefit of it.' Bozo Hindley had us chanting pages from Kennedy's Shortbread Eating Primer. 'You've got to get these into your heads,' he said, 'otherwise you won't be able to make sense of the rest of it. And it's good stuff.' It was the kind of learning that was like putting up the scaffolding so the building, proper, could start.

We were always tested on what we had been set to learn. Even in Rα, Greek and Latin lessons usually started with a ten minute test. There, in a chance investigation of the drawers of Willie Graham's desk, where we were playing shove-ha'penny, Taylor discovered a well-worn note-book of lesson plans and tests. It detailed week by week a programme of classwork, homework and – most useful – the tests to be given in season. It was treasure trove indeed, and not to be spent, but hoarded for the future. We copied the tests out, week by week, striving always to be one or two weeks ahead in case he should remember to lock his drawers, but he never did. We held it as a sacred trust that such knowledge should be handed down to successive generations. And so it was, as I heard at a reunion dinner, forty years on.

Despite the formality of homework and tests, I thought we learned more by a process of unconscious absorption than by being actually taught. We belonged to a society where knowledge was prized and effort applauded, and eventually, when I came to study modern theories of education, I was amazed that I had learned anything at school. Proper teaching, the Professors declared, involved explanation and practice, pupils should be encouraged to assimilate and understand rather than memorise. Then, it was assumed, learning would happen in the normal way. The sort of teaching we had at MGS made learning into a sort of game in which there were no boundaries. It was presented as an adventure, like entering a strange country and daily discovering something new, or climbing a mountain, so the higher we got the further we saw, and the summit was always just over the next ridge. Certainly there was drudgery – what else is a Latin prose but hard work with dictionary and grammar – but it was presented as part of a process, like digging the garden to plant potatoes. We were taught that hard work paid off, and we saw that it did, for there was always a reward, if it was only in the feeling that we were acquiring material for future use. 'You may not believe this, Davidson,' Willie Graham said to me as I was slogging through the sixth book of the *Iliad*, 'but one day you will read this stuff for pleasure.' And he was right.

We were always given lots of written work and our marks were collected in class, so we all knew who had done well and who hadn't. Homework was handed in to be corrected, but in class our exercise books were handed to the boy behind for marking, In iiiα Bedson did mine and I did Franks'. Bedson was scrupulous, even to bothering about a comma or a dash, and never gave me benefit of the doubt. I reckoned he cost me dozens of marks. I hated him. Franks always disagreed with my marking of his work. He was obstinate and persistent and would argue individual cases with me at break-time. Occasionally he carried the dispute to arbitration forcing me, for I was never very sure of myself, to defend my decision. This strategy succeeded for a while, but one day Artie Moore brusquely and forever dismissed him. 'You're wasting my time, Franks. Davidson is usually fair, and he doesn't come snivelling to me about Bedson's nit-picking.' It was a glorious moment, crowned by my realising that he'd noticed how severe Bedson had been.

Failing to turn in work usually meant a PS but we were seldom punished for bad work, only made to feel uncomfortable, even ashamed. We were expected to do well and our shortcomings were regarded as temporary lapses, not what was expected of us, and clearly demeaning. 'You have let yourself down,' said Artie Moore, handing me back a shoddy piece of work. 'I don't like to see you in this light.' And this spurred my endeavours better than any penalty.

3. ME AND GOD

As a child I knew religion was very important to some people, but I couldn't understand why. Although we didn't go to church, in the Lakes I knew lots of people who did. My Aunt Dodie, who taught me to read and died when I was small, believed in God. When I asked her what it meant she said, 'the hope of better times to come'. Did that mean Christmas or the summer holidays, I asked. 'Not quite,' she said, 'but something like the warm glow you get thinking about them, and other times when you're happy.' At the time, I thought I understood, for everything seemed to be upside down. We were losing the war; it was bitterly cold and we were short of fuel; my father was away most of the time and my mother was always busy. Aunt Dodie herself often hurt so much that she wasn't able to read to me. She died in the middle of *Our Mutual Friend* just when Lizzie Hexham went to live with Jenny Wren. Aunt Nan often said, 'These are bad times.' Aunt Dodie got me to say my prayers, and for a while I said 'Our Father' when I got into bed, and at Aunt Nan's suggestion added on, 'Please God make Aunt Dodie better,' but it didn't prevent her from dying and so I stopped .

I was puzzled by the kneeling and the praying which seemed to be done to stop something terrible happening. They were like standing in the squares so the bears couldn't get you, except you knew there were no bears. Reverence, which was clearly very important to some people, I thought of as a sort of respect, like listening quietly and patiently while your elders were speaking. Good manners generally seemed to be a form of reverence. But saying prayers was like talking to someone who wasn't there, and in a strange language. I enjoyed singing hymns in Prayers, but often struggled to understand what they meant. What was 'the panoply of God'? (by Rα I'd learned enough Greek to work it out, but I didn't go into Prayers then) and 'my strongest gain I count but loss' seemed a denial of striving and competing, which were drummed into us as great goods. 'Gladly the cross-eyed bear' I liked because it could have come out of *Alice in Wonderland* and might be the start of a good story.

At school were the Crusaders, very strong on God. They wore little white shields in their lapels, with a red cross on them, and preached at us fiercely. One who travelled on Bowker's used to sit next to me when there was room and ask uncomfortable questions about home, whether I had brothers and sisters and if we ever said prayers or went to church. He said, 'God is watching us all the time, you know.' I didn't know. And I didn't like to think he was. Not so much because he was God, as because I didn't like the idea of being watched. Anyway, I felt God ought to have much better things to do. 'Whatever you do is noticed,' he said. While he spoke I could see him out of the corner of my eye, looking at me closely as though he were standing in for God. Shortly afterwards I met Caddy and McElvie and they rescued me. After that the Crusader left me alone. McElvie said I should watch out for him because he was 'very pi'. I wasn't quite sure what 'pi' meant, but I caught the sense of the warning.

Most of us were northern, urban heathens and embarrassed by talk about religion. It was a part of the private life we kept separate from school. The morning assembly was called 'Prayers', but we didn't do much praying. We sang a hymn and listened to a Prefect reading one of a dozen or so familiar passages – the Prodigal Son, Consider the lilies, the Good Samaritan – then passed quickly on to school notices and the Chief's observations – too much litter, a good turnout for the Music Festival and, ominously, 'All those who travel on the four-twenty from Victoria Station to Rochdale, stay behind.' There was a separate assembly in the Lecture Theatre for Jewish boys, which according to Harris was 'v boring'. They also had a separate table in the refectory.

An hour's RI featured on our timetables, but it didn't mean much to me until the Sixth when it was taught by the Chief. Before that it was spent either in a loose sort of discussion about contemporary issues, like Capital Punishment and Why God hadn't stopped the Holocaust – although it wasn't called that then – or bits of ancient history with a biblical flavour. I remember a splendid lesson about Babylon and the Tower of Babel and what language Adam and Eve might have spoken in the Garden of Eden, with Simkins at his best. Actual bible study didn't take place until Rα, when Willy Graham introduced us to the Greek of the New Testament and surprised us by showing how different it was from the Authorised Version.

Willie Graham was one of the properly religious members of staff and once kept the whole form in for a special PS, because someone chalked IHΣ on the front of his desk. With Mr Moreton we'd had a fair amount of the Bible in both English lessons and RI – the chapters about Samson and Delila, Abraham and Isaac, bits of the Song of Songs and Ecclesiastes. I remember him with his gravelly voice, which was half groan and half whisper, reading Ruth's words to Naomi, 'Whither thou goest, I will go…' and closing the book with a snap at the end of the passage, just as the bell rang. 'Beautiful, beautiful,' he growled. 'Now, get out, you unappreciative little beasts.'

I was aware of other divisions and faiths, and could hardly be otherwise in a school that had separate Jewish prayers and dinners, but I wasn't quite sure whether Catholics were Christians or not. I was mistrustful of Catholics, on account of what I'd read about the Spanish Inquisition and Torquemada. I remembered Sir Richard Grenville in mortal peril crying, 'Sink me the ship, Master Gunner, / Sink her and split her in twain. / Better fall into the hands of God / Than into the hands of Spain'. That had quite clearly put God on one side and Catholics on the other. Apart from that, I saw them as a threat, partly because of my reading and partly because of a disturbing experience with a priest while on holiday with my aunt in Tynemouth. She told me that the man with a strange hat and a black cloak was probably a priest. I didn't tell her any more about him. Otherwise, actual knowledge of Catholics at that time was limited to McInnes in 1c, whom I'd been shown one break. When I asked what Catholics were like, Broadhurst took me along the corridor and pointed him out leaning against a radiator. I was surprised that he looked much the same as everyone else, for I'd half expected some distinguishing feature, like the priest's long black cloak that he'd wanted me to come under.

Later on, in iiα when I travelled home by train, I made friends with two boys from De La Salle College. They were burly rugby-players and looked to me like thugs, but proved not to be when I got to know them. They were only potential thugs: their violence was always imminent but never actual, they threatened but didn't strike. They were always going to 'beat me up tomorrow'. When they got out, at the station before mine, their parting words were usually, 'Tomorrow, we're going to beat you up.' I came to look on it as a sort of Catholic 'Goodbye'. They talked a lot about sin, a word that didn't figure at all in my vocabulary, and had frightening tales of public beatings by someone called Father Benedict, whose name they always mentioned in hushed tones.

4. JEWS AND CHRISTIANS

I was only just becoming aware of religious differences. Something, I knew, kept Church and Chapel folk apart, but of the differences in kind I was largely ignorant. Even in Catholic Lancashire, parts of which might never have accepted the Reformation, I'd grown up thinking of Catholics as enemies. On the other hand, I knew a lot about Jews, both from my reading and from Jewish friends. When I got round to finishing *Our Mutual Friend* I'd warmed to Lizzie Hexham's friend, Riadh, and in *Ivanhoe* I sympathised with old Isaac of York, agreeing with Mr Moreton that Ivanhoe married the wrong girl. Shylock was difficult to weigh up, but in the end I sympathised with him, largely because he'd been done down by Portia, who was the worst kind of smarty-boots and reminded me of my bossy Barrow cousin.

There were few Catholics in school but something like a third of the pupils were Jewish. They weren't noticed as being in any way different. In our early years we would chant, 'And the Lord God said unto Moses / All Jews shall have hooked noses / Excepting Aaron, / He'll have a square 'un.' In iα, Abrahams, a burly, amiable figure whose clothes always seemed to hang on him, and who had a large bulbous nose, was often the uncomplaining object of its recitation. And Cohen and Silverman and Harris who had ordinary-sized noses would join in the chant. By iiα we'd grown out of such childish practices.

The horrid revelation of the Concentration Camps when I was in iβ gave me the first inkling that to be Jewish was to be something quite different. As the extent of the Nazi persecution was revealed and the horrifying details of the Concentration Camps emerged, sympathy grew for the Jews and all things Jewish. After sixty years it is hard to realise the feelings of anger and revulsion that grew as the full horrors of the Nazi persecution were disclosed. 'Why,' I asked the form's Crusader, 'did God let this happen? You say he can do anything. Why didn't he stop this?'

At first I found it hard to believe the pictures and the stories which filled the newspapers and the Pathé News Reels. I couldn't understand how people could do such things to each other. In "King of the Khyber Rifles", the death of Gunga Din had disturbed me for weeks, despite its being obviously phoney. But these photographs of real people in real situations, not soldiers or rebels or old fashioned 'baddies', but harmless, ordinary folk whose only fault seemed to be that they were in the wrong place at the wrong time, distressed me deeply. Shots of matchstick creatures with lemur-like eyes, crouching beside mounds of decaying bodies, seemed scarcely credible. One newsreel, which I saw twice in one week with a mixture of horror and satisfaction, showed how an American colonel had rounded up all the Germans living nearby and marched them round the camp to see the atrocities that had taken place there. A telling sequence showed the lady from the Schloss in her fur coat and boots complaining of the way she had been

treated, actually *made to walk* and look at the piles of bodies
and the emaciated children, too weak to eat the food that was
now within their reach.

At school, one effect of the opening up of the Camps was
to emphasise Jewishness. It was difficult to be openly
sympathetic, boys of eleven aren't usually good at any such
display, but there was a great deal of subdued talking about
what had gone on. Some wore yellow or striped shirts with the
Star of David sewn on them, but such displays were frowned
upon rather than approved. They were seen as a cross between
bravado and sentimentality. Only the very brave or the strongly
individualistic made them. I remember a break time, in one of
the little groups that formed in the Refectory, when someone
affecting a Public School drawl said, 'I say Abrahams old boy,
fearfully bad show what these German Johnnies have been
doin' to yore folk. It's just not on, that sort of thing. Just NOT
ON...' It was part embarrassment that such things had to be
said and part inability to find the proper register in which to
say them.

In iβ I had a Jewish friend with whom I sometimes stayed at
weekends – I could never get him to stay with me. 'I can't,' he
said, 'you don't keep the Sabbath.' He did once visit us in the
Lakes with his family, when we arranged a picnic down by the
beck. It wasn't a success, because they weren't used to sitting
on rocks and eating out of doors, and the flies were a nuisance.
When I visited them it was like going into a strange country. I
was received very warmly and was fascinated by the gentleness
and formality of his life at home. Unlike mine, where the
atmosphere was agitated and tense with my cousins rushing to
get to work in the mornings or get out at night and everyone
wrapped up in some private concern, David's family seemed

to lead a quiet, orderly life, despite the unconventionality of his clever elder brother who wore a yarmulka at home as well as the Star of David. (When he was seventeen he won an open scholarship to Cambridge)

In our house we had no such exceptional being and everyone did different things. We each went our own way, meeting only once or twice a week for meals, and then it seemed by chance. At David's, on Friday night, we ate a formal meal together. There were candles on the table, I was given a yarmulka to wear, and before we ate his father read from the Torah. We had spicy fish-cakes, or chicken – which was always a treat – with rice which was only served as a pudding at home. The vegetables were baked and spicy or sweet rather than tasteless and soggy. Afterwards we had fruit and coffee. On the Saturday we sat altogether in a big lounge and read or played chess with his father, while his sisters and mother played the piano or did jigsaws. His father said, 'Yesterday we work, tomorrow we work, but today, we do nothing.' What we had to eat had been made the day before and the only cooking was boiling water for the coffee. On Sunday, everybody was busy again and I was given a lift home.

My father would have liked the Harris' household because he could have done his Guardian crossword there in peace, and had someone to listen to Tosca or La Bohème with – apart from me playing with my soldiers behind the settee. Here on winter afternoons, I listened to Grand Opera, ranging from Pagliacci to Die Meistersinger. My father, lying back in his chair, would conduct and sometimes join in the singing.

Even now, I seem to hear these pieces in four-minute sections punctuated by the clicks and clunks of the auto-change. Still, they subconsciously interrupt my listening.

5. SUTTON

Outside classes, discipline was maintained by the Prefects. They patrolled the corridors during the dinner break, often in pairs. Sometimes they were effective quellers of incipient riots, but mostly they were subjects for ribaldry and ridicule. They had authority to impose lines and order persistent wrong-doers to go to the Prefects' Room where the Head Prefect had powers to beat them, although as far as I knew he never did. I was sent there once for cheeking the newly appointed George Davenport, whom I'd known from Bowker's days. Their room was next to the Gym, looking out over the playing fields and with a little sunny sitting-out place with deck chairs, very jolly and informal. The Head Prefect laughed at me for taking George seriously, as though he had that trouble himself; after all, George was just a year and a bit ahead of me and only slightly bigger.

In the quads and on the playing fields there was rarely any trouble. We played cricket using piles of bags for wickets, and football with heaps of jackets for goals, and sometimes side by side. The presence of members of staff taking the lunchtime air might temporarily impose restraint, but there were no regular patrols. On one personally memorable occasion the Chief himself had intervened to check our 'insensitive behaviour' regarding the newly painted door, but generally we were left to do unchecked what we wanted to do.

However, Mr Sutton, the school porter, sometimes took it upon himself to prowl the corridors in search of malefactors. He was a lean and angular figure with something of Groucho Marx about him. It was partly the way he moved and partly the way he looked. Even before I was in the Sixth and an

afternoon habitué of the Tatler cinema and an aficionado of
the Marx Brothers' films, I thought that all he needed to step
into a remake of *A Night at the Opera* was a big cigar and a
lecherous wink. Customarily dressed in a long frock-coat with
frogged fastenings, Sutton had Groucho's stoop and black hair,
swept back from a frizzy front, and small spectacles through
which his eyes gleamed with apparent malevolence. Even now
I don't think I exaggerate. He exuded mistrust and dislike for
the creatures he had to do with, and guessing this they behaved
badly towards him as a matter of course. Furthermore, noticing
how he smarmed up to authority while coming down heavily
on them, they made sure his life was difficult. To us it seemed
that he spent his time at breaks roving the corridors in search
of petty wrongdoers, whom he hurried away to be 'dealt with'.
Few lunch-times passed without him driving some wretch to
the punishment station outside the Staff Room door.

His room was opposite the Cages where the coats were kept
and next to the pair occupied by Pansy Mason and Cuthbert
Seton. It was crammed with mislaid items, books and balls,
odd gymshoes and abandoned clothing. During breaks seekers
of lost property would wait outside his door. He had a snappish
manner that made him unpleasant to deal with and it was never
clear whether he should be treated as one of the staff – which
he patently wasn't – or in a joshing, off-hand but respectful
way like the kitchen ladies. Once I left my gym things on the
radiator outside Simkins' room and they were 'handed in' by
the cleaners. All sports thing should have name tapes on them,
and mine hadn't – but I told him what was in the bag before he
opened it. Still he said, 'How do I know they're yours. They
could be anybody's.' He fished them out and held them up.
'Decent enough gear. Good enough for Wood Street,' which
was where the Hugh Oldham Lads' Club was. 'I'm just making

up a parcel for them. They'll be glad of these.' He kept me in agony while I reckoned not only the expense of new ones but their cost in coupons should he be as good as his word.

While I was in iiiα the school was rocked by series of practical jokes. They were rumoured to be the work of L5b, a frankly un-academic class noted for producing formidable entrepreneurs. In one of his morning commentaries on the State of the Nation, and MGS in particular, the Chief referred to these activities as 'outrages' and certainly much of what the jokers did was delinquent if not downright criminal. They got into the backs and nooks of the building; they clearly had a pass key and could come and go as they pleased, even at weekends. They removed the inside knobs of classroom doors along the Maths corridor, so once inside it was impossible to get out. Then they fixed the lights so the fuse blew when they were switched on. This they did intermittently for the best part of a month until the cleaners refused to touch the switches 'in case they banged'.

They regularly invaded Sutton's room and reorganised it. On one occasion they moved everything out of it into the Cage opposite and jammed the lock, on another they left a cat in his room over the weekend with food and water but no cat-litter. However, their final stroke against him verged on the criminal. In his room was a hatch through which he rang the bell for the start of afternoon school. Its ting-ting-ting set us jog-trotting muddily back to school, hoping the ringing wouldn't stop. The jokers looped the rope round a brick in the shaft, and when he rang the bell the brick came thundering down towards him. He might have been killed.

The following morning after Prayers the Chief electrified his audience by sketching the possible consequences and stressing the likely fate of the culprits if the worst had happened. The case of Neville Heath, recently hanged for murder, was vivid in the public eye for the papers had been full of the case. I remembered reading frightening accounts of the murderer's progress to the gallows. With such an example we were made to see that capital punishment was more than the subject for a debate. The whole episode gave us an uncomfortable feeling that by condoning, if not applauding, the activities of the jokers, we were all guilty. Crime and Punishment were part of our lives and the jokers had been living in the shadow of the noose.

The gang's last and greatest coup, which did something to mend its reputation, was the Spider in the Hall. One Tuesday morning as the school was dutifully engaged in the morning hymn, the juniors on the steps behind the Chief slowly stopped singing. Row by row, they fell silent, mouths gaping, heads moving from side to side, as something slowly descended from one of the gratings in the ceiling of the Memorial Hall. Those at the far back of the hall were next to see it and likewise stopped singing. Those directly below sang lustily on, puzzled by the fading choir and the sense of something happening. I like to think that they were singing, 'New mercies each returning day, Hover around us while we pray,' but I don't suppose they were. The creature came to rest in the air just in front of the Chief and on a level with his eyes. It was more like a giant dragon fly than a spider and as it swung and spun its celluloid wings flashed in the lights, its pipe-cleaner legs seemed to twitch. Its tubular body, sprigged with feathers, was painted a vivid luminous green. Pants Acton at the organ, with his back to the spectacle, played on as though celebrating the creature's descent.

The Chief behaved as though nothing extraordinary had happened. He glanced round meaningfully at the choir and, obedient to the sound of the organ, the singing took up again at the start of a new verse. Meanwhile, the creature began to turn and swing as though the hot currents of air rising from the open mouths below had given it life. Morning Prayers thenceforward continued almost as normal, though the lesson was gabbled and the notices given out in a hurry. All the while the Chief remained silent, gazing balefully at the thing which had descended on his school. As soon as the daily business was done, he rose and swiftly led the way out of the Hall, which, for the first time since his arrival, broke into an excited babble.

And that was that. No one was found, and it was the gang's last act. At the time there had been a bustle at the back of the Hall as someone set out to see what was going on. But it was too late. The door at the back of Harry Plant's room was still ajar, but the roof-space it led to was empty. Round the ventilation grating the dust had been disturbed and the winding gear lay across the mesh, but those who unwound it had quit the scene, even, I guess, before their creature had stopped swinging.

Forty years on – again – one night in a Lakeland pub I heard who had done it and how it was managed. The names were only names, as often happened in a school as big as ours, and I was particularly sorry I'd never known them.

6. GLIMPSES OF THE WIDE WORLD

In iiiα I gradually became aware of the good and interesting things that Manchester provided for free. Until then, the city had been a place I had admired only in passing. First fleetingly from the windows of Bowker's, then breathlessly as my cousin, now gone to South Africa, hurried me up to Albert Square.

In the afternoon I was always in a rush for the train. Missing it upset my afternoon routine and left me until 4:43 to loiter uncomfortably on Platform 4 where I was exposed to the jeers of schoolfellows travelling on the Middleton, Rochdale and Littleborough line.

As I got older, I lost the urge to get home from school as quickly as I could. I dallied in front of interesting buildings, went into shops, explored the alleyways off Deansgate and marvelled at the half-timbered overhang of the Old Shambles, then facing the cathedral across an acre of rubble. Instead of dashing through Cheese Alley to the portals of Victoria Station, I sometimes strolled round Long Millgate and gazed at the gaunt façade of the old MGS. It was the same in the mornings, except Mondays and Thursdays when it was imperative that I join the home-workers' co-operative on the School Bus.

From my earliest days I took to dropping into Willshaw's Bookshop in John Dalton Street, just before they opened officially at nine. I would be their first caller, a small, talkative schoolboy, loitering among the books and asking questions about them. I suppose I was an engaging child, ready to talk to anyone and capable from an early age of conducting a conversation. I got on well with the city gents who travelled on the train, and had no trouble talking to strangers – which got me into one tight corner with a Scout Master and another with the priest. Willshaw's manager, Mr Buckley, and his assistant, Miss Spencer, might have discouraged me, at a time when they were preparing for the business of the day. But they were kind, and interested in my being there for a few minutes, two or three times a week. They fostered my interests and when the school library couldn't produce *The Adventures of Gerard,* they got a second hand copy for me. Then, when I was held spellbound by the Swallows and Amazons, they kept me up to date with them as they were published.

The books on display there always caught my attention. A large, coloured edition of *Alice in Wonderland* held me for days, in the course of which, I learned 'The Walrus and the Carpenter', 'Old Father William' and 'Jabberwocky'. Some time later I was taken in the same way by the monologues of Stanley Holloway and for weeks would bore my friends and family with 'Sam! Sam! Pick up thi musket...' and 'There's a famous sea-side place called Blackpool...'. My father was always prepared to give me money for books, and I usually spent at Willshaws the tokens I got at birthdays and Christmas, so I was, in a small way, a regular customer.

At the other end of the day, I found I could give the city half-an-hour before setting off home. For a while, I took to visiting Kendal Milne's and Lewis's, where there was fun of a sort on the lifts and escalators but I soon became bored with the simulated luxury of glitter and shine, the vast displays of things which I neither wanted nor admired. So I deviated no more into Deansgate but went straight down Cross Street where the windows of Stanley Gibbon's, receding from the street in a kind of a tunnel, had minimalist displays of valuable issues. They were usually shown in blocks of four, mounted on small white cards backed by black velvet, and priced exorbitantly, thus glamorising the whole business of philately. The thought that something of their ilk might turn up in my bumper packs of unsorted British and Colonial often lured me to the windows and eventually into the shop itself, where I had a sympathetic if discouraging reception. It was much the same at Basset Lowke in Corporation Street, where the shiny models of steam trains and motor cars with their delicately precise modelling cried out to be held up and inspected. I ached to hold them. There, too, from being merely a spectator, I ventured inside the shop to inspect the cabinets and chat with the shopmen, who were generally kindly disposed towards a talkative thirteen-year-old.

But of all these attractions, it was another bookshop, Sherratt and Hughes on the corner of St Anne's Street, that held me, even until it was time to rush for the 5:20, which was always uncomfortably full of office workers. I was especially drawn to the second-hand department in the basement. Here, the windows on a level with the pavement, showing only the feet and legs of the passers-by, cast light down on rows and rows of leather-backed volumes with ribbed spines and gilt lettering. I coveted them from the first and I don't really know why. But the weight of them and their smell and sight of the old black print drew me, perhaps in the same way that an enraptured neophyte is entranced by the fumes of incense and the lure of powerful mystery. Attracted by the title of the first poem, I spent my Christmas book tokens on an edition of Spenser, one pound ten shillings, six octavo volumes with decorated spines and gold titles. "The Shepherd's Calendar" didn't turn out to be quite what I expected; the shepherds weren't at all like the shepherds I knew. The volumes containing "The Fairy Queen" remained closed until I was at Oxford, and then only read under direction. However, the set of six, squat and golden-brown, sat comfortably on the top of my bookcase through the rest of my schooldays and it made me feel good only to look at them.

Apart from bonanzas at Christmas and birthdays, I was usually short of money, but could generally get some for a book. Daily expenses I helped myself to from the loose change in my father's trouser pocket, telling him what I needed, and what I had taken, as he eased himself into consciousness. I never needed very much: a couple of shillings, eight pence for bus fares and a shilling for lunch, unless I had a dinner ticket. My train fare was covered by a season ticket. From time to time he would accuse me, in a half-hearted way, of taking more than I needed. This deeply offended my sense of honour, but sowed seeds that sprouted and when he had a pocket full of loose change, I would help myself to an extra bob. I'd always been led to believe that anything over the necessary costs, I would lose or 'fritter away', a favourite phrase of my father's. So I felt it always a duty to spend whatever I had left before I got home. The Tuck Shop or the Pie Shop on the Meldon Road estate could always gobble up a spare sixpence, and on the way home there was a bake shop in Fennel Street – just opposite the entrance to Cheese Alley – that sold cream cakes for fourpence.

I was never really interested in money – it still bores me to talk about it or consider ways of getting it – and although there have been times when I could have done with more I never really considered its lack to be an embarrassment. It was inconvenient sometimes to be short, but that was all. I was made aware that as a family we were not rich, but I never felt poor or went short of anything I needed. My father was a local government official, a Medical Officer of Health, and as far as I could see he led a pleasant, unstressed life, attending clinics, inspecting schools, going to meetings. None of these seemed to interfere with what he really wanted to do, like going to Old Trafford in the afternoons, or taking a week off in September to go fishing. I made up my mind then, that I would follow his example and get taken on by some benevolent organisation which would largely leave me alone while it paid me to do the things I was good at and enjoyed doing. Whatever it was, I knew it would have to be about books.

7. MUSIC

In iiiα I was introduced to the Music Society by Satters, tall, thin, bespectacled, anarchic, who had suddenly become a close companion. Looking back at him through the tunnel of the years, I see him as a sort of cultured barbarian, an educated vandal who quite fittingly went to Balliol. We must have been in the same form since iα, but he didn't rise above the horizon of my consciousness until the third form, when I found out that his family came from Ulverston. That made him a link with home, for he usually spent his holidays in Furness. He became my musical mentor and fellow delinquent, and in time, we managed to re-organise the Record Lending Library to our own satisfaction.

('What shall we do with these recordings of the Wolf-Ferrari songs, Davidson,' he said. 'No one takes them out.' He paused. 'Steal them, perhaps?'

'Oh, I'm not sure about that, Satters. Not yet, anyway.'

'My catalogue says they're quite valuable. Forsyth's might be interested in them.'

'Maybe we could swap them for the *Brandenburgers*. They would have a better circulation.'

But that was when we were blasé sixth formers.)

At Michaelmas half-term I'd gone to visit him when he was in Ulverston. In between talking about fishing and Broughton Mills and how much better it was than Bolton, where there was nothing to do at weekends, I mentioned my father's addiction to opera.

'That's what I do on Saturdays,' I said, 'loll on the settee while my father plays his opera records – Verdi and Wagner mostly.' Satters, not much interested in fishing, perked up.

'Opera?' he said. 'Not my pigeon. I'm more for symphonies. Beethoven's the jockey for me. Marvellous stuff. Hits you in the pit of the stomach. Does your old man have *Fidelio*?'

'What's that?' I said.

'Beethoven's opera. He started another one but never got much further than the overture. You like Wagner, you say. I think he always sounds a bit belchy. All trumpets and timpani. But if that's the sort of thing that grabs you, you might like Beethoven. He does it very well. We're playing the *Eroica* at the Mus Soc next week. You should come along and find out.'

My father was always sniffy about Beethoven – which I felt, even then, was a bit like talking down Shakespeare: you were so strongly expected to like him that it seemed a grave error not to do so. Father justified his position by a series of potted judgements: 'Echoes of Haydn and glimpses of Brahms. Neither one thing nor the other, but interesting stuff. Part of the necessary development between Bach and Wagner, I suppose.' Like a lot of his off-the-cuff remarks, I only caught the general sense of what he meant, but it was clear that Beethoven had only his grudging approval. Thinking about this view some years later, I felt it was a bit like accepting Galileo as a minor but necessary step between Ptolemy and Newton.

Nevertheless, the 'great Ludwig' – Satters' phrase – wasn't entirely foreign to me for I'd heard the Hallé play the *Pastoral* at one of the Sunday afternoon concerts my father took me to. I'd been swept away by the swelling tide of sound as the woodwind gave way to the violins at the beginning of the first movement. That was in the days when the Hallé played in the draughty King's Hall at Belle Vue, where the Christmas circuses and wrestling matches were held. It was beyond the botanical gardens and adjacent to a great field of black cinders where we parked the car, then picked our way through rows of other vehicles to reach the entrance. Inside there were tiers of wooden seats looking down onto the platform. We were always high up

– 'That's where it sounds best,' my father said. Certainly the hard benches around us were always fairly full of what seemed to be discerning listeners for some of them had scores. There, I would sink down and let myself be engulfed by the music, closing my eyes and concentrating on the sound. The orchestra itself was a huddle of dark shapes thirty yards away, shot with silver and golden gleams from their instruments. The players were so far off that it was difficult to tell who was playing what. Only the percussionist, standing to one side surrounded by his pots and pans, remained visibly distinct. I couldn't imagine how those who went to wrestling matches or the Circus ever managed to see anything.

From the first I was bowled over by the sound of a full orchestra: the clarion of the brass and the sweep of the strings, the clear piping of the woodwind. It bothered me that the musicians were too far away for me to distinguish who made which sound, and the whole effect was magically puzzling. I would struggle to adjust the music to the programme notes and wonder how the words could relate to the sounds. It was easy enough to see the connection between the *Ode to Joy* and the exultation of the chorus, but I couldn't work out which passage in *Till Eulenspiegel* was meant to represent his affair with the merchant's wife and while the surge of the sea was clearly portrayed in the opening of the *Overture to the Hebrides*, the 'exultation of divine vouchsafement' in the horns of the third *Brandenburg Concerto* was not convincingly apparent to my agnostic ears.

The Music Society met on Tuesdays after school in Johnny Lingard's room, opposite which I used to loiter on truant trips to the loo in Prep 1 on the off chance of him having one of his famous 'turns'. Satters' enthusiasm encouraged me to go the next meeting where the man himself received me courteously. The secretary entered my name in the list of members and told me I needn't pay my subs until next week. I found a desk by the window among the half-dozen or so ordinary members, while the committee members and officers had seats round the table with the gramophone. In command position next to it and lolling in his armchair was the famous Johnny Lingard, lean and sharp-faced with flashing spectacles and a shock of yellow hair that he would fling back with a toss of his head. I could well imagine him 'throwing a wobbler', a phrase which our Australian airmen used to describe the fits of near hysteria they teased my cousins into. He supervised the changing of the records and sharpening of the needles which were made of thorn or fibre, for the Mus Soc would have none of the steel ones of the kind which had got me into so much trouble in iβ. Occasionally as his acolytes were at work, he would provide programme notes, like: 'Watch out for the change of tempo in the coda,' or, 'The richness of the orchestration in this next section will make you swoon.' 'Swoon' was a favourite word of his.

I remember that first meeting well. It was a cold November day with a cloudless blue sky and a bitter east wind which harried the weather vane on top of the clock tower. I half lay on the desk top with my head on my folded arms and watched the light fade across the rooftops. Beethoven bore me away again, the changing themes and varying rhythms enchanted me. Rossini, Mozart, Verdi, even the 'great Richard' himself, paled into insignificance and I was lifted out of the bare classroom into regions of pure sound. Satters was vindicated, and the 'great Ludwig', too. The divine voices of Galli-Curci, Patti, Melba, the purity of Gigli's tenor, were all relegated to the level of the crooners my cousins played when it was their turn on the gramophone. My father's taste seemed callow and his heroes, Wagner, Brahms, Puccini, Rossini, second-rate fellows. I resolved to buy a recording of *Fidelio* for his birthday which was, I remembered, next week. Satters would know where I could get one and I was sure my mother – and my cousins if I could reach them – would chip in.

After that I became a regular attender at Mus Soc meetings. My musical horizons widened as I was exposed to Bach and Vivaldi, Mozart and Schubert, Mahler and Sibelius, whose second symphony was almost as much of a revelation as my first hearing of the *Eroica*. I suddenly became aware that MGS was a very musical school. Without my realising it before, there were always virtuoso musicians performing in the lecture theatre or the Memorial Hall: singers, fiddlers, organists, wind players and innumerable pianists, some of whom went on to be international successes. Scarcely a lunch-time went by but someone was giving a recital, even if there was no one listening.

The affairs of the Mus Soc – never known as anything else – extended into lunchtimes when a few enthusiasts would meet impromptu in the cubby-hole at the back of the library where the Society's collection of records was kept. Here, among out-of-date gramophones with monstrous horns and racks of heavy records, even rolls, knowledgeable members would affirm that Gieseking was better than Paderewski, or Menuhin than Kreisler, or Satie was rubbish. My musical education was extended in all sorts of exciting ways as I listened to these pundits laying down the law, damning and exalting – nothing was done in moderation.

Satters was much better than I was at knowing what was going on, and to further our musical education, we took to visiting

Forsyth's Music Shop on Deansgate. Skirting the displays of pianos on the ground floor, we made for the basement. There, we would commandeer an audio-booth and listen to records we were pretending to buy. (Having managed to raise the money for an edited version of *Fidelio*, I'd established my authenticity as a bona-fide customer for one occasion at least.) I guess we were something of a nuisance, and occasionally, after asking for something impossible to listen to, like *Das Rheingold,* we would be eased out. But perhaps because we came at the tail-end of the afternoon when business was slack, the staff were not only tolerant, but informative and indulgent. Maybe they recognised us as the seed-corn from which future harvests would be gathered. In the same way that Mr Buckley and Miss Spencer at Willshaws indulged me, they humoured us by pointing at what was new whilst unobtrusively repairing the gaps in our knowledge of what was old. Again, I guess we were sponsored by our little metal owls.

Even in the bleak days of austerity after the war had ended – during the times my father despaired – it seemed that the city was throbbing with music. At the Central Library there were lunchtime recitals in the little theatre in the basement, and at the Royal Northern School of Music on Oxford Road there was always someone performing. Later on when I was free to ramble in the city in the evenings, I went to hear travelling opera companies at both the Palace Theatre and the Opera House, where I was entranced by Vittoria de los Angeles as Carmen. And after I had left school, I remember the newly ennobled Sir John in the newly restored Free Trade Hall, turning to face the audience, until we were all were seated and attentive, before he raised his baton.

8. FAT FREEMAN

Fat Freeman was a hate figure. Made up of provocative attitudes and manners, physically unattractive, he seemed made for persecution. He wasn't really fat, just stocky and squat, but 'Fat Freeman' was a name that tripped off the tongue. It was coined on his first day, and it stuck. He joined the school late, having 'chickened out of the war' in New York where he'd acquired a grating, American accent and a lot of un-English habits. He spoke as though he was playing a part in one of the gangster films we sometimes saw on Saturdays. These disadvantages he improved by being a crushing know-all, also he was oily, fawning on people when he wanted something, and curtly dismissive when he didn't. He boasted, he wore a ring, and he walked with a swagger. Only to meet him in the corridor, swinging his hips and swaying his shoulders, was to dislike him. These habits may have won him respect in Manhattan, but in Rusholme they cut little ice.

That he had managed to avoid the war was the real and insurmountable bar to his being accepted. While we were sleeping in air-raid shelters and suffering air-raids, living off dried eggs and potatoes, getting sweets once a month if we were lucky, he was steak-fed and candy-stuffed, so he said, and living in a 'Dooplex' apartment overlooking the Park which was full of entertainments and attractions that were so 'noo an sophisticated' as to be beyond our comprehension. It was irritating beyond belief that he always expected us to be impressed by this parade of luxuries – 'You might a seen them in the movies, 'cos I guess there's nuthin like 'um over hee-ur.' We weren't impressed: we were disgusted, even though we had only the vaguest idea what he meant. I thought 'duplex' was the name of a fancy gear change that some chaps had on their bikes, rather than the Sturmey Archer three-speed that most of us desired. And by Park he seemed to mean a fun-fair rather than the public gardens most towns had. This dissociation of sensibility made everybody loathe him, and all the more because he didn't notice it. He was the only Jew I knew to be persecuted, and most of his persecutors were Jewish. David Cohen said, 'What a bore you are, Freeman. Why don't you drop dead?' Levi would simply shake his head and sigh. Big Abrahams, a thug in his own right, said, 'Sod off, Freeman. You smell like my sister.' And so he did, being strongly perfumed with deodorant and talcum powder, in a society where most of us quite rightly smelled of dubbined football boots, carbolic soap and boy.

As Satters observed, Freeman had the 'social skills of a rhinoceros at the watering hole.' 'Hey, guys,' he would say, barging into a group, 'you wanna see my noo Biro...' He would produce one of those ink-sticks which Simkins preached against and Artie Moore forbade – Freeman had his homework rejected three times before he recognised the ban was absolute. At other times he would produce his brother's Fraternity pin or a waterproof watch, something he was sure we wouldn't have. He would butt into conversations, confident that what he had to say was more interesting than what was going on. 'Wassat ole football you on about? Yew shud a seen the Noo York Yankees play. I knoo the Cheer leader before we came over here. Wow, there was a babe.' To those of us discussing Bert Trautmann's keeping or Nat Lofthouse's headers for goal, these interruptions were not merely crass, but disturbingly offensive. He would be invited to 'Get lost,' to 'Take a long walk on a short pier,' or 'Drop Dead.' Satters would snap his fingers an inch from Freeman's nose and tell him that as far as decent, honest people were concerned, he'd had it.

But he never 'got' any of this. Bewitched by the magic of his own presence, he just couldn't accept that people weren't glad to see him. He would say, 'Aw cummon, you fellas. Youse guys sore or sumpn? Here, I got some candy. Less all have some candy.' And taking a handful for himself, he would pass the bag to someone else. His constant bragging about the parcels from America which gave him much more of most things than we had, only served to widen the gap that separated us. He tried hard to use these goodies to 'get in', but they availed him little for, true to the traditions of the Empire, we took the bribes but didn't let them affect what we had made up our minds to do.

What became increasingly irritating was his refusal to be squashed. No matter how much he was put down, he always bounced back. His exposure to life in Manhattan seemed to have made him unsquashable. We heaped on him all our feelings of deprivation: food-rationing, blackout, hand-me-down clothes, make-do-and-mend, family disruption and loss. We made him into a repository of our grievances, a kind of scape-goat. I guess those affected by the obscenities of the concentration camps still being revealed found his thick-skinned optimism particularly hard to put up with. It made matters worse that he was such a sleek and self-satisfied goat. It irked us mightily that he wouldn't go off into the desert and die, but cheerfully remained to remind us of our guilt.

He couldn't believe that we loathed him and he regarded our attitude as part of 'that crazy sense of humour' we Britishers had. 'But you're British, Freeman,' said Satters with a cruel gleam in his eye. 'You showed us your passport. Remember?' And so he had; in his first week; when, despite his determination to be different, he was trying to prove he was one of us. 'But you're chicken British,' Satters continued, 'because you ran away during the war. You just like to think you're American. Well, you might just as well be, because Americans stink. And so do you.'

And that was our general attitude to the USA just then. From being our glorious allies, brothers-in-arms, purveyors of cigarettes and candy, nylons and silk nighties, they had become truculent, self-important bullies who strolled the streets as though they were in an occupied country. At weekends, droves of them came into the city from the Air Base at Burtonwood. Besides our smartly turned out squaddies they looked like tourists, with loose jackets and flapping trousers. Loud-mouthed and overbearing, they were insensitive to the point of brutality. Furthermore the girls loved them. What better grounds for our hatred? Also there was much disquiet amongst our elders about the atom bomb and its continued development. The American tests at Los Alamos and Bikini Atoll were ample reasons to fear that they would use such weapons again if there were another war, like the one that was brewing in Korea. Also, there was growing and increasingly authoritative opinion that there was no need for them to have dropped a bomb on Nagasaki. The one on Hiroshima would have been enough.

Fat Freeman occasioned the only time I remember being beaten at MGS – that is apart from the taps that Billy Hulme used to administer for minor faults in grammar or spelling: two taps from Little Dot for missing an accent. Those were more in the way of public entertainment than punishment; but this was in earnest and it stung. A few of us were in Punishment School for some group misdemeanour which I've forgotten about, perhaps because I was ashamed of being a part of it. We were in Harry Plant's room – where Spiderman got into the roof space above the Memorial Hall – a disgruntled, disaffected group, waiting for the master-in-charge. Hargreaves and I were sitting together with Freeman just in front.

I had recently made myself a cosh. At that time, 'Cosh boys' figured in the Press as the latest evidence of our degenerate times. 'Coshes' were what American gangsters carried in the detective novels of Peter Cheyney which I was reading at the time. Mine was made from a length of rubber gas-pipe that I'd bent into a hoop and hammered a piece of lead into. It was carefully bound with string and wrapped in a two layers of broad band elastoplast from my father's medical stores. It was about nine inches long, bulbous and white. Slightly floppy, it looked like an erect penis just beginning to wilt and as I was showing it to an interested Hargreaves, he pointed out the similarity.

'What's it for?' he said.
'Hitting people. It's a cosh. You must have heard of them.'
'Where do you hit them?'
'Here,' I said, and swung it round to catch Freeman at the back of the ear. 'Like that.'

Just then the master-in-charge appeared, stern-faced, laden with marking and the Punishment Book. Freeman gave a theatrical scream and collapsed over the desk. The man in charge seemed not to notice and carried on to the desk where he carefully laid out his things and started to rummage in the drawers. This took a minute or two, during which Freeman kept whimpering and I tried to merge with my background. Finding what he was seeking, Nemesis stood up with a large gym-shoe in his hand. He caught my horrified eye and crooked his finger. No words were spoken, just a sign. Mesmerised, I crept to the front, where without speaking, he turned me round. bent me over the front desk and gave me two stinging blows on the tight of my pants. Still not a word was said, and we returned to our respective places – he to call the register, and me gingerly to sit down.

9. SPORT

I never liked Games and I never wanted to be on a 'team', or even part of a gang. Groups of two or three were what I liked; Caddy and McElvie, David Harris, Hargreaves, Satters. As a member of a group, I always felt swept along and put into positions where I had to do what I didn't want to. I never had a sense of 'team spirit'. This had been recognised early. In a meeting à propos my failure to shine in ways expected of me, the Chief had told my father: 'Davidson is an individualist who only does with reluctance what others do'. This was a view repeated in my reference for Oxford, which so intrigued the college admissions board, according to my tutor, that I was offered a place almost on the strength of it.

In earlier days, this disinclination to be part of a group was most obvious in my dislike of Games. In Prep 1 and 2 I thought I ought to like football – it was usually presented as a 'good thing' in the books and comics that I read, although I noted that it didn't figure in *Swallows and Amazons* – and at first, I turned out on Games afternoons, hoping I might enjoy whatever we were going to play. However, the weather was generally cold and nasty, and I never seemed to get a kick at the ball. Warned not to chase after it, which seemed the sensible thing to do, I stayed in the position I'd been allocated – left back, as a rule – and waited until the play came to my quarter of the field. Then, as the hearties who knew all about it bore down on me, passing the ball between them, I was flummoxed, so was the goal keeper and usually the ball was 'lodged in the corner of the net', as they put it in *The Rover.*

'Why didn't you tackle him,' our captain hissed as we formed up for yet another kick-off.

'I couldn't catch him,' I said. 'He dodged past me.' And adding in regretful tone, 'It was the only chance I had of kicking the ball since we started.'

'You've got to keep up,' he snarled. 'Support the half-backs and be ready to feed the forwards.'

What did he mean: 'Feed the forwards?' How could I when the ball never came near me? Much later on, when I became a half-hearted supporter of Manchester City – the Blues, by far the most popular team at the time – I realised what I should have done, but even if I had, I knew my heart wasn't in it.

MGS was a sporting school for those who wanted it to be. Whatever it was, you could play it: soccer, rugger, lacrosse, athletics, cross country running, swimming. With so many potential players it was possible to encompass all sports, and once in the main school you could choose. I was no good at ball games, and apart from disliking the hurly-burly of the football field, I hated being out in the cold and the wet. The Chief had done away with the old House system which separated the school into groups comprising all ages, in favour of Divisions which were composed of the forms in one year, so Division One was made up of all the first forms. On Games afternoons I met my peer group, and I didn't like it.

The school didn't have a sporting ethos. There was no general or popular adulation of games, no looking forward to important matches or admiring the heroes who would triumph in them. Colours were awarded to those who represented the school, and their names were announced in the general business transacted after Prayers, but that didn't seem to give them special prestige. Sport was much celebrated in the comics we read – *The Rover,* especially, was devoted to sporting heroes, but in the *Wizard* and *Hotspur* they were still fighting the War or engaged in "Adventures". We were all encouraged to play something every week, but in iiiα at least, there was little enthusiasm for sport. By that stage I had acquired an antipathy to football of every kind and opted for swimming or running on Games afternoons. Running seemed to me the least painful; after all I ran a mile most afternoons, from school to the bus and from the bus to the train, usually carrying my bag and my coat. The only difference was that on games afternoons I changed into shorts and pumps.

Apart from cricket, that most individualistic of team games, which I loved passionately without having the slightest aptitude for it, I had no taste or skill in games of the kind we were expected to play. The sporting spirit inherent in *Tom Brown's Schooldays* was to me not so much mystery as anathema. My sports concerned solitary country skills, I was a keen fisherman in the becks and rivers of home and I was finding out about roach in canals, tench in ponds and pike and perch in the flashes of South Lancashire.

In iiiα Claude Rayne set us a homework essay with the title: "Sundays". 'Let your imaginations roam,' he said. '"Sundays",' he paused as if to savour the word, 'what does it *mean* to you?' I knew what it meant to me and I let myself go in three sides of lyrical effusion. When the work was returned, I was shocked to discover I'd got nought out of twenty. Claud Raine, unmoved by my complaining, justified his marking.

'The subject of the essay was *Sundays,*' he said. 'Your essay was about fishing.'

'But that's what I do on Sundays,' I said.

'You didn't make that plain. It may be a reason but I don't accept it as an excuse.'

I was mortified, because I was used to doing well at essays. Was I not the winner of the *Ulula* Prize for the best article in the School Magazine? My last piece in it had been about fishing. The book I chose for a prize was about fishing.

My interest in Field Sports had recently grown as I was learning to shoot. For Christmas that year I'd got what had been for ages my heart's desire: a BSA air rifle, and I realised that I'd made my last visit to the Irwell Rubber Company for catapult elastic. The ballista had been replaced by the cannon. In the summer I'd had the supervised use of a .410 shotgun and licence to wander over a hundred-odd acres of wood and fell and field. How could a grubby game of football compare with the excitement of that? I noted that in *Stalky and Co*, another favourite, the only sports they seemed to allow were running and swimming, which were all right with me. Furthermore, their idea of a fine afternoon was to disappear into the countryside with something to read and to smoke, which matched largely with my ideal, except I hadn't yet taken to tobacco. With the departure of Mr Cuggy, I had taken to swimming at lunchtime, when there was half an hour of free-for-all. I liked the easy camaraderie of the baths, no one was striving for anything, the atmosphere friendly and good-humoured, and apart from the dedicated souls who trudgeoned up and down the pool dodging the dive bombers, there was a general lack of any purpose but simple enjoyment.

Otherwise, when faced with a choice between team sports and running, I ran. Although we were just across the road from the Rusholme Sports Ground, where national running events took place, there was little emphasis on running. Our course was simply round the school. Leaving the Rectory where we changed, we ran up to Old Hall Lane, then down it to the houses by the Gym, round to the Memorial Hall then back to the Rectory – twice if there was time. Half of this was what I was accustomed to run at 3.40 on my way to the bus. Perhaps as a result of my daily training I was found to be quite good at running and I enjoyed it, generally managing to keep up with the leaders. Then, much to my annoyance, I was picked for a school team in a Cross Country run. I was horrified: my sacred Saturday was marked out for something I felt ought to be happening during the week. It was part of a Manchester Schools event and the course was somewhere out towards Stockport, impossibly difficult for me to get there from Bolton, I argued, especially on a Saturday morning. I sought to be excused from this honourable but onerous obligation. Artie Moore listened in a kindly but unsympathetic way. 'I know it's difficult,' he said, 'but you ought to go. The team is depending on you, so you must make the effort. Catch an earlier train, perhaps. Arrange to go with another member of the team. Ask to meet someone who's travelling from town and go with him. I think you must try to be there.'

There was the glint of steel in his kindly, practical advice, and put in that way it all seemed so simple and un-arduous I could only comply. And so, full of resentment at the thought of a spoiled Saturday, I rose early and caught the strangely empty 8.20 into Manchester. I hadn't arranged to travel with anyone and I had only an address to guide me and instructions from someone who'd run there last year. 'You catch a 53 from Piccadilly,' he said. 'Get off at Penny Hill and follow the crowd. You'll probably see someone else from school. There'll be lots of runners. Stick to them.'

I dawdled a bit on the way up to Piccadilly, spent some time looking in the window of Stensby-Pickford, and it was well after nine when I boarded the 53. When I tendered my fare, the conductor had no knowledge of Penny Hill. 'No hidea,' he said. 'Sure it's on this route? Sounds like a girl. I'd better book you through to the terminus and you can get off when you like.'

The fare was more than I'd imagined and ate into my store of money. My father had given me half-a-crown, 'in case of emergency' but I'd already marked that down for a new Penguin at Willshaw's together with a plausible reason why it had had to be spent. Now I might have to sacrifice the post-race pie from the shop in Fennel Street. The bus limped its weary way down Stockport Road without my seeing anything like a running track or boys who might be runners. Nor was there any sign of open ground big enough for a cross country run. My watch told me that whenever I found the stop it would be a race to get there in time. Soon we dropped down into the dip which I knew was Stockport. The white Town Hall gleamed in the winter sunshine. I looked in vain for a bookshop then caught the 53b back to Manchester. It seemed to go a different way back and half way it stopped for longer than usual. I looked up from my book and saw it was filling with boys, red-cheeked and tousled, carrying sports bags. Amongst the crowd waiting to board were the other members of the Cross Country team.

'You!' said my captain. 'Where were you? We had to run without you. You lost us our chance in the Relay. We couldn't compete without you.'

'Got lost,' I mumbled. 'Couldn't find the right stop. Ended up in Stockport.'

'You're a wet,' said the Captain, a tall fair-haired boy from S3F. 'You'll never get picked again.'

That's a relief, I thought, and tried to look disappointed.

10. SCHOLASTICS

And so the year went on with Greek grammar and Latin proses; Cuthbert Seton on the Industrial Revolution, Turnip Townsend, Coke of Holkham, the Corn Laws: 'Draw me a picture of a turnip drill,' he ordered. English with Claude Rayne: *Essays of Elia* I think and Leigh Hunt and Rupert Brooke. Every day incomprehensible maths with Ernie Cropper. I was stuck in the bottom maths set, surrounded by strange faces with nary a form-mate to share my burden. It was all dry as a bone, except the bones our dogs had were always slimy. Dry as dust, except we moved about so much it hadn't time to settle.

In English we also learned about clichés. They were non-contentious and usually expressed some tacit agreement about the nature of things. They helped the discourse to flow along in unsurprising, agreeable ways, without 'frightening the horses', a phrase of Satters, which he said was often used by his grandfather who used to be an ostler. 'He looked after the horses at The Sun Hotel in Ulverston.' Satters and I devised conversations which were made up of clichés. Viz: 'How goes it, Satters?' 'Tip-top, old bean. And yourself?' 'Oh, Quite well, you know. Mustn't grumble.' 'And your lady wife?' 'In the pink, or is it in the red?' 'A trifle cold for the time of the year, what?' We always came back to the weather and finished, in unison: 'Most inclement,' pronounced 'ink-lemment'.

Perhaps it was because so much of our time was spent learning lists of verbs, theorems, grammatical rules, that we played words games like this which in themselves were tests of what we could remember. Apart from Greek, which was new and special – only the alpha forms and Classical VI did Greek – we marched along well-trodden roads, slogging along with shouldered packs, preparing for the battles that were to be fought next year and the year after, and the year after that. Matriculation was next, our first struggle with the outside world, then Highers, then Oxbridge Schols, then Mods, then Schools, the list seemed endless. In Rα we would start on the exam syllabus, meanwhile, it was essential that we acquired the 'grounding' – an undefined but significant quantity, whose value had been regularly asserted by both Simkins and Artie Moore. 'A good grounding in vocabulary and syntax is essential to your mastering Homer, Xenophon, Caesar and Ovid,' they said, and they might as well have added: St John, Horace, Shakespeare, Kipling, conkers, ice-skating, flirting and all the skills that were necessary for "getting on" towards whatever ends the Fates had in store.

Somehow, what we did at school had become more important and instead of being just an unpleasant but necessary adjunct to home, where the real living was done, it became the other end of an axis. Two stations held for so long in equipoise became part of a continuum. What we did at school acquired significance and importance and seemed less of an imposition than a necessary training for the real games we would eventually be playing. The weekends were no longer spent in isolation from what I did in the week, but gradually became extensions of school life and I was involved through it in the cinema and theatre and concerts and all kinds of exciting and mind-expanding pastimes the city could provide.

School influence and affairs reached further and further into what I thought of as my other life. Even the journey to and fro which I'd considered part of it became subsumed in the all-embracing reach of school. For instance, the school bus involved its passengers in various interesting and unexpected ways. It left Cannon Street just after nine, and it was usually a rush to catch it. Nevertheless, as the morning traffic built up it was often late reaching school, thereby giving those without a Late Pass a perfect excuse for missing prayers, and like Bowker's creating a community of its own which cut across the formal divisions of age and class. School bus chaps acknowledged each other with a wink or a friendly cuff on the shoulder in passing. Like the discretion of shipmates who tell on shore nothing of what happens at sea, what took place on the bus was kept in a closed book. The Prefect removed his cap when travelling to show that as far as he was concerned, what we did was *ultra vires*. Not that much illicit occurred – a little smoking on the back seat, perhaps, the occasional rag which the conductor was quick to stamp on, much late homework and a great deal of fraternising with the High School girls.

In iiiα the three of us who were regular School Bus men set up a discrete working party devoted to vetting our homework. On Monday mornings, Satters and Hargreaves and I would pool our attempts at the weekend's Latin prose and in the course of the journey agree on the best version. Then we would decide the scores, awarding high marks in rotation and allotting errors to avoid any hint of collaboration. There was often a wrangle.

'No, Satters, you'd better have three mistakes this week.'
'But there were only two in my rough copy.'
'That doesn't matter, you had full marks last week. You can't expect to do well all the time.'
'Why not?'

'Because you're not Todd, and this is a co-op,' said Hargreaves, from Rochdale.

We liked the idea of outwitting Artie, and it wasn't copying because we all started with versions of our own. We acted as a committee with dictionaries and grammars to hand, and puzzled out a fair copy. Rarely did it differ in more than a couple of points from Artie Moore's. Sometimes the process continued at break, just before the work was due to be handed in. Then, anyone simply trying to copy was driven away. 'Piss off,' was Hargreaves' way of dealing with an upstart trying to muscle in with an eager pencil and a clean sheet. 'Boil your own cabbages.' These Monday and Thursday morning conferences had great educational value. Arguing about the differing versions, fighting to defend one's own in the face of sharp criticism and speculating what might be the best, taught me more about Latin and Greek, verse and prose, than ever I learned in class. There it often seemed as if the top of my head was taken off, raw knowledge poured in and then left to ferment or decay as it proved useful or not. As the year progressed and we advanced in our study of Greek, the co-op was useful again and another morning a week was taken up with joint studies.

This interfered with another unintended benefit of the school bus, namely the girls from the High School in the bay opposite. Passengers from both buses took a keen interest in each other and there were frequent exchanges of notes. More, it seemed to me, from them to us than in the other direction. Sometimes a bossy girl prefect would interrupt and intercept them, but despite her efforts meetings were sometimes arranged. The more impetuous and daring arranged to rendezvous at lunchtime in Platt Fields, which adjoined the girls' school, although it was out of bounds for the girls. After-school appointments were not uncommon, but most meetings were arranged for Saturday mornings. Then, over coffee in the Kardomah, a visit to the cinema might be negotiated with the promise of a couple of hours in the dark.

I'd progressed little in my knowledge of sex and girls since the days when Caddy and McElvie and I used to speculate just what it was that Pickup and his girl were up to on Mosley Common. Despite my encounters at home with frank and forceful Cumbrian lasses, I was still in their eyes very much a booby. 'Wat's use o' Greek if tha kna's nowt about furtlin?' was one contemptuous view of my academic life. In the hurly burly of catch and kiss I was as fastidious as I was with football.

The bold makers of assignments were in the fifth or sixth; to me in the lower school girls were still a mystery. Although the Macinnes family I'd lived with before we came to Bolton had two daughters, I still thought of them as the cats and myself as a dog. I saw Marion and Marjorie quite often for our families were close friends and they went to the High School, but I was still for them a figure of fun, to be teased as a matter of course. When we met, as we often did on the way to our respective buses, they would smile at me in that superior way people have who have seen you in your underpants. I knew that they would never be able to take me seriously. But just now, these old connections were useful in establishing communication between the buses, for where I sat became a marker, a sort of range finder. Thus, a note could be addressed to 'The boy in the window two seats up from Ian Davidson'.

As I later found out, it was not unusual for the chosen one to turn up supported by a couple of friends, as happened to me when I was in the first year sixth. At first I was staggered to see how different they looked out of school uniform. Had they not approached me I might not have recognised them, so much did they seem to be of the same generation as my cousins. I was immediately horrified at the prospect of having to buy them all coffee and buns, but the friends calmed my fears by scuttling off to a table on their own, from which they watched us closely and seemed to be taking notes. In this instance I found them an asset for I could ask about them rather than fumble for a conversation about us.

11. AND SO TO Rα

Artie Moore gave way to Willie Graham and almost as one day follows another I found myself in the Remove, my last year in the lower school. Now was the time for serious effort for this was when we sat the School Certificate, the fearsome Matric, which I already knew something about from my Barrow cousins. They had presented it as an ordeal on a level with Torquemada's inquisitions, but only half as bad as the torments of the next stage, the Higher School Certificate. These exams were part of a system that was about to be replaced by the GCE, and the first step in a process, still apparently in train, of making it easier and easier to get an academic qualification. The exams we were being prepared for were almost the last of the old kind and those we took two years later were the Advanced GCEs, the first of the new régime.

Willie Graham was tall and bespectacled with the look of an ascetic. He made me feel that life was a grim and weary business, and I didn't take it seriously enough. His voice was high-pitched and rose almost to a shriek when he was exasperated. Unlike Artie Moore, who made us sit in alphabetical order, Willie G allowed us to choose. In the free-for-all of the first day of term, I bagged the desk by the radiator on the next to the back row. It was also next to the window. Here I was on the edge, out of his line of vision and on sunny afternoons I could experiment with a little burning glass while the serious work of the class went on around me.

In Rα we became real Greek scholars, progressing from the exercises we did with Artie Moore translating sentences like, "Pericles summoned the generals to the Agora" and "O, Demosthenes, will you teach the boys to orate', to the real Greek of Xenophon's *Anabasis* and Book Six of the *Iliad.* To my surprise I began to enjoy the subject. I felt something of the drama of the ten thousand marching north because it was the only way they knew to get home. At first, when construing Xenophon, I would pronounce "Cyrus" as though it rhymed with "cirrus", which I knew as the Latin for curl, and had a short "i" sound as in "syrup". Willie G, would patiently correct me, 'It's a long "y", Davidson. 'Think of "sky".' And so I tried to, but the connection between "sky" and cirrus clouds – which we had learned something of in geography with Toby Cantrell – confused me. One morning I was pulled up so sharply that I was unnerved and the name became a stumbling block. As I proceeded, it recurred two parasangs later, and I was so unsettled by the sight of it that I said again, "Cirrus". Willie G exploded, waving his hands and rising to his feet. 'Sye-russ!' he shrieked. 'Sye-russ! Sye-russ! He was the king of Persia, not a meteorological phenomenon.'

Our form room now was at the end of the short passage leading to the balcony and at the foot of the steps up to the Art Room, where Mr Broadhurst had encouraged us in iα to pursue a life of art and craft. My friend of those days, Mr Tunnicliffe, who suggested I tried drawing with my other hand, had gone back to his proper job. (That Christmas I got a copy of Negley Farson's *Going Fishing* which he'd done the drawing for.) One afternoon as I sauntered along the corridor that stretched between Prep 1 and Rα I reflected on the changes that had taken place. I had started with Mrs Gaskell round the corner at one end and I now I was round the corner at the other. In between there had been seven years of learning and change.

There was no Prep Department now and no Bowker's, but I tried to visualize myself as I was then, waiting at the end of the bus queue, buttoned up to the neck and bound round with satchel straps, just as if my mother had prepared me. As I passed each door voices echoed in my mind. Mr Moreton's low, plummy tones as he read the adventures of Gerard, Tommy Stott's abrasive judgements: 'Go to PS or write an essay'. Simkins' level voice, valuing bun pennies almost as if he were speaking to himself. Bozo Hindley chanting, 'And Pompey ad a rat.' Sloppy F's First War reminiscing in a little voice, 'Biscwee Mussyer.' And Miss Robins thumping the piano and joining in as we sang, 'Better far be woad.' My early life passed before me and I felt I was coming to what seemed an end.

There was nothing beyond the Art Room and the door to the balcony was usually locked – after Hartley jumped from it trying to prove he could fly. Clearly, progress from Rα would involve us all in an almost mystical transfer into another region, perhaps we would be dissolved and then reconstituted into other shapes, or forms – which came to pass, for some of us were transmogrified into Classical Sixth formers, some into History Sixth formers and some into Maths Sixth formers and some even into workers of the world.

I found Willie Graham a fractious and difficult man to deal with. One foggy morning when I arrived ten minutes late to his lesson, he quizzed me closely about my journey. He was right to do so for, banking on the excuse offered by the weather, I had loitered in Willshaw's. Unfortunately for me, the dense fog of the city centre was considerably thinner in Rusholme, and far from being the yellow miasma that choked me in Albert Square, what Willie G could see across the playing fields was little more than early morning mist. He wanted to know what time my train got into Victoria, and how long I waited in Albert Square; how thick was the fog; why had it taken me so long to walk half a mile. I struggled to present a credible time sequence.

'There's twenty minutes missing, somewhere,' he said.

'It must have taken longer on the bus,' I faltered.

I knew I had been convicted of dawdling and was estimating the penalty when a tap at the door heralded the entry of Hargreaves, sprightly and ready for work.

'Gosh, sir,' he said. 'The fog in town's unbelievably bad. My train was late and the buses are scarcely running.'

Willie G turned from me like an old dog disturbed at its dinner.

'Where have you come from, Hargreaves?'

'Rochdale, sir. It's unbelievably bad there. And when I got to town I couldn't believe how bad it was there.''

'I'm a credulous man, Hargreaves, but I draw a line when it comes to believing the likes of you and Davidson. But in this case I suspect there may be a backbone of truth in what you say. You are both intrepid travellers. It's a wonder that you got here at all. Go and sit down.'

The form was disappointed. The instant theatre offered by my public execution, set to run to another act with the arrival of Hargreaves, was summarily shut down. No more play today.

We shuffled to our places, grateful for the reprieve and opened our books.

'Where had you been?' I asked him at break.

'That fishing shop in the Old Shambles. I never have time to go there in the afternoon. Bloody hell! The fog was so thick I nearly stayed there all day.'

Although we did not know it, Willie Graham was suffering from a painful ear ailment which affected his balance as well as his temper. Perhaps it was one of the symptoms of this disorder that he imposed on us a "lock out" halfway through the autumn term when someone chalked IHΣ on the front of his desk. Most of us were downright unbelievers, not yet wise enough to be sceptical, and despite our progress in Greek, few of us had any idea of the significance of the letters. The Crusaders in the class were disturbed and murmured amongst themselves. They knew where the inscription was most frequently to be found. The Jewish members were not likely to know.

Willie G was accustomed to shuffle into the room and plant himself at his desk, where he stayed and so it was several days before he noticed that it had become a temporary altar. By this time the letters had started to fade. The brushing of our jackets and trousers as we leant over his desk during the break-time shove-ha'penny football had almost erased the letters, but at a distance one could still discern their ghostly shape. Even those who knew their meaning were surprised by the storm when it came. Willie G. had come to the front of the class to collect our exercise books, and on turning to put them on his desk he saw the letters. He gave a gasp of horror. 'Who, who ...' ('Like an owl,' someone remarked later) 'Who did this?' Wild-eyed and aghast he faced the class, pointing behind him and repeated, 'Who did this?'

I fancy that all of us were stunned by the fury it plunged him into. Had it been an act of deliberate sacrilege, instead of a casual gesture of irritation it could not have provoked a stronger reaction. Todd, one of the few who actually understood the true significance of the cipher, was sent for a damp cloth to wipe it out. The rest of us were treated to a diatribe outlining our shortcomings. We were not directly threatened with the pains of hell-fire, but it was strongly intimated that those who'd perpetrated this outrage would suffer for it at the Last Day. 'Remember,' he piped, 'remember the third commandment, which you break at your peril.'

Our immediate punishment was to be locked out. The privilege of using our form room during breaks was much valued. It had been often denied lower down the school when we were still barbarians, but by the time we reached the Remove, it had come to be regarded as a right. Being locked out in the wet and nasty days of November was a great inconvenience and meant a daily half-hour of misery as we waited, hunched against the radiators, leaning against the walls, constantly exposed to the scorn of passers-by. Worse still, our access to the Note Book of Tests was limited to what we might gather at breaks.

After Christmas, Willie Graham went to have his ear seen to and our new form master was "Claude" Rayne. He was quiet and diffident and took everything that happened in class with equanimity and was thus sharply in contrast with Willie G, whose volatility had become quite disturbing. We knew Claude well for he had taught us English in iiiα – I remembered his enthusiasm for Rupert Brooke and how Hargreaves and I were suspicious of his singling out for our appreciation the phrase, 'rough male kiss of blankets'. Claude was a newcomer to the school, one of those who had been through the war and resumed – case-hardened and battle-scarred – their former careers, almost as if five years of fighting had been an advanced course laid on by the Ministry of Education. Life in the forces might have inured him to any kind of outrage that we were likely to commit. He was rumoured to have been in the Air Force and his face was scarred as though it had been mended by plastic surgery. He was unlikely to have been upset by the IHS. Under him we continued to read the Greek Testament in RI but were more concerned with what it might mean than making a just translation.

During one of these lessons I glimpsed the magic inherent in words, and as one becoming gradually aware that he had some talent in using them, I was deeply interested. In a discussion of the first verses of St John's Gospel, we were directed to the beginning of Genesis where God said, "Let there be..." and something stupendous happened. 'What,' we were asked, 'does that imply about the power of language?' I saw the same idea repeated in the opening of St John, where " the beginning was the Word". I knew that words weren't things but I also knew that words could make things happen, and that sometimes things existed only by virtue of the words that described them. It was a moment of epiphany when I had a dizzying glimpse of what words might do.

12. LEARNING

In my early years at school we were treated as though our heads were like bottomless buckets which would take whatever was poured into them. I learned without thinking about it. In those days I didn't ever consider the process of learning or its purpose, beyond satisfying the requirements of the inevitable test. Masters set us tasks and we did them, because that's what we went to school for. The lists of verbs and nouns that Bozo Hindley had us chant were part of a game, as were the kings of England or Greek paradigms. 'You're making bricks, now,' Simkins said. 'It's always a boring business. But soon you'll be able to build something, and that can be fun.'

I think it was only in Rα that I began to be interested in what I was taught. Before that I was little more than an acquiescent receiver of what my teachers broadcast, and still mildly sceptical at hearing that I might one day read Homer for fun. Despite my rooted antipathy to doing what I was told, and my first belief that Homer stank, once I got beyond the difficulties of the language and came to the story, I began to see that the Iliad was not what it seemed and I was fascinated by the ironies and contradictions in the text. Here was a tale of a war where the Greeks and Trojans were as ruthless and bloody as anything I read about in Scott or Conan Doyle. The celebration of the heroic ethos when Glaucon and Diomedes meet as enemies and part as friends was as noble as any struggle Waverley or Gerard were involved in. But the focus kept changing in Homer, for pictures of the glories of war at the spear's point gave way to scenes from home, of worried wives and frightened children. The valiant Hector, guardian of Troy, foresees his own death and the inevitable downfall of the city, even to the extent of visualising Andromache as a slave fetching water from the well. As he bends to kiss his infant son, the child shrinks back into his nurse's arms, terrified by the nodding plume of his father's helmet. What value the panoply of war if it serves only to frighten children? What was I to make of it when κορυθαίολος Ἕκτωρ, Hector of the glittering helm, was reduced to a bogeyman?

I saw these episodes as vividly as pictures from my own time. In particular they reminded me of those other images of war which disturbed me so much: the boy with the bundle, the shattered bedroom. They lingered in my memory generating the worrying thought that, despite our victories, things don't really get any better. I glimpsed a world of uncertain fortunes and perilous times, and I realised that my cocoon of middle-class security was beginning to split. It all added force to my father's insistent reminder, 'You must never forget how lucky you are ...'

Thus about this time I realised that the classics were no longer a joke, where Caesar adsum jam forte, or adventures where chivalric warriors did exciting deeds of honour, but often dramatic and disturbing observations of the stupidity and brutality of the world. I began to see the irony explicit in the Homeric epithets which all too often derided the heroic ethos they were supposed to be celebrating. As I write this I wonder how much of its drift is the result of a lifetime spent in academia and how much was revealed at that time. Impossible to untangle: but the germs of critical awareness and the sense that there was more to the story than the story itself derive from that time and those mentors. At that time I had yet to encounter Catullus' versions of the grand passion which agitated the Romantics.

Another striking picture from that period was of Xenophon's soldiers counting the parasangs as they headed for what they hoped was the sea. Deeply into the story and eager to find out what happened, I bought the Penguin translation and read beyond the set text to where the armies reached the coast. That moment and the cries of the soldiers, passing down the weary files, passed down the centuries and into my dreams.

From this time my teachers ceased to be ogres and task masters whose function was to dragoon us into acceptable habits of mind, and became individuals, fellow human beings. A new kind of master appeared as the armed forces were disbanded and their members were released into their old occupations. They were younger and free-er in their relations with us. The old divisions between 'them' and 'us', masters and boys, were largely broken down and I recognised in 'Claude' Rayne and 'Basher' Bailey a readiness to tease us, be familiar and friendly and treat us with a kind of amused condescension that admitted a gradually developing sense of equality. I felt I was no longer of the genus 'Boy', but an interesting, developing individual capable of being extended.

'Basher' Bailey taught us the set books for the English Matric and through a series of dramatic presentations, brought them alive. Through his eyes, I began to see the mole-like Silas Marner as more than a pathetic creature, damned by his religion but saved by love. Through Bailey I discovered a new way of looking which gave colour and perspective to the outlines of plot and character. Hitherto they had just been scenes, leading to the end which was what the book was about – William Brown triumphing over Mrs Bott; Robin Hood defeating the Sheriff of Nottingham; the Saint outwitting the Tongs. Bailey showed me for the first time that these stories were more than a recital of events leading to a satisfying conclusion, but coded commentaries on the way of life we live and the sort of creatures we are. From him I learned that there were stories to be told about the tales, and these were often much more interesting than the tales themselves. He called them parables and showed us how us to discern in them the hidden significance of apparently ordinary events.

13. LUNCHTIME PROMENADE CONCERTS

At the beginning of the Spring Term Satters drew my attention to a season of concerts by the BBC Northern Symphony Orchestra, under the direction of Charles Groves. They were on Friday lunchtimes in Manchester Town Hall and they were free.

'We could go to these,' he said. 'Nobody would know if we cut Gym. Nasty Mister Saunders doesn't know us and so long as he's got three lines of monkeys jumping on the spot, he's happy. We'll be in town by half-twelve and back here by ten to two. A piece o'cake.'

And so it was. We slipped out of school in the confusion of change-over and met at the Pie Shop to buy lunch. Satters said, 'I went out past the lecture theatre. No one noticed. Except Old Hugh – and he winked as I went by. How about you?' 'Past the Science block and stinks alley. I don't think anyone saw me, either.'

Capless and hiding all signs of school, we skulked by the shops until the bus came, then scampered aboard. Eating our pies as the bus bumped townwards, we wondered what the programme might be and just where the concert would be held. Satters had been inside the Town Hall to look at the Ford Madox Brown murals. 'They were in a sort of council chamber,' he said. 'You couldn't have a concert in there.' I'd been in love with the Town Hall ever since my first glimpse of it on the day my cousin led me to the tram stop in Albert Square. In those days it was sooty black, defended with sand-bags and shutters.

We passed under the high arch by the Central Library and followed the signs: To the Promenade Concert. Admission

Free. As we went we were handed a programme which told us that the concert would be broadcast live and that an audience would give the performance authenticity, and the bodies in the hall would help the acoustics. But we must 'please refrain from talking loudly between items and only applaud at the end of each piece'. It seemed to make us part of a programme that was to be heard by thousands – millions, maybe.

Following a train of people through the great doors and down a dim, echoing passage, I found the inside of the building as thrilling as the outside. Grand stone stairs ended in high assembly rooms with murals and gilded furniture. Richly patterned floors led down long shadowy corridors past echoing chambers and small committee rooms. The concert hall itself was ornate with wooden screens and traceries under a decorated ceiling. Light streamed down from tall lancet windows. At the back was the orchestra, connected by a web of wires and microphones with the BBC engineers who were positioned at the other end, head-phoned and crouching over their gear, gesticulating at their colleagues. The audience almost filled the space between these two groups of adepts each about to work its own particular magic. Breathless with haste and excitement and heedless of advice about where was the best place to listen, we pushed our way through the crowd until we were directly under the orchestra.

The hall was quite full of what I took to be office workers in their lunch hour and small groups of old-ish retired music lovers, such as I saw at the Hallé on Sundays. A web of wires and dangling microphones swayed above our heads. On the platform the orchestra tuned up, making exciting sounds which rose above the hubbub of the gathering audience. Behind them a fan of gilded organ pipes rose to an ornate ceiling. Deaf to

Satters protesting that the best sound was at the back, I insisted on staying where we were. I wanted to see and be near the musicians, to watch them play as well as hear them.

This was far more thrilling than the Sunday visits to the Hallé with my father: not only did it have the taste of stolen fruits, it had immediacy and a sense of being involved. We, the audience, were necessary. It said as much on the programme: our presence made the music sound better, we were necessary to the broadcast and we mustn't talk. In the King's Hall at Belle Vue, there was no doubt about our status, we were listeners at a distance. Here we were almost part of the orchestra. The players sitting on the platform above us were close enough to talk to, the brass and the timpani ranged on the steps rising up to the organ pipes were open to close inspection. Directly overhead towered the burly, ginger-haired figure of Charles Groves, so close that we could see the beads of sweat on his forehead and hear the boards of the rostrum creak as he swayed to his work. And just as we arrived he set to. We had scarcely unbuttoned our coats before he raised his baton and with a flick of his wrist launched the whole orchestra into the opening bars of Auber's Overture, *The Bronze Horse*. I almost fainted with pleasure.

The magic of that opening never really dissipated. Always, as he raised his baton, at the beginning of a concert I could feel the hairs rising on the back of my neck, and I let out in a subdued gasp the breath that I didn't realise I'd been holding. Over the next six weeks I watched spellbound as he whipped the players into a frenzy over rousing overtures like *The Thieving Magpie* or *The Merry Wives of Windsor.* Sometimes he reined his players in behind a soloist, sometimes he gathered them all together for the full orchestral effect demanded by Brahms or Tchaikovsky. He controlled the violins with a flick of the wrist, so their bows rose and fell in a sweep of sound and movement that made my heart turn over. On the steps behind the woodwind, the brass sat hunched in a row, with their instruments between their knees, almost like batsmen waiting to go in. Maestro Groves would raise his arm and they would obediently take up their instruments to deliver a blast of sound, brazen and full-throated, that thrilled me to the core. That done, they would cease to be angels and become cricketers again stooping in a line, glancing at each other out of the corners of their eyes as if to see who had farted. Only the woodwind, demure and patient with their instruments resting on their lips, were docile, playing when called upon, but for the most part quiet and still, like well-behaved children at a party, stuck between the wild romantics in the strings and the rough pit-boys of the brass.

The programmes ran strictly to form: an overture, a short symphony by Haydn or an early Mozart, sometimes a concerto, and then a short piece for the finale, *The Fountains of Rome* or *L'Arlesienne*. Thus the programme covered the fields of the classical, romantic and faintly modern repertoire. Occasionally there would be a piece by someone frighteningly modern and English, like Frank Bridge or Delius or Vaughan Williams. The programmes were at once daring without being adventurous, introducing us to the new, while reminding us of the old. They widened my musical horizons and made the weekly diet at the Mus Soc seem narrow and old-fashioned, Sibelius and Mahler notwithstanding. I came away soothed and thoughtful, wondering how and why this music worked on me the way it did, and why, even, it was so different from my Sunday visits to the Hallé with my father. I mourned my lack of musicianship and spent hours tinkering at the piano, regretting the music lessons I'd abandoned years ago.

14. EXAMS

At the end of our year in Rα was the serious exam. I knew about it through my cousins, and about its even stiffer successor, the Higher School Certificate. Conversations with them would go: 'Now then, young Ian, how's things with you? What's happening at school these days? School Cert this year! Now you're up against it. I remember ...' and they would be off on a tide of reminiscences. Cousin Sylvia had been told that she would have to go and work in a shop if she didn't pass, but if she did she would have a bicycle. Memories of Highers haunted them even more. Cousin Hughie hadn't slept for a week. As it turned out they all got through, harried and coaxed, threatened before and praised after, yet even now on the other side of the ordeal they still regarded it as the stuff of nightmares.

Something of their urgency and apprehension showed in certain of my classmates who confessed to having been warned and bribed. Bicycles were the usual carrots and the World of Work was the stick. My folks eschewed both penalties and rewards – I suggested a new fishing rod. My father said, 'But we expect you to do well. You've got a good brain. Now's your chance to use it.' As ever at these critical stages in my growing up, my mother tried to raise in me a sense of urgency. 'You ought to be more concerned about your matric than fishing,' she said. 'Why don't you worry about these things?' But to me it seemed that they happened as a matter of course, like Christmas or birthdays. I was five years younger than Sylvia so scarcely aware of what was going on when she sat the exams, now she was in her second year at University and still worrying about exams. Was there no end to them, I wondered?

193

At first I was largely indifferent, borne along in the general stream, thinking no further ahead than the next homework conference on the School Bus. After Christmas the importance of the exam came home to me as I noticed the growing anxiety of some of my classmates. Hargreaves was a bit tetchy. 'Bloody School Cert. You'd think the world depended on it. The Old Girl says I've got to spend Sunday morning "doing your homework properly". She stopped me going fishing for tench last weekend. When I told her we did it on the bus, she nearly went hairless.' Satters also was living in straitened circumstances, but he was more phlegmatic. 'You've got to keep them happy on the Home Front,' he said. 'I'd be jankered for ever if they knew half of what goes on.' His father was a schoolmaster and more in tune with the songs we were supposed to be singing – Hargreaves' father was only a Bank Manager and didn't know about these things, but Hargreaves' Grandma had promised him a new bike if he did well. 'But she won't say how well I've got to do.'

Form mates began to talk about inducements to work hard and the rewards on offer – so much for a credit, so much for a distinction, there seemed to be a regular tariff. Until then I had only thought of the exams as another hurdle to be cleared, a bit more of unpleasantness to be gone through before the Summer Holidays. It was only when I heard my mother talking about it with Tom's mother that I knew something important was about to happen. Tom was now in Lower 5b and sitting the exams for the second time. 'I've tried threats. I've tried bribes,' she'd said. 'I've even locked him in his bedroom. His father's talked to him seriously, but nothing seems to have any effect. He just daydreams his time away thinking about football. And he can't get into the team there.' My mother clucked in sympathy and said nothing, seeing I was within earshot. 'He spends plenty of time with his books, but nothing seems to stick. And he must get his Matric or they won't let him take his Articles. As Jack says, the Association won't accept anybody unless he has a Matric.'

"Serve the sod right,' I thought, 'if he can't become an accountant.' And I remembered how he'd gloated over me once about not having to bother about University because he could go into his father's office and make lots of money. But his plight did make me realise that Matric was important, and as the weeks went by even Satters talked about it.

'I've been promised lots of record tokens,' he said, 'if I get five Credits, but that's easy. Fifty percent's a piece of cake. It's Distinctions that count, anyone can get Credits.'

'What about Passes?' I said.

'Passes are for peasants. We're the élite, my boy. Didn't you realise? The cream of the School's intellect's gathered in Rα. We're the Prize Pupils. Distinctions are what we're after.'

This revelation came as a shock. I'd never thought of us as being special or even clever. But then I remembered the time the Chief caught four of us kicking a ball against a newly painted door and how he nearly doubled the punishment because we were in iiα. Mrs Grindley, too, at the same period raged at us because we refused to be serious about biology. 'It's about Life,' she said, emphasising the capital letter. 'You're clever boys and you could learn it standing on your heads. But you just won't try, because you don't think it's important.'

I'd never thought much about intellectual differences. Boys who were good at some things weren't any good at others. I knew I could learn quickly and easily. Getting up word lists, memorising declensions and conjugations was no trouble at all, and I'd only to read a poem twice for it to stick, and I was good at writing essays. But I was rotten at Maths, couldn't draw at all and not much good at sports. Also I was slow on the uptake, only grasping the significance of situations and conversations after everybody else had understood and reacted. At home among my peers, who valued quickness of wit and physical ability, my standing was very low. 'Nay, Ian,' Dot Tyson said when I'd angered her father by standing on a hen's nest, 'will tha nivver larn?' I thought of the time Tom's mother had set me to learn 'Forty Years On' and didn't believe I could have done it so quickly. 'Why, Tom was at it all morning and then couldn't manage without prompting.' Sucks to Tom, I'd thought, my wrists still sore from the Chinese Burns he'd given me. Now I was being given my revenge. Tom was stuck in the lower school, and I'd be going through to the sixth next year.

Most of us were fifteen when we did the Matric, some only fourteen. The school had a reputation for driving its brightest, perhaps due to the Chief's influence, for under his leadership it had increasing academic success. At Oxford and after, I remember defending both him and the school against those who decried MGS as a forcing factory which drove some of its best brains to nervous breakdowns – suicide, even. In the five years I spent under his general direction, the school seemed as pleasant and easy-going an institution as any would-be idler could wish for. Certainly we were kept at it. Work was assigned and collected, corrections were carried out and further assignments made, but I felt no pressure to perform. I was stretched but not racked. We were expected to do well, get high marks, be interested and perceptive. This was the ethos of the school and we accepted it. There was no force, or sense of compulsion, nobody nagged or hectored and the worst reproach I had was Artie Moore's sad rebuke, 'You have let yourself down.' It stung more than a lashing with scorpions' tails.

14. SCHOOL CERT.

I don't recall much about the exams themselves. I've better recollection of the run up to them and the aftermath, which lasted for weeks – until the results came out. I know we sat some of them in the Gym and some in the Art room, and some, which were special to us, like the Greek, in our form room. The Art room was just above our form room. 'Up the steps to the scaffold,' Satters said, as we set out for the Latin exam, except it was a mass execution, for Rβ was with us.

We poured out what we knew onto sheets of official paper, then went out into the sunshine of what seemed to have changed from Judgement Day into something quite ordinary. I remember a tremendous sense of liberation as the warmth of outside swept over me after the chill of the high exam rooms. 'And the rest of the day to yourselves,' somebody said in an Irish accent. It always seemed sunny when we did exams. The rooms where we sat them were cold, airy cages. In the Gym, the light inched across the floor made shiny by the co-ordinated movements of thousands of feet. The Art Room, with sky-lights slanting north, had a sepulchral air, emphasised as much by the funerary nature of much of the art work as by the gravity of the invigilators. They passed slowly up and down the rows, handing out more paper when needed, while the Inquisitor in charge sat at a raised desk so he might take in the whole room with one glaring sweep of his x-ray eyes.

Afterwards, outside, I was filled with a strong sense of having escaped. It drove me out and away from the groups gathering, question papers in hand, to discuss answers, questions, omissions. To me it was like probing fresh wounds; sufficient to the day are the exams thereof; they were part of life's unpleasantness, best got over and forgotten as soon as possible. With Satters and Hargreaves and other town-bound boys, breathless with haste I sped to the bus and freedom. Only on the upper deck of the 42, bound for Piccadilly, watching the familiar landmarks pass by, Dickenson Road, the Whitworth Art Gallery, the University, did I begin to feel easy again. Then in the comfort of the Albert Square Kardomah, I might relax.

There was no holding post-mortems. That might have had us agonising over missed opportunities and fatal blunders. Better abide by the verdict of the examiners than repine like the gang round Todd and Robinson, mouthing and chewing over old question papers like my father's terriers with an old slipper. We preferred a flippant dismissal and a harking forward to pastures new.

> 'Which question did you answer on *Richard II*, Satters?'
> 'Can't remember. Both of them, I think.'
> 'It was an 'either … or' question. So you've failed.'
> 'Oh, well. There's always that job in Woolworths …'

Why was it always 'working in a shop', that we were threatened with? Was it to do with the professional middle-class scorn for Trade? Perhaps our parents, familiar with the world of Kipps or Mr Polly, had a sense of horror at the thought of a life spent behind the counter. It was all right for David Harris, leaving at fifteen to go into his father's business, and mentally challenged Tom, hoping to go into his father's office. It was no good, though, going into a shop. Perhaps a book shop would be all right. I'd always thought that the people who worked in Willshaws and Sherratt and Hughes had a decent sort of life. And the assistants in Forsyth's were all right because they knew all about music and how much better Gieseking was than

Kempf, and which recording of the Brandenburgers was the best. At home, one of my Broughton mates had just got a job working in the Farmers' Supply and he seemed to have a high old time cheeking the customers as he sold them bags of feed and sacks of cement.

PART IV -

LIFE IN THE SIXTH

1. HISTORY SIXTH DIV III

In the sixth we were split up into groups of specialists. Most of Rα proceeded into Classical Sixth, but there were a few renegades who went elsewhere: History Sixth, Maths Sixth and one, at least, into Science Sixth. The twenty-eight or so of us who'd been together since we were eleven dispersed into those fields considered best for their talents or careers, and for all that we saw of our old class mates, we might just as well have moved to another country. Apart from those considering a career in medicine or science, it was never suggested that we follow courses linked to any vocation. Our education here was an end in itself, the broadening of the mind, refining the sensibilities, making us aware of what was 'proper to our common humanity' – which was what the whole process was for, according to Simkins.

I chose History Sixth because there I could 'do' Eng. Lit as well and French, which I enjoyed. I'd decided that higher Latin and Greek were not for me. I wanted to be a writer, and it seemed to me that studying the masters was essential to becoming one. All my life I wanted to write for a living, but it was forty years on when I started, and then I was a retired man. Back in 1950, though, I was intoxicated with the idea of getting shot of school and retiring to the Lakes, where I might live on a pittance and write. All through my time at Oxford I was still animated by this ideal, and when I took my first job – a temporary teaching post at the local grammar school – it was intended to be only a stop-gap, a momentary blockage in the flow of the deathless prose that I would turn out when I had time left over from being me. Little did I think then that the job would lead to more teaching, more study, further involvement in education until it became easier and pleasanter to make a living talking about books as a journeyman academic, than actually writing them. And now, when I have got down to it, I miss the talking.

Although I was glad to turn my back on the Classics I missed my old classmates and, chiefly, Hargreaves. In Rα we grew close, spending a lot of our holidays and weekends together learning about life. He'd taught me how to catch tench and I'd taught him how to catch trout. We pooled our knowledge of other fields, like girls and sex and what to read next. We went to Old Trafford in the summer and in a half-hearted way followed the fortunes of Manchester City football club. Now I only saw him in the holidays. However, the shift to H6 firmed up my relations with Satters who wanted to be a Historian. 'Stuff the classics,' he said. 'Anyway, you've a better chance of an Oxford place with History. Everybody goes for the Classical Schols and I'm fed up with Greek.' It was the first time I'd heard anyone talk about 'Oxford Schols'. Even Hargreaves, staunch anti-intellectual that he was, mumbled, when questioned about his choice of sixth form, 'Well, there are some closed Classics Schols. Open only to entrants from MGS. Be a pity not to have a shot at them.' I realised that he and Satters had been 'got at', for I'd never before heard either of them voice any opinion about what might happen after school. With a shock, I remembered my father's throw-away remark as we drove through Oxford on that dreary January day in 1947 or 1948. 'One day you might come here,' he said. Now it seemed I might make his casual prophecy come true. Just as the end of my school days was in sight, I glimpsed further avenues of education stretching beyond and there seemed no end in sight. However, Oxford sounded fun, and whatever I did next, I wanted to have lots of that.

H6 comprised an interesting group of students. It was a melting pot of boys from the Classical, Modern and Science sides of the lower school, brought together by a general interest in Arts subjects. In this case they were History, Latin, English and French or German – and they provided entry to most Arts courses at University. The syllabuses followed in the other Sixths were much narrower, intended to qualify those following them for specialist degree courses, mainly in science or medicine.

'What are you going to do with a degree in Latin and Greek?' Satters asked Hargreaves. 'You can't go out and govern India now. They've given it away.'

'Oh, I don't know,' he said. 'Manage a Bank, perhaps. Or run a Shipping Line. Or something. Anyway, that's years off. There's National Service to do before then. I might stay on there and become a General. What about you? All you can do with a degree in History is teach.'

'Is that so?' said Satters, raising his eyebrows. 'I might go into the Church and become a Bishop. They seem to do all right.'

Joining H6 was like starting anew, for more than three-quarters of the class were strangers, faces I'd passed in the corridor, figures from the playing fields, vaguely remembered voices from Prep 2, gruffer and hairier, but basically the same. We met on the first day of term in Bunn's room which was on the ground floor under the Art Room. It was also at the end of the Maths corridor and therefore on the other side of the school from where I'd spent my academic life so far. Moving there was almost like crossing a watershed into new country. I was saying goodbye to my homeland, the region where I'd spent the days of my boyhood, the rooms I'd waited outside, the windows I'd frozen under, the desks I'd dreamed at. The very atmosphere, diffused through the bright exhortations of Miss

Robins, the booming voice of Mr Moreton, the dry cackle of Artie Moore, had permeated my being during the last six years. Life there had been so different from what it was becoming now that I made a list of the things which had characterised life there.

The floors, for instance were a composition made to look like marble - a mottled surface flecked with black and grey and orange. They were just the same as the floors outside Bunn's room, but then, shoes we wore in the austere post-war years had soles of a synthetic leather which allowed us to slide on the surface of the corridors almost as though we were on ice. The walls were covered to head height with emerald-green tiles which imparted a ghostly glow to their echoing reaches. The classrooms, apart from what idiosyncrasies of decoration the inmates might make, were identical. Six rows of five, lift-the-lid desks with tip-up seats attached were flanked on one side by windows, opening only at the top. On two others, shoulder height panelling of honey coloured boards faced rows of rarely used lockers on either side of the platform where stood the master's desk. Our way out to home and freedom was down the stairs by Artie Moore's room and past the Library into the windy arcade that led ultimately to the Gym. To the left was the quad where the footballers played their balletic lunchtime games contrasting so starkly with the tightly ordered square of figures on the other side, where Dicky Radford drilled the Cadet Force. It was only in the Sixth that I recalled and valued these features – the backgrounds to so much of my conscious life – and set them against a growing outside world.

Life in the sixth was much free-er: the sense of bondage, of being constantly supervised and directed, had been replaced with an atmosphere of laissez-faire. We had free periods to do largely what we liked with, we were not constrained by the general rules of coming and going. As a further improvement of our living conditions and as a sign of our growing responsibility, we were given the freedom of the library. Hitherto available to us only at lunchtimes, and just for the return and exchange of books – I recall in those days feverishly searching the shelves for more of Brigadier Gerard and only finding Sherlock Holmes – it was now our common room. At the top end, where it extended in two opposing recesses, were long tables where we were free to lounge and even gossip quietly during our free-periods. In a small side-room the Music Library was housed, nerve centre of the Mus. Soc., although Johnny Lingard's room still remained our Concert Hall. Satters and I as minor officers of the Society sat here often, while we appraised the record collection and considered larceny.

As masters became more human, their names and natures seemed to change and they became People. Before this they were 'sirs' – 'Please, sir'. 'Excuse me, sir'. 'Sir, may I …?' Then they were primarily representatives of authority, and in most cases identified, if at all, by the special names we gave them. Boys who had been on Trek with them or joined the School's Summer Camps said they discerned traces of humanity – like Billy Hulme reciting, 'Sam! Sam! Pick up thi musket …' or Simkins heading for his morning dip in the river in the rain – but normally there was a barrier between master and boy as wide as that which kept the Belle Vue monkeys on their island. After the Remove the relationship changed. No longer ogres, they appeared as individuals rather than the stereo-types suggested by their nick-names, whose derivation I began to ponder. 'Sloppy' Hyslop was easy to understand and its abbreviation to 'Sloppy' H to distinguish him from his brother 'Sloppy' F. 'Toby' Cantrell and 'Billy' Hulme were particular, and inventions based on their initials, I guess. But why was a first name given to some masters and not to others? Simkins was always 'Simkins', Bunn was always 'Bunn'. I never heard of Mr Moreton by any other name, although his initials were H.V., I think. 'Pansy' Mason was somehow appropriate for he was willowy and slight and minced as he walked. He was balding and what I thought of as 'moon-faced' with round spectacles to match, and a reedy sort of voice, quite unlike the booming of Mr Moreton or the dry, clear snap of Artie Moore. Pansy's room was next door to 'Cuthbert' Seton, who was precisely articulate, with an antic manner that enlivened his teaching. He made us draw diagrams explaining the Three-Field System, pictures of Turnip Townsend's seed drill – or was it Jethro Tull's? and Macadam's road-building technique of impermeable surfaces. He advised us to be empirical. 'Spread your breakfast toast with treacle,' he said. 'Then hold it under the tap. It's a scientific experiment.'

On my first day in History Sixth I noticed a change in our status. As we sauntered into Bunn's room, big and high-ceilinged under the Art Room at the end of the Maths corridor, Bunn was waiting for us. The room was like a study, with tables and chairs instead of desks, bookcases full of books and there were pictures on the walls. Bunn was seated at a large untidy desk. 'Good morning, chaps,' he said. 'Good morning! Come in, come in.' Smoke rose from the ash-tray on his table. When we were all gathered he rose to address us, a tall, thin, donnish figure – as I realised later when I got to know my tutor. They both had an inquiring, discursive manner, gently questioning, always prepared to make interesting digressions. I characterised them as 'What if ...?' people, whose un-aggressive enquiries led into broader fields of understanding, rather than tying one down to precise explanations.

Bunn was a historian, but always ready to digress into painting or music, literature or contemporary politics. In one lesson, Satters plotted his progress from 'Metternich to Massenet to Monet, then back to Vienna via Ruskin and Rousseau'. I remember one lesson which he based on Constable's painting of Salisbury cathedral under the rainbow when he drew together Anglicanism, and Patriotism, the Corn Laws and the Chartists, Industrialisation and Pastoralism in a way which gave coherence and illumination to mid C19 England. 'Next week,' he said, 'We will go to the Whitworth and look at some Constable drawings.'

Bunn's History lessons-lectures-discussions were complemented by Pansy Mason's spirited excursions into the literary backgrounds of our Eng. Lit. set texts and culture in general. He took us, or urged to go, to the theatre – Wolfit's *King Lear*, *The Ascent of F6*, *The Way of the World*, Machiavelli's *Mandragola*, which was closed down by the Watch Committee before its week was out. He encouraged us to go to the cinema, not only for the latest 'releases', like Olivier's *Hamlet* and *The Third Man*, but classics like *The Battleship Potemkin*, *Modern Times*, *Un chien Andalou* which the school Film Society showed, and Cocteau's *Orphée*, *La Ronde* and *Bicycle Thieves*. Together, he and Bunn pushed us towards the lectures at the Library Theatre; and insisted that we visit the Picasso and Matisse Exhibition which exposed Modernism in Art to our astonished, northern eyes. In between these cultural treats – of which there were lots in Manchester – we read *Vanity Fair* , analysed John Donne's poems, read *Antony and Cleopatra* and *Hamlet*, Tennyson, the Prologue to *The Canterbury Tales*, *Absalom and Achitophel*, *Major Barbara*, *Pride and Prejudice* and an Anthology of Romantic Poets. We also learned from him the rudiments of literary criticism.

The third leg of our A level course was French, taught by a new master, Mr Courtenay, in what used to be Mrs Gaskell's room when I was in the now-defunct Prep Department. The memories I had of those days – bartering with Lewis, keeping brisk by deep breathing – were quickly overlaid by expositions of *Eugénie Grandet*, *Hernani* and French poets of the nineteenth century. I was quite good at French,
and the literature was new to me, but its writers didn't engage my attention as closely as the English. I wasn't really interested in Balzac's *Comédie Humaine* until later life, when I'd had time to savour something of it for myself. *Hernani* I liked, but the rest of Hugo, hélas, sank beneath my intellectual horizon, never to reappear, unlike the other poets who became subjects of increasing interest and continue to fascinate. I loved the scabrousness of Baudelaire and Rimbaud, the effrontery of de Nerval, the tantalising glimpses of meaning in Mallarmé and realising that my not understanding didn't matter. Most of our literature lessons were taught in French. Like Billy Hulme, Mr Courtenay – he never in my time had a nick-name – wanted us to become accustomed to the sound of the language. After Christmas we had the advantage of a French Assistant, a pale, diffident figure who was not much older than we were, and whose rapid, colloquial French was almost impossible to understand. However, he sharpened our ears and our tongues, and when we went to Paris at Easter, I was delighted that I was able to understand the natives, and both gratified and surprised when they understood me – in a limited way, of course.

2. SUNDAYS

Restoring the petrol ration livened up the weekends. Most family cars had been laid up 'for the duration'. Propped up on wooden blocks in garages, with the wheels stacked against the wall, they provided hideaways and dens and places for secret assignations. On Sunday mornings my father and I often went to Belle Vue. He said it was something he used to do when he was a student. 'Nash and Brothwood and Cummings and I would walk across from Brunswick Street, to get rid of Saturday night's fumes. It restored our vitality. We used to feel that visiting the Zoo put us in touch with nature again.' I could well imagine them on these mornings as they rambled round the Botanical Gardens, nursing their hangovers and arguing about where they should go for lunch.

I'd come to know these friends of his student days quite well. Now prosperous medical men, they were scattered around the country, but two or three times a year they came to Broughton for Poker Weekends when they would revive their student days by playing cards and drinking until dawn. My mother loved it. They called her Mrs Nackle, after the nagging harridan in *Love on the Dole* – another memory of their student days. She was good at poker, or perhaps kept a clearer head than they did, for in the mornings there was often a little heap of her winnings on the sideboard: shillings and sixpences and threepenny bits, from which she would give me something for crisps and a bottle of sarsaparilla. Mrs Harper who used to clean for us was scandalised by the signs of their debauchery for she was a strong Methodist. To protect herself from these manifestations of the devil she would sing hymns as she cleared away the empty bottles, and Nash, who had a fine Welsh bass and a Chapel upbringing, would sit up in bed and join in.

On our visits to Belle Vue my father would always insist that we 'take a little exercise round the botanical gardens', then we would visit the Zoo. There everything of interest was behind bars and short of room. A pungent smell of ammonia and damp straw pervaded the enclosures where the animals were penned next to each other as though they might take comfort from being together. A famous exhibit was the Tygon – a cross between a lion and a tiger. It looked a desolate beast and seemed to spend its time immobile in the corner furthest away from its neighbour and the spectators, as though it didn't know what to make of itself or what to do. The lion, on the other hand, had a much stronger sense of identity, though it too was a sad creature with a tattered mane and hairless tail, pacing its cage, six strides forward, turn, six strides back. I would watch the muscles moving under its patchy hide and regret the frustration of so much energy. After that, it was a relief to watch the monkeys playing with each other and themselves. At least they had room enough to roam and rocks to climb, even if the lack of cover gave them nowhere in which to be modest, even supposing they had a sense of propriety. They openly gave the lie to the Puritan view that sex was shameful and showed it to be a joyous, public activity to be practised whenever and wherever there was the opportunity.

A group of us used to go to the Speedway on Friday night. For a time we became fans of the Belle Vue Aces but I didn't really enjoy it and only went to keep company with those who did. I always found it a bewildering experience for the noise of the bikes and the violence of the riders disturbed me. They were clad in leather and masked so they might have been creatures from another world bent on domination of this. Their machines were like weapons of war. At the start the bikes threw up fountains of black cinders from their wheels, and when they went round corners they sprayed the spectators with bitter-tasting grit that got into the eyes and hair and stayed there. The visiting teams were always accompanied by aggressive supporters, demanding to know which side we were on. I was scared of these strong partisans who would give you a bust on the nose as soon as look at you, and I made sure I was always with friends.

To our unsophisticated eyes Belle Vue represented the world of entertainment. Apart from the Speedway, there was the Greyhound Racing Stadium with meetings three times a week, but it was several years before I ever went there. Then it was with a South African friend from college who was a serious gambler. In the sixth week of each term he would set aside enough money barely to survive until his next cheque. Then he would go to the dog track at Littlemore and try his luck.

A third venue was the Kings Hall which I knew from Sunday visits with my father to listen to the Hallé, but at other times featured other musicians, like Les Compagnons de la Chanson, the Blackburn Choral Society and Black Dyke Mills Brass Band. Also, and to my eyes sacrilegiously, there were World Championship boxing matches and weekly wrestling bouts where local heroes like Kiss of Death Kelly met the Black Doctor who came from Accrington. At Christmas we went to see Sid Field's Circus which played for a whole month. I remember a couple of visits to the wrestling, where hooded and masked hunks of muscle threw each other about a small roped-off enclosure. Their contests seemed to be so violent that it was always a surprise at the end of the contest to see the antagonists walk unaided out of the hall. I was equally staggered to see that the ringside seats were largely occupied by stout middle-aged women, some of whom were big enough to be contestants themselves. They screamed and swore furiously during the bouts and were often in tears at the end of the fight. I was amused to recollect that these barbaric rites took place on the little bit of stage where John Barbirolli stood to conduct the Hallé.

3. HAUTE COUTURE

In the sixth we were no longer treated as boys – that generic term for the 'troublesome and inconsiderate, dirty, noisy, lying and idle' – Billy Hulme's words. In the sixth we were 'chaps', or 'fellows', which we enunciated in a grossly affected way accompanied by a wave of the hand. We started to realise ourselves as individuals and although it took a week or so to get used to our new status, by half-term we had comfortably settled into being aesthetes or hearties or dedicated scholars or just plain sixth formers. Then we acted out for a scene or two whatever roles we felt best suited the personalities we were hoping to develop, and then settled for the one that seemed most acceptable.

As we were no longer required to wear school uniform, we began to dress in subtly different ways and notice what each other wore. I was quite startled when one of my new class mates – a product of U4a – asked me what I thought about the 'cut' of the 'sports' jackets that most of us now wore instead of blazers. Until then I'd thought of clothes, only recently de-rationed, simply as things I was given to wear and therefore almost entirely my mother's concern. How I looked was up to her, she might nag me for looking scruffy, having long hair and shoes that needed polishing, but the actual garments were what she fished out of drawers and carried away to be washed when I took them off. Until iiiα a lot of my clothes had been hand-me-downs from the wretched Tom, and until quite recently new clothes involved coupons and making do with what was 'in stock'. Now it was possible to go out and buy new, from a widening selection of stuffs and styles. Just at that time I was reading as much of Wodehouse as I could lay my hands on, and I realised that when Jeeves wasn't sorting out Bertie's social problems he was moderating what he wore. I hadn't for a moment considered how such matters might affect me, and here was Buckley, on the 42 bus going to Piccadilly, talking about cuffs and buttons, vents and big lapels and what did I think about 'bum-freezers'.

Also, there was a growing interest in hair styles as we rejected the short back and sides of our lower school days in favour of luxurious growths that were brylcreemed into a quiff that stood out over the forehead, or waved over the ears and swept up at the back in a 'duck's arse'. However, it was important not to look like a 'spiv' – one of the idle black-marketeering layabouts that figured so often in the cartoons of Osbert Lancaster and Ronald Searle. Thin and stooped and with a Ronald Coleman moustache, they were supposed to stand at street corners offering for sale gear that was hard to get – nylons or fancy ties, or whatever was, at the moment in 'short supply' – a phrase from the war that still had general currency.

It was possibly the first time I'd been brought to consider how I might look, apart from not wanting to be different from everyone else. Again I wondered what was the 'real' me and remembered the Duchess' advice to Alice. Trousers were no longer 'pants' or 'britches', but fashion items, tight-fitting and tailored into 'spider legs'. Only recently, patches and darns had been acceptable evidence of thrift and expediency, showing how patriotic we were with our 'Make do and mend'. Now newness was the fashion and what my father called 'fripperies and fol-de-rols' were matters of serious discussion. Buckley and Ernie Booth once spent a free period discussing 'turn-ups' and fob pockets, decorations hitherto forbidden for reasons of economy. Now they had been reinstated and were clearly essential features of what Buckley called 'a decent pair of bags'.

Shoes were also matters of concern to the fashion-conscious sixth former – not me, nor Hargreaves, still less Satters who, according to Hargreaves, generally wore his clothes like 'a flag pole on a windy day' and had boots 'fit to go ploughing in'. The standard black lace-up brogues of our early years which we all wore were abandoned almost as though they were marks of servitude. In their place we wore various forms of footgear. Until it became cold and wet many chaps came in sandals or gymshoes, some favoured 'desert boots', made of untanned leather and high in the ankle presumably to keep out the sands of Libya. A bit smarter, and no doubt reserved for leave in Alexandria, were thick rubber-soled 'brothel-creepers', in brown suede. Most of us were still not quite clear what a brothel was – knocking shops we knew about, but brothels sounded foreign – was the "th" soft as in "thatch", or hard as in "thee"?. These styles were for the casual dresser, but smart, slick types verging on the raffish favoured black ankle shoes with elastic sides, sometimes with the pointed toes that we called 'winkle-pickers' and always worn by spivs.

It was an uneasy time. Still in the shadow of the last war, already we seemed heading for the next. For those of us who only had vague memories of life before the war, things were getting slowly better, but the discontent of our elders was clear. My father had only just stopped implying that things couldn't have been worse if we'd been defeated. People were looking forward to the approaching general election, which seemed to herald the end of the Labour administration and the start of the 'good life'. But our widening interests and growing consciousness was hedged by fears of an approaching apocalypse. The horrific pictures of the concentration camps were complemented by even more atrocious scenes from Hiroshima and Nagasaki, which were the result of our own side's barbarity. We were told that although we had defeated Germany, we were already threatened by the dangers of nuclear war that might be unleashed on us by the red-Russian hordes, or the gum-chewing Americans whose trigger-happy generals seemed to cherish the idea of 'nuking' Moscow. 'It's the Yanks we've got to worry about,' said Satters. 'They've never had war. They don't know what it's like and they're itching to drop another atom bomb.' My father was equally gloomy. 'The Americans, boy, they're the ones to worry about. The Russians have enough on their plates clearing things up at home. It's the Americans to watch out for. They'll drag us into another war if we're not careful.' I thought of the fat, gum-chewing Colonel we'd had to stay, whose only reading matter was a book of comics, and felt that father might be right.

It was an uneasy time, conflict was in the very air we breathed and we were all militarised by National Service. Two years in the Forces, recently increased from eighteen months, waited for us all.

4. WORKADAY WORLD

I found the work in the sixth exciting. For the first time I came to see the connections between literature and history and realise that one ran into another, except Woodward wasn't as interesting as Conan Doyle. It was not quite the same with music and painting, although Delius and Debussy almost made it seem possible. Satters thought he understood. 'Think of the Siegfried Idyll,' he said, 'or L'Après-midi d'un faune. You can almost hear the colours.' But I couldn't yet see how music and painting were related to when they were composed. In the lower school subjects were mostly kept separate. There were obvious connections made between Latin and Greek, and it was easy to see, there, how one civilisation had led to another – although the eight hundred year gap between the Iliad and the Aeneid was never explained. And I never understood why it had seemed necessary to change the names of the gods.

As Bozo Hindley and Simkins said, our learning in the early stages – the endless vocabulary lists, the columns of irregular verbs to conjugate – was making bricks with which to build palaces. I began to see what they meant: then we began to lay the foundations, now the buildings were starting to rise. French ceased to be a series of word lists and grammatical rules. I began to make sense of the sounds our French Assistant made – much quicker and more vivid than the way Mr Courtenay spoke. I realised, almost with a shock, that Baudelaire was a kind of French Keats and Balzac as compelling a story teller as Thackeray. Satters used to talk of our days in the lower school as the time when we were 'in the Sweat Shop'. He said, 'In those days we were grinding away, dear boy, grinding away...' Now, I thought, we could begin to benefit from what we had ground.

We were bright boys in Rα and we'd been well taught, we'd got our Matric as a matter of course: no one failed anything, everyone got a bicycle and we'd all gone into the sixth. But advancement was not open to everyone. The wretched Tom had failed again – in maths, especially important to one aiming to be an accountant. I met him from time to time, avoiding my eyes as we passed in the corridors. My mother said, 'Tom doesn't seem to be doing so well. His mother's at her wits end about him.' Ungracious and vindictive where Tom was concerned, I couldn't resist a sneer. I had just read a story about a bishop, anxious to ease his conscience, writing to the boy he'd bullied at school, seeking forgiveness. A fortnight later he got his reply on a postcard. Fraught with memories of boyhood loneliness and despair it read: 'Can't forget, can't forgive. Sorry.' It was clearly a cry *de profundis* far deeper than any I'd experienced but it spoke to me of the anguish and desolation I'd experienced in the first weeks of Prep 1. I suffered mainly on Bowker's, but each night I returned to the comfort and security of the family. Nevertheless, the feeling of helplessness and isolation had made its mark, and I glimpsed the abject horror of a state where such conditions lasted for weeks on end.

I discussed this aspect of early school days with my cousin John, who was now in the sixth at Epsom College, which he still assumed was far superior to MGS, even though their results weren't as good, and its headmaster had nothing like the standing of the Chief who was on his way to becoming a telly-star. A propos his early days, John said, 'It was a bit lonely at first. But one soon made chums. And there was an exeat once a month when you got back to see the folks.' I'd experienced enough of his family life when we were together at Prep School in Dumfries, at the beginning of the War, to realise that John's family life was very different from mine, and reflected that for him school might have provided a more congenial background. His not doing as well as I had in his Matric had been a great and uncharitable joy to me, so accustomed was I to stories of his academic prowess in an institution he said was clearly a cut above a "mere grammar school". A renewed connection with McKelvie, who'd transferred from iiβ to Rugby – a much posher place than Epsom – convinced me that the Public Schools were not all they were cracked up to be. 'They're mad on Sport,' he said, 'and full of bum boys.' He didn't explain what bum boys were, and I didn't ask. John was staying with us in Broughton when the results came – telephoned from home, I think. I remember he got his about lunchtime and I mine some hours later during which he lorded it over me, speculating on my possible-probable failure. We were helping with the hay when the news came, delivered by hand on the back of an envelope. It was one of the sweetest moments of my life so far when I showed him that I'd done better than he had.

After the lower school, life in the sixth seemed quite leisured, although I see now that it was because we were allowed to 'get on with it' by ourselves. That was Bunn's phrase: 'Don't ask me, just go to the library and get on with it. You can find out these things for yourselves.' And so we did. We went to plays, the latest films, the galleries and talked forever in the coffee bars and libraries that were now our common rooms. The Whitworth and the Mosley Street galleries, the Rotunda of the Central Library, the exhibitions at the John Rylands. Todd, on the strength of a signed chit from Simkins, even got into the chained library at Chetham's. It was all learning without effort. We scouted the cultural riches that the city laid open to us, spending almost as much time in there as we did at school, most of it concentrated in the Albert Square Kardomah, or the coffee lounge of the YMCA next door to the bombed-out Free Trade Hall – both too near the Central Library to be kept away from.

Satters developed an interest in Pre-Raphaelite paintings and I followed him through the galleries as he moved from the "Hireling Shepherd" to the "Light of the World", which wasn't far. For a while we haunted the Town Hall examining the Ford Madox Brown murals in the Great Hall. We studied "Work" while Satters speculated about the identities of those figures which hadn't already been identified. 'That shoveller in the foreground – he must be someone. The vicar, perhaps. Or his local MP.' Bunn was a great expounder of paintings, but refused to be drawn into the discussion. 'A barren kind of anthropomorphism, turning paint into people. What does it tell you of the times? That flower seller with the broken brimmed hat, or the woman with the child: what about them?'

We read voraciously, passing round with enthusiastic recommendations what we'd just finished: *Point Counter Point, Antic Hay, The Heart of the Matter;* Auden and Isherwood, Eliot: *Notes Towards the Definition of Culture;* Webster and Marlowe, Steinbeck and Thurber, Carlyle and Stephenson, Hemingway, Scott Fitzgerald, Faulkner, Maurois, Gide and Rimbaud. One of the German speakers from U4A got us interested in Hesse. He passed round *Steppenwolf* and *Klingsor's Last Summer,* which was an attractive read because it had a racy cover of a couple asleep on a rumpled bed – far more erotic than any *Health and Efficiency* or the tattered Hank Jansons that were passed around. *The Naked and the Dead* puzzled most of us, seeming to be little more than descriptions of atrocities in language we would never dream of using. For a while, after reading it, Jammy Chambers – another transfer from U4a – would enliven mornings while we were waiting for registration by sitting on his table with an imaginary machine gun and 'hosing down the beaches' to eliminate any of the enemy who might have crept up on us in the night. 'Gotta be done every morning,' he said. One day Bunn loomed behind him in full fusillade and waited, like a dark question mark, while he panned the room with appropriate sound effects. 'Got 'em all?' he said. 'Good! I'll just have a roll call of our guys.'

5. THE CHIEF

In the sixth the Chief took us for the one period a week that was labelled RI. He had a broad view of what constituted Religious Instruction and would engage us in conversation about religion and philosophy, economics and ethics, or simply the main leader of that morning's *Manchester Guardian* – which he expected us to have read. All this was very different from the previous year's RI when Willie Graham took us verse by verse through the Gospel according to John. This was satisfactory for the Crusaders and disturbing for the orthodox Jews but felt to be something of an imposition by the working majority of us Anglo-Saxon heathens. Nevertheless, we would agree that it looked up when Claude Rayne took over.

I found the Chief's classes very stimulating, for apart from the occasions when I'd listened to my father and his friends, it was the first time I'd encountered free-ranging discussions of this kind. They were good enough to miss cricket and coffee for, and they made me think in new and exciting ways. The Chief had a strong sense of the absurd and a nose for paradox. 'Better a truth come out of a wrong than a wrong remain undone,' he said. He spoke from what I conceived was a scientific standpoint, giving reasons for the conclusions he drew and often digressing into physics or chemistry which persuaded me that they too could be both speculative and uncertain. His manner contrasted valuably with the Blessed Bunn's, who had a discursive way of teaching which fired my imagination, linking as I have said seemingly disparate topics in a way that was often startling, on one occasion making connections between pre-Raphaelitism and *Mary Barton* and the American Civil War.

The Chief made me puzzle over the supposedly unquestionable verities of religion, and reconsider our general uncritical acceptance of Christianity as a 'good thing'. I remember with delight his engagement with a militant member of the Crusaders. After a brief account of the Crusades and the almost hysterical fervour they seem to have generated, the Chief went on to discuss the fanaticism of the Christian martyrs who seemed to prefer death to life. The Crusader comfortably suggested that as believers they were headed for a better state, what matter if it came sooner than later? 'In that case,' said the Chief, 'they were utterly selfish. If man has a duty, it is to other men. To seek your own salvation at the cost of what you might do to help your fellows is a kind of selfishness.' He pointed out the paradox of a religion that sought with force and the edge of the sword to bring peace on earth and goodwill to men. At a time when Might seemed to be Right – after all we'd just won a war against unmitigated evil, he declared: 'Christian soldiers wearing the panoply of God are just another manifestation of Fascism.' All this was strong meat for boys to digest who'd passed their adolescence hating Hitler and all Germans.

It was of the greatest intellectual value to be brought face to face with religion this way. Although most of us were indifferently religious we were children of a region that was strongly aware of its religious roots. Non-conformism had flourished here from its earliest days and according to some historians the Reformation had by-passed large parts of Lancashire. Cuthbert Seton had been fond of pointing out that Bonny Prince Charlie recruited a regiment of Lancashire Catholic Gentlemen. My upbringing on the extremity of the county had kept me in such ignorance, that I hadn't knowingly seen a Catholic until MacInnes was pointed out to me. But now my travelling with the boys from De La Salle, as well as a general widening of horizons, had made me aware of a pervasive Catholic influence. The large towns on the northern and western sides of Manchester all had Catholic centres. Bolton and Blackburn, Wigan and Preston, each had its notable Catholic School, and just down the road from MGS was Xaverian College, whose blue-capped boys mingled with us Owls as we travelled to and fro.

The De La Salle boys I travelled on the train with were fearfully religious. A strong consciousness of evil seemed to dominate their lives and they went day by day in fear of slipping unwittingly into a state of mortal sin. Worrying about it kept them awake at nights and it appeared always to be mixed up with 'impure thoughts'. This they would admit, but no more, and try as I would, I couldn't get them to talk about it or explain why it made them so fearful. 'It's sex,' Hargreaves said. 'A good blow-through is what they need.' This man-of-the-world attitude was born of his experiences with the girls from the Convent who didn't seem to let their religion interfere with their natural urges. Mixing with them had made him something of an expert – or so he would have it appear. I understood them to be even more determined than the forthright Cumberland lasses I spent my holidays learning how to deal with. The chaps from De La Salle were reticent apart from remarks about being pure in thought and deed. They were in terror of a kind of Chief Inquisitor whose name was rarely pronounced. I supposed it was in case it caused him to appear, like the devil, and felt sure it was Father Benedict, the famous flogger they used to talk about – again in lowered voices – when we were in the third form.

At this time I also became aware of the area's many non-conformists churches and on Walking Sunday had a comprehensive view of their strength as they paraded down Cheetham Hill Road. These Whitsun Walks were not only demonstrations of faith but excuses for much jollity. Satters and I went to see the fun. Originally, I suppose, intended as a simple witness when congregations would walk through the town together, they had become a sort of muted carnival. Certainly they had all the signs of providing a good day out. On this occasion they filled the road as they came down the hill towards Victoria. As far as my eye could see there were ranks of embroidered banners declaring church and faith. Amongst them were floats decorated with flowers, many with tableaux and surrounded by ranks of girls in white, holding streamers. Church elders and their minister walked behind. Brass bands intervened in the procession, some riding on floats, some walking and, beside the walkers in the actual parade, groups of supporters, all in their best, kept pace on the pavement with their own chapel. As they swayed down the hill towards the city, banners held aloft on poles and spread by ribbons in the hands of their attendants, they looked like a flotilla of square rigged ships in a regatta. Wesleyans and Low Anglicans, Methodists, Primitive Methodists, Unitarians and Congregationalists, Baptists and Plymouth Brethren, all seemed to have shelved their differences for one glorious day of solidarity – after which they no doubt went back to accentuating their differences, forcing schisms and defending their own private, peculiar worlds.

Often the Chief's musings on religion strayed into philosophy and he would talk to us about seeing and believing, sense data and logical positivism, the nature of reality and all in an allusive, discursive way that served to whet our appetites for what was to come at University. He made me wonder about the way I thought and the way I was. What proof had I that anything existed outside my head which made sense of everything? He also made me aware of what I came to know as the mind body problem, by calling on us to consider the difference between what we thought and what we felt and how far the irrationality of the one could be regulated by the formalism of the other. I seldom left his classes without feeling stimulated in a different kind of way from any other lesson.

6. GROWING UP

The first year of H6 laid open my mind to worlds hitherto undreamt of. For the first time, school and what developed from it were more important than what went on at home. The daily rush to catch the train became a dawdle, as I browsed in the Central Library, or lingered over afternoon tea in the YMCA. Often a group of us would remain in town for a concert or a play, holding out in a corner of the Albert Square Kardomah. There we were indulged by the staff, and only hurried away when the early evening rush began. They tolerated our occasional extravagances – or parsimonies – in the shape of two coffees for four of us lasting an hour and a half.

For the first time in my life I felt the need for money. Not for big things like records or fishing tackle which came by saving-up and begging, but for day-to-day running expenses. Until now all I'd needed was bus fare and dinner money. Now there were coffees and tea-time buns to stop me feeling hungry until I got home – often I would stay in town to see a play or a film. Money was always short, and already I could see its lack becoming a perennial problem. Most of us came from middle-class professional families and were amply but not lavishly supplied. Money was not discussed – my mother's laying into my father for his financial ineptitude one New Year's day was the only time I can recall the subject being mentioned, apart from occasional grouses of my father about what he saw as unjustifiable extravagance – like my mother buying new curtains for the bathroom, which occasioned a tremendous row. Even the Jewish members of our group who were supposed to be good with money came from families of musicians or lawyers and were fixed pretty much as the rest of us.

Of all my acquaintance the hapless Tom was the only one with any interest in amassing riches. Scraping the necessary Maths O-level at the third attempt, he left school at Easter and went to work in an office off Cross Street. I sometimes met him carrying letters to the Post, while I was on my way to scan the shelves at Sherratt and Hughes. He was as stony-faced and supercilious as when I'd been the recipient of his cast-off clothes, but the haunted look of conscious failure that hung about him at school had given way to an insolent swagger. Now he was on his way to becoming a successful business man. When he saw me he would clap his cigarette to his lips and give me the shortest of nods. 'Poor Geraldine,' my mother would say if Tom's name came up. 'She had such high hopes of him – Cambridge and the law and being called to the bar – none of them will happen now. Still, I suppose he'll turn into a fat, boring accountant like his father, and make lots of money – which will please her.' Here she would sigh, as if my father didn't make enough.

The YMCA was cheaper than the Kardomah in Albert Square and slightly nearer the Library. But there we sometimes encountered smooth men whose zeal to ingratiate themselves discounted their willingness to buy our coffee. At the Kardomah, unless it was a busy time of day, we were generally left alone. I was often short of money but not cripplingly so. Father's pocket was still at my disposal and I financed myself each morning from his loose change. Half-a-crown or five bob was usually there for the asking, but to get folding money needed a formal request with a well prepared justification for such extravagance. Penguin supplied most of my books at one and sixpence or two shillings, the same as a seat at the Tatler.

I reckon my pocket money of five shillings in 1950 had something like the purchasing power of ten pounds in 2010. At Christmas and Birthdays when I got a ten bob note from my Great Aunt, I felt rich beyond the dreams of avarice. For as long as I could – about ten days – I would keep it in the corner of the mirror in my bedroom where it caught my eye in a comforting way as I came and went, and especially as I sat at my desk. Beer and cigarettes, those great drains on a young man's purse, didn't yet figure in our budgets. Smoking was all right for nascent bucks like Tom, mixing daily with proper business men who would pass round the fags as a matter of course, but for most of us it was something we weren't quite sure of. It 'spoiled the wind' – not that many of us were sportingly inclined – and, what was worse, made the breath smell, which we were told would put the girls off. One hapless member of the newly assembled H6 was already known as 'Dogbreath', and his ostracism was a warning to us all. Satters was almost neurotic about whether he was tainted or not. He had a test whereby he would gasp into his cupped hands and snuff up the exhalation. 'I can still smell it!' he would cry. 'That gasper I had on Saturday night. Oh why did I succumb?'

Adepts in some fields – precociously knowledgeable about music and books, for instance – we were still children in others. Sport and Politics we knew little of, despite the imminence of a general election. Our supposed support of Manchester City lapsed as we found more interesting ways to spend Saturdays than standing on the terraces at Maine Road. In the summer it was different. I was a keen cricketer but absolutely devoid of skill. I couldn't catch, I couldn't bat and my bowling was so slow that any competent batsman had got its measure after three deliveries and howked the next three over the boundary. Still I loved the game and played whenever they would let me – which was only when there was no one else. I dreamt of belonging to a team, but mostly I was only a keen spectator for I was a junior member of Lancashire County Cricket Club, which gave me free entry to Old Trafford for all matches.

My father, himself a member, would leave his work in the early afternoon when there was a County Match and often I would join him after school and together in the Ladies Stand – for juniors were not allowed in the Pavilion – we would watch the last two hours of play. I loved the sense of privilege as I waved my membership card at the gateman, and relished being able to walk round the ground and sit anywhere. My favourite place was in the Hornby Stand, behind the bowler's arm and just below the scorer's box. At times there I could hear the commentator describing what I was watching for the benefit of his radio listeners.

From this vantage point I got a comprehensive view of the field of play. Not only could I study the bowler's art, see how much turn he got and how the batsman managed, but also I could see how the field was arranged after each over, to accommodate the bowler and the known propensities of the batsman facing him. When Washbrook, for instance, was at the crease there would always be a deep square leg and an extra cover point. It was a pleasure to me to watch the field changing between overs, to guess the remarks that were passed and feel that I was in a small way a part of the match. It was from the Hornby Stand that I saw the great Don Bradman bat twice. Each time he was dismissed before he'd got going by Malcolm Hilton,

Lancashire's smart new bowler who was not much older than I. In the Test match the Don again scored badly, but became enshrined in my memory for the execution of a perfect late cut. He seemed to lean back and merely kiss the ball as it bounded to the rails. Nevertheless, there were honours enough for the England side, when an injured Denis Compton scored a magical century and a half and Lancashire's own darling boy, Cyril Washbrook, scored a century before the match was rained off on the fourth and fifth days.

Girls were the great mysteries. Prickings of the flesh and urgings in the blood were vindicated by *Women in Love* and the much read French copy of *Lady Chatterley's Lover* that circulated amongst the cognoscenti. Enlightened by films like *La Ronde* and *A Streetcar Named Desire* we were encouraged to confront the monster that was beginning to dominate our secret lives. As Frank Sinatra began to supplant Bing Crosby we became suffused with a desire for romance that titillated our senses and gave us immoral longings. The morning traffic between the school buses became a frenzied trade in names and directions and often resulted in actual assignments, which were fully reported and meticulously analysed. The keen interest of both sides to become deliciously involved made it hard to tell which were the hunters and which the prey.

The start of the spring term was bothered with debates about the forthcoming election. I suppose it shows how much I was absorbed in the life of the sixth that I can't recall much about them or it. It was a time of great political ferment. Dissatisfaction with the Attlee government was expressed in my father's view of the times. 'Things,' he said, 'just aren't getting any better.' To those of us who couldn't remember anything else it didn't seem too bad, but among our elders the sense of disappointment was almost palpable. Many, like my cousins, fled the country, and two from my father's side went to Canada and Australia. My father's great friend from Broughton, a middle-aged farmer, sold up and went to Tasmania to start again. 'This country's buggered,' he said. The Labour Government's radical moves to alter the shape of society upset more and more people, and to many returning from the war, life in the colonies, as they were still known, seemed an attractive alternative. My father, whose orange-backed copies of the Left Wing Book Club were my first reserve when I ran out of reading material, became more and more disillusioned. Sometimes when I got home late and starving, I would find him in deep discussion with one or other of our neighbouring friends. I would be ordered to make myself a sandwich and join in as they mourned the state of the nation.

The Welfare State was just coming into being. As a medical man my father was interested in how the National Health Service would turn out – most of his colleagues seemed to be against it. Internationally, the Allies were starting to quarrel. America was flexing its muscles like a prize-fighter at the end of a successful bout and looking for another contest. Russia was busy growing its own atom bomb, judging, perhaps rightly, that the one dropped on Nagasaki had been more to impress them than cow the Japanese. To me the next production at the Library Theatre or next week's Hallé programme was far more important The election took place in February, and as I rack my memory, the most I can recall is Satters wearing a big yellow rosette – it might have been on polling day – as he pursued a startled Ernie Fox, trampling his blue rosette which fell off during the chase.

7. SUMMER OF 1950

At the end of my first year in the Sixth I reckon my whole perception of who and what I was crystallized into the being that I am now. I acquired a sense of having grown up, not merely because I was treated differently but in my growing understanding of the world outside of school. I felt a change of mood from passive to active – I could do things now rather than be done to. I was becoming an independent being, no longer a robot to be programmed by school and home.

Instead of being a piece of flotsam washed here and there, I acquired a little momentum of my own and began to move slowly and roughly in the direction I thought I wanted to go. Not that I had many definite ideas about that – except I was going to be a writer – and of course, live in Broughton Mills. My last piece in *Ulula* had been a poem, powerfully influenced by *The Waste Land*, especially by its terse, dispassionate, desperate view of a world so similar to ours in appearance but so different in spirit. Verse seemed now to be the stuff to produce and, encouraged by a kind of efflorescence of poetry evinced by Dylan Thomas' readings on the radio and the production of verse plays, like *The Lady's not for Burning* and *The Cocktail Party,* I directed my creative genius into a kind of rhythmical prose – sometimes it rhymed, sometimes it scanned, but you could tell it was poetry by the way it was set out on the page. Verse was less bother than prose, somehow it didn't require as much effort, and it was a better way of dealing with those powerful feelings that cried out for expression. Already I had a file of fragments, mere jottings marking my teenage angst, many in the manner of the masters – 'Imitation,' said Hargreaves, 'the sincerest form of flattery. Except yours is probably insulting,' – but however hard I tried to be serious, cheerfulness kept breaking in and as I wrote I unearthed a vein of scurrility which would out.

The file grew in size for I added to it most nights, and during the day's idle moments, I would think about how the current piece might be extended or improved. My father's secretary offered to type out any finished pieces when she had 'a spare moment'. Many of these were elegiac – I daren't show her the scabrous lampoons and bawdy ballads – 'More Byron than Wordsworth,' Satters said. I remember a sonnet's opening line: 'A dead leaf on the lawn, and still July.' Written while snow was still on the ground, it suggested that I already heard the rumbling of time's chariot. My father was always interested in what I was doing and saw what Mary typed out for me, but he wasn't much good as a critic, mainly because I didn't trust him. 'Too sombre, boy. And not enough substance.' Who, at seventeen, believes in his father?

Mostly I kept private what I had written, really because I felt I had to. But one day while I was scribbling in the library Pansy Mason caught sight of my file. 'Your works?' I mumbled something about "jottings" and "diary". 'I should feel privileged to have a look,' he said. In an impulsive moment I passed it over; after all, he did know about these things. Remarks he'd made about my bits in *Ulula* were judiciously complimentary while being guardedly critical, as though he'd admired the plant and didn't want to stunt its growth. 'Mm,' he'd said. 'Quite promising. Be better when you've found your own voice.' Which I took to mean – all right for a lad, but too much like Eliot. As I handed my file over I babbled explanations about its personal nature, and how it functioned more as a diary and commonplace book than a collection of finished works, and how he really mustn't take anything seriously.

He kept it for about a week, during which I felt bereft, and handed it back with a wry smile which showed he'd read the poem about his teaching style. 'Some good stuff, there,' he said. 'Stick at it. It may come to something. I've taken the liberty of putting a pencil note on some of them.' And indeed he had, gently deploring some of my extravagances, but adding a faint schoolmasterly tick besides the bits where he thought I had succeeded. I was both gratified and encouraged.

Meanwhile, life at home had suddenly become quite different. Until now it had been a maelstrom of social activity as my cousins, teased by my father and egged on by my mother, conducted their various tumultuous affairs. When they left to do what Betty called 'some real living', my mother, short of someone to organise, cater for and play with, got herself a job managing the practice for my father's friend, whose surgery was next door but one. Also she took up bridge, long a passion of my father's, and soon they were spending three or four nights a week, and most weekends, at the Bridge Club.

As a result, most evenings from seven onwards, I was blissfully and luxuriously on my own: the lounge was empty, the best arm chair was at my disposal, I had time to read whatever I liked and free choice of records on the radiogram. It was the sort of existence I might have prayed for. I played the operas my father dismissed as 'frivolities', like *Paggliacci* and *Carmen* – which I came to know by heart. I listened to the radio a lot and as the *Radio Times* arrived I would scan it and mark with one, two or three stars those programmes I ought not to miss. Television had not yet entered the house, although my father shamelessly squatted on our neighbour to watch Wimbledon. When my mother suggested that this might be an imposition, he said,

'Well, Alec imposes himself on my whisky often enough...'
Which was true.

I relished these solitary evenings and when the bridge players
had gone I would heave a great sigh of relief. I was now free
and alone and the evening stretched out before me to do just as
I pleased. I spent a lot of it listening to the Third Programme:
Bertrand Russell told me about the pleasures of idleness; A.
J. Ayer explained logical positivism – well, almost, but they
complemented what the Chief had said; also, by listening hard,
I tried to make sense of Stockhausen. I remember a production
of *Medea* in Greek, which I managed to follow with the help
of Loeb, and a performance of *Axel* by Villiers de l'Isle Adam
which intrigued me with the idea that it might be better to die
at a moment of exultation than endure a life of disillusionment
and decay. To 'die upon a kiss,' to realise a moment of supreme
achievement where, 'now more than ever seems it sweet to die'
was a consummation I understood and admired without actually
wanting to experience. 'Living!' cries Axel. 'Our servants can
do that for us.'

However, life had too strong a hold on me ever to consider
relinquishing it – even, I think, if I had achieved all that I dreamt
of. But I admired the idea, just as I could sense the despair of
Eliot's 'burnt out ends of smoky days' without ever wanting to
share it. Living was too rich, the streets were full of excitement,
there was so much to read, to see, to listen to. Hargreaves had
just introduced me to Gieseking and Beethoven's piano sonatas.
It was the summer when Ramadhin and Valentine triumphantly
beguiled the England batsmen and helped the West Indies beat
Lancashire, twice, and by an innings. Gorgeous Gussie Moran's
lace knickers brightened up the Centre Court. In the outside
world, the Americans and the Communists achieved another

confrontation, this time in North Korea, and committed us to another war. National Service was extended by six months. It was confidently asserted that the Americans wanted to 'Nuke the commies'. Apart from Gussie's knickers, the news was black except that petrol rationing ended and I fell in love.

8. FLIRTS

Until now, girls and sex had been more of a nuisance than fun. I realised without properly understanding, that these things were regarded differently at boarding schools. According to cousin John, and McElvie, the chaps arranged things amongst themselves. Girls for them, too, were also much of a mystery, but lust was manageable. Each in his own way offered to show me but I wasn't keen. They both seemed to regard girls as a different species, cousin John in particular treating them in much the same way as my father treated the dog – petting it when it obeyed him and being severe with it when it didn't. The girls at Broughton almost loved him for it. 'That cousin of yours,' Katie said. 'He ought to be in a museum. He makes you seem almost human.' McElvie they called 'the professor' because he always spoke to them seriously and politely. At least I had daily experience of the sex and learned how to deal with them in a limited way. But I lacked the confidence to forge ahead in the same cavalier way as Peter Seddon, and envied his panache which often led to tremendous success.

Still, as the first year of the sixth progressed, the 'problem of women', as Hargreaves called it, occupied us more and more. As usual in our class we took our lead from literature and after *Antic Hay* had been passed around our little reading group, 'Where the hormones there moan I' became something of a slogan. About the same time the flirty note-passing between the buses became a much more significant activity. In iiiα it had all been a joke; we were the call boys, the messengers, accosted as we got on the bus, and frequently the earliest readers. But the business sometimes became serious, and the notes touched what Satters described as 'the raw nerves of adolescent passion', although Hargreaves regarded it as simply, 'feeling horny'. Whatever it was, the recipients of these notes were sometimes pale and tight-lipped when the scrap of paper was delivered into their trembling hands.

At that time our ideas of romance were mostly derived from the books we read and the films we saw. At the cinema there was on the one hand the wholesomeness of Hollywood and on the other the raffishness of the Continent where sex was something much more serious and disturbing than the sanitised, sunshiny business portrayed by Judy Garland and Veronica Lake – although according to Hargreaves, a night on Veronica Lake was every fisherman's dream.

I had a foothold, so to speak, in the other camp by my connection with the Macinnes girls. They interested themselves in my affairs and promoted a liaison with Wendy, an impossible connection since she lived in Mossley, twenty un-negotiable miles from Bolton. She was the one I hardly recognised when she turned up at the Albert Square Kardomah, accompanied by two friends who kept watch from a nearby table. We went to the Tatler, I don't think they followed us, and held hands stiffly for an hour and a half. When we stumbled out into the sunlight of Oxford Street she said, 'I've got to go home now,' and ran off to catch her bus. We met again twice and then it was the summer holidays and I came to love another. She would nudge up against me when I bought the tickets, pushing her one and sixpence towards the cashier, who took my three shillings and passed me Wendy's money as change. So it was as if I'd paid for her, but really I hadn't.

Conversation of any kind was difficult. Apart from what we did at school, and I suppose a kind of general unspecified lust to discover ways of proceeding, we had no common ground. We always did the same thing – met in the Kardomah and went to the Tatler. Over coffee she would talk about how awful her friends were and how embarrassed she was by their coming with her on our first date. I suspected they were only there because she asked them and said so – being frank and frontal. Then she asked what I did at school and so we were off on a discussion about Baudelaire and Mallarmé which was not what either of us wanted, but seemed at the time the only common ground. Where she lived seemed impossible to reach, so anything other than a Saturday meeting in town was virtually impossible. Satters lived in Mossley but when I suggested that he might profit from our connection he said, 'I'm not taking in your dirty washing.' Those who lived in South Manchester had a much easier time of it socially with Youth Clubs and Tennis Clubs. Bobby Newton from Sale could walk part of the way home every night with his girl-friend. 'Like Derby and Joan,' Jammy Chambers said. 'She even carries his books for him.'

Wendy was very different from the girls at home who were used to Pete Seddon's 'rough and fumble approach'. This was quite physical and close in, so his courting, which was often in public, sometimes became a wrestling match. His opponent usually gave as good as she got and occasionally was actually victorious, in any case both sides end up flushed and excited. His girls were nearly always beefy and as quick with the tongue as they were with the hand. 'They're all up for it, you know,' he told me once, licking the blood off a scratch, 'they like the physicals but try to hide it.'

I usually found them less than willing, but then perhaps I didn't try hard enough and they were different with me, less forward but pointed. Somebody said I was 'better talking than doing'. They were always ready to turn my words into something I didn't mean, like making a simple remark such as 'I think she's nice,' into a full blown declaration of love. My standing amongst them was rocky anyway, partly because I was away a lot of the time, and partly because I was clearly ill at ease amongst them. Pete didn't help by making fun of me, like declaring that my new pants, which I was quite proud of, were 'like a small hotel.' So that when Katie raised her eyebrow for an explanation he could say, 'Because they've got no ballroom.' Katie's reply was a dig in the kidneys so sharp that it made him wince. But it was clear she did it because she liked him. This was the northern way. If she fancied you she would hit you or maul you about, otherwise you'd be ignored. It was an attitude that left me cold and embarrassed and annoyed because I didn't know how to deal with it and didn't really care to find out. It was only after I'd been seriously smitten myself that I began to get on with girls and that summer of 1950 gave me my first real taste of romance. It was as corny as that but it was also an eye opener and almost impossible to describe in anything other than clichés. My world was turned upside down and I swung between exhilaration and despair. At the end of the summer I was a changed man.

My summer job was at Seddon's farm doing the kind of things I'd been doing casually in the holidays since I was big enough to hold a shovel or a rake. But this year it was a regular job, five days a week at one and six an hour. The £3 a week it realised was wealth beyond my wildest dreams. I didn't tell my mother for she would certainly have impounded at least half of it for 'savings'. Most of my Broughton friends worked, for at that time University was seen, there, to be only for those wanting to be doctors or vets, or girls aiming to become teachers. Pete Seddon was being kept unwillingly at school, but John Fletcher was in the solicitor's office, and George Newton in the Bank where his uncle was manager. They only got thirty shillings, but then, they had jobs 'with prospects' and went to work in a collar and tie and were inside all day. For a month, I donned my shabby old cords at seven every morning and strolled across the valley to have fun with Pete, barrowing shit or scaling hay under the tutelage of old Jack Hutchinson, in what he called 'the Huniversity hov Life'. Everything we did was in a spirit of fellowship and fun that made even the most boring of tasks seem interesting, although it was hard to be enthusiastic about weeding a field of turnips.

This life of quasi-independence had a deep effect on me, and I felt I grew up in the space of a month. I was judged big enough to look after myself and my parents, busy at home in Bolton, only came at weekends, and not always then. I was king of my own castle, and as a young buck with money in my pocket, at the weekend I was ready for anything. Shows, Sports, Dances, Jaunts. Since I was now a working man I was largely treated as grown-up and I enjoyed it. There was a great difference between Ian, the doctor's son and 'Ee as works fer Seddons'. On a Wednesday, Martin might say, 'Na then, Ee, wheer ur we gaain this wi'kend?' And I might reply, 'Nay, I'se nert bothered. Best ax Seddy.' And we might be off to the dance at Chapel Stile or pictures in Ambleside, with fish and chips in Coniston on the way home. Nobody bothered if we smoked or if we drank pints of shandy and bottles of Forest Brown. We were what were known as 'gallus young lads', and such things were expected of us. There was a dance every weekend somewhere within reach, usually costing half a crown, including supper of sandwiches and a whist pie or two. Twenty Woodbines cost a shilling and beer was ten pence a pint. Only on Saturday nights if we ventured to try a rum and pep or two before going to the dance, were we ever warned against the demon drink. I loved the life and felt if this was being grown up, I could hardly wait to do it properly.

In those days everyone smoked – and those who didn't were regarded as eccentrics. Maybe girls started later than boys, but to produce a packet of Players and invite one to 'have a gasper' was an acceptable approach to some unknown fair. The brush-off was a dead pan, 'Don't smoke'. However, if she said, 'Go on, then...' you had grounds for a conversation. It was a ploy that worked in Broughton, but I hadn't the opportunity to use it much in Manchester. Wendy hadn't smoked, and I was still at the stage of wondering whether I liked it or not, experimenting on the train in the mornings, trying hard at the weekends. On the school bus where it was not unknown for someone to light up, the would-be sophisticates would sit in the window seats wreathed in smoke and wave their fags at anyone who cared to look at them.

Bunn's room always smelled of Balkan Sobranies which were his preferred brand. I see him now like some seer or vatic priest expounding the principles of his mystery, a nebulous grey figure with the afternoon sun glancing through the airborne wisps of smoke that coiled around his head. It was the same in Ernie Cropper's room where we were allowed to keep our things, there was the lingering smell of his pipe, which he smoked while marking books, but unlike Bunn, he didn't smoke in class. Perhaps it was different when he taught in Maths Sixth. In a characteristic flight of fancy that managed to combine showing-off with fantasy, Satters said the whiff of Bunn's cigarettes lingered like the faint smell of sewage in the Marais where we'd stayed on one of our Easter trips to Paris.

In Bunn's we sat at tables with no storage space and were given desks that could be locked in one of the Maths rooms just along the corridor. So I found myself again in the room from which I had been rescued by his secretary on the morning I first met the Chief, and where I had struggled to understand algebra. Ernie Cropper – a much more benign figure now – would be sitting there some lunchtimes as we came in and out. If he recognised me he didn't say. Some mornings when they didn't fancy going into Prayers a couple of free spirits would stay there, hiding behind the desks at the back when the 'seekers' came round. Their approach was always heralded by the banging of doors as they came up the corridor. I fancied they 'lit up' more as an act of bravado than to get the refreshment of a good smoke.

There wasn't much smoking at school, as far as I knew: no secret lunch-time club in the basement or desperate gang behind the bike sheds, which were directly in view of the Master's Common Room. The smokers were found in the parks like the gang of desperadoes I used to meet at the decaying playground in Birchfields Park. But then, how was I to know what went on throughout the school? There were so many of us: nameless faces that passed in the corridors, anonymous figures on buses and in Prayers. Perhaps if they'd been members of Old Trafford I'd have known them. Twice at Oxford I was introduced to chaps whose time at school had exactly matched mine. Harris's clever brother squinted at me when I saluted him in Broad Street. 'Don't tell me,' he said. 'You're an Old Manc.'

9. THE LAST DAY

I went into the second year of the sixth with a strong feeling of discontent; more and more I felt the confines of the classroom. The summer job, the taste for money in the pocket, the freedom of living on my own – if only in a supported and temporary way – had combined to give me a sense of what it was like to be independent. More than ever I felt that Broughton Mills and the Lakes were home and they must be lived in. The landlord still refused to sell the house to my father, and as he and my mother came up less and less, I had a paralysing fear that they would give up the lease before I could take it on myself. This was a powerful incentive to enter adult life, which was already offering delightful sensations, like looking after myself, being treated as a working man, whizzing off to dances on the back of Gerry Babb's motor bike, or racketing around the Lakes in Terry Moorat's sports car, and swooning in the first phase of love. Life was fun, and while going out after supper and coming back home at dawn was part of a new found independence, being accepted as a reliable member of a working community was another. The offer of being articled to one of the town's solicitors, a cousin of my mother's, was momentarily attractive, until I saw that it would place me in the same ranks as the wretched Tom.

Yet this longing to return to my roots didn't spoil my appreciation of what was on offer elsewhere. By now I had come to see that Manchester was more than MGS, and that the city offered daily a multitude of interesting experiences it would be almost sinful to miss. As well as its cultural attractions it provided an interesting social life as a group of us took to passing long afternoons in the YMCA at the top of Peter Street. The coffee lounge seemed to have been purged of last year's importunate smoothies and was now frequented by interesting people: Hallé musicians just come from rehearsal, visiting actors resting for the night's performance, fighting men just back from the war. We listened to them as they gossiped about love, life and literature and bought us coffee. It all went to create an air of unconventionality and hedonism which was quite different from the slightly uncomfortable atmosphere produced by those earnest men with familiar ways that we'd become wary of the previous year. Sometimes in the early evening, smoking Gitanes, and swearing a little, we would adjourn to the little bar in Mount Street and brave the quizzical stare of the barmaid.

The return to school in September had found me in a particularly awkward mood. Nothing seemed to make sense, what I was doing seemed a waste of time. I wanted to be out and part of the world. I wrote on the cover of my precious file, 'Good time is wasting with the doddering fools, / Who talk about draft plans but never of tools'. In this mood I struggled to the end of the autumn term, tormented by thoughts of what my beloved might be getting up to while I was away. I was upset because she only replied to half of my letters – but then I did write often – and I was worried about the brother of one of her friends, a young farmer with his own car. To allay my justified fears I took a long Christmas break, thereby missing some of the mock A levels and incurring much just censure. I guess it is a mark of the school's tolerance that I wasn't put out there and then.

I found the Easter term just as wearying as its predecessor, and although I found classes interesting, I felt certain I might manage better on my own. We had finished the set books and were now involved in extensive revision. Bunn stopped digressing, Pansy Mason stuck firmly to the texts. Only in French, learning Parisian argot from Monsieur Philippe, did we seem to be learning something new. I took to missing classes and spending days in the library. My relations with the Chief were not always cordial despite his regard for my pieces in *Ulula* and my enjoyment of his RI lessons. As I became bored – after all, it was my ninth year as an Owl – I grew blasé about attendance, sometimes leaving after registration to be in time for morning coffee at the YMCA, and as the year drew on, to be at Old Trafford for the first over of the day.

One morning before break, the Chief sent for me again – he'd left it too late the previous day. We had a brief discussion of my present approach to education.

'You're using the school as a club, Davidson,' he said.

What could I do but agree, for I was hardly a model pupil?

'But,' I replied, feeling the need to keep my end up, 'as far as I know about these things, it's a good club.'

'That might well be so, but I'm cancelling your membership.'

So I packed my bag and left that very day.

It was a shock and as I said my farewells in the library to such of my friends who were not on their way to Old Trafford or coffee at the YMCA, I was conscious of having crossed a kind of Rubicon. I knew I was leaving forever a select community that was both privileged and demanding, composed of intelligent and assiduous contemporaries for whom the second rate was not acceptable. They argued about Existentialism and atonal music, Russell and Ayer, Americans and their hankering to drop another bomb. They weighed the merits of Balliol against Trinity as though admission was theirs just for the asking – perhaps it was. Nevertheless, I felt it was time to be off. I was almost eighteen, National Service loomed and I'd already had a taste of the adult world.

I was allowed to come back for my A-levels, although some thought it a waste of time. I'd managed to mitigate the fierceness of the storm at home by setting to work seriously and steadily on my own, and fortunately my exam results were gratifyingly good. I returned to school the day they were posted and on my way out, looked into the Chief's office. He was just leaving.

'What do you want?' he said, brusquely.

'I've just come to say goodbye.'

'Come in.' He turned back into his study. Then facing me squarely he said, 'Don't put things off. You procrastinate and you're something of a dreamer. You tend to live in a world of your own. That may be all right, but don't ignore the other world. Do the things that have to be done. And do them now. Remember, the most important things in life are only learned by doing them. Now, I'm in a hurry. Goodbye. Good luck.'

That ending I recall vividly: the Chief, a slight, dapper, balding figure emanating authority, the austere, shadowy room in which we stood, the two of us momentarily arrested on the verge of doing something else. Outside, the corridor echoing with the cries of exultation and despair, now seemed to lead to a world of confusion and doubt. 'What now?' I wondered. 'What now says Plato's ghost?' And as I walked down the drive to Old Hall Lane, I thought that maybe this was how Adam felt when he heard the gates close behind him.

Three years later when I got a place at Oxford, perhaps on the strength of an enigmatic reference which my tutor told me about much later, perhaps because of something Pansy Mason had added, the Chief wrote me a friendly letter of congratulation. Under the neat signature, Eric James, he had printed: DO IT NOW.

In after life, I noted with pleasure his knighthood, then his appointment as Vice-chancellor of the new University of York, and finally his elevation to the peerage. I felt he had become justly recognised as the great man we all knew he was. The last time I saw him was on the top of Coniston Old Man sometime in the 1960s. As I gasped to the summit I saw a familiar profile inspecting the view that stretched from Scafell round to the Langdale Pikes and beyond. It was shortly after he was appointed Vice-Chancellor at York. I reintroduced myself and he remembered me. 'Ah, Davidson,' he said. 'At last we meet on your own ground.'

EPILOGUE

They say we should never look back, but I don't agree. Plato thought man travelled into the future backwards, having only the long vista of the past to give him some idea of what's to come. In a way, Virgil agreed with him, viewing time as a stream against which man had to row hard just to stay in the same place, and when he stopped he was borne helplessly back into the past. Nevertheless, the ancients tried hard to look into the future. Priests at the great Oracles made fat livings out of divination. Vast sums went to the Vates at Delphi, and no Leader seemed able to go to war without specialists in the business of augury such as Ornithomants and Haruspices to tell him whether it was a good day for a battle or not.

In the Christian era, confident that Heaven was our destination, we looked forward to a better life in another world: this being a sort of testing ground to see who was fit to go on. Nevertheless, time's ever rolling stream bearing all its sons away was something we often sang about and, generally, to this day retrospection remains a popular pastime. The blue remembered hills have always been in sight but out of reach. Considering where we came from, and what we were, may help us to understand what we are and perhaps gives us confidence to travel into the future – which is another foreign country.

But what of trying to go back and visiting the places we haunted years ago? It's an eerie experience, I can tell you. Quite recently two of us, form-mates in that other life, returned to MGS and were shown round the school by an informative sixth former. It was a hot Saturday afternoon, the click of ball on bat came faintly through the windows as we paced the familiar corridors. Rounding a corner, I imagined the shuffle of retreating feet down the stair-well. As a classroom door opened, a faint gust of boyish laughter seemed drowned in the creak of the hinge. From behind closed doors I thought I heard the drone of an instructing voice. As in Kipling's strange story, "They", about a house and garden littered with the traces of children who never appear, there seemed to linger in those empty corridors and classrooms the echoes and shadows of what we once had been.

' "O mihi praeteritos si Iuppiter referat annos",' I said to Hargreaves. 'Wrong,' he said, with the ghost of Simkins at his elbow. 'It's "O mihi praeteritos referat si Iuppiter annos". It won't scan otherwise.'

We saw a lot of new buildings, that day. The school as we knew it had extended on every side. The bike sheds had become a Music Department. The library now stretched over the area where Dicky Radford used to drill the Cadet Corps. The Science Department had grown out towards Birchfields Road. And at the other end of the school new blocks of classrooms housed the revived Prep Department which I belonged to in 1942. The playing fields still stretched down almost to Wilmslow Road and nothing was lost of them. We didn't visit the Rectory and its dank basement where we changed for games, but it was still there. However, the old elms we used to swing from by the cricket field had given way to a cricket pavilion built in the 1950s.

The core of classrooms we inhabited and the school offices are now much the same, physically, though in some cases their functions have changed. The room where Cuthbert Seton told us about Jethro Tull and his seed drill is now an office, as is next door where Pansy Mason infected me with a delight in

Eng. Lit. Opposite them, the cages where we hung our coats have been given over to a bookshop, an art display area, the Ian Bailey Archive Room and the Development Office. The quad outside the refectory, once the site of lunchtime football games, has been built over to provide well-deserved accommodation for the staff. Transformed is the dingy cave at the bottom of the main staircase, where malefactors caught by Sutton waited for judgement. That has become the Reprographics Room and Drama Studio. No more does a cloud of tobacco smoke billow out from the opened door and across the stair-well, where we infants in the Prep used to fly our paper aeroplanes.

What is now the official entrance to the school, through the double doors facing the arch and the drive to the gates on Old Hall Lane, was in our days a hallowed place of memorial to Old Boys and we were kept out of it. We flowed in and out through the entrance by the side of the Memorial Hall, or through the cloisters by the refectory. Car-parking, which was never a problem in our days, is now reserved for important visitors beneath the clock tower in the quad where it is supervised by the amiable gaze of Hugh Oldham. He used to stand in a niche by the way in from Birchfields Road, where he was next to the Late Boys' Entrance, and I always imagined he gave me a wink as I went in with my forged Late Pass.

My renewed experience of the school as a functioning organism is limited to a few recent visits. On one, bewitched by the changes around me, I stumbled and fell. Almost before I had time to recover my breath, I was hoisted into a wheelchair and taken to a fully equipped and professionally staffed Medical Room. There I was examined and questioned closely before I was allowed to go. "Be careful," I thought, "one careless word will land me in the X-ray Department of the MRI – just to make sure." Had it happened to an elderly visitor in my day, I'm sure, he would just have been dusted down, given an aspirin and advised to look where he was going.

Services like this show how the composition of the school has changed enormously. There are many more female members of staff and many more administrators. Apart from the kitchens where Mrs Bedford held queenly sway, Mrs Grindley and the librarian – who could have passed for a sixth-former – the place was wholeheartedly male. Now, everyone not distinguished by his blazer or a sixth-form tie wears an identification tag. The community I belonged to, composed of white Anglo-Saxon heathens civilised by a substantial Jewish presence, has now become a multi-racial society. White faces are balanced by the black and brown and yellow of their classmates. There is an air of purpose in the groups and individuals who pass me in the corridors; even the small ones in the revived Prep School seem to have an air of self-sufficiency. The one I talked to looked to be about nine and was both confident and articulate, and would, I'm sure, have told me which Oxbridge college he was aiming for, if I'd asked him. At his stage, I was a mere cipher, the shadow of an academic entity, borne like flotsam in the tides that washed around us.

Today's generations seem composed and sedate, whereas we were rough and rowdy as we trooped from one classroom to another. Like refugees, clutching our belongings to our chests, we pushed and jostled, while the corridors echoed to our cries. Now orderly groups process, muttering to each other, more like novitiates in a seminary than the schoolboys we were. Even so, the building nowadays seems busy, even between lessons. There is always movement about the place and a sense of quiet endeavour. It was not what I remembered; for when

I sought to alleviate the boredom of a lesson by asking to 'be excused', the long corridors, ghostly green with reflected light, were always empty and quiet so I could hear my footsteps on the composition floor. But the air, then as now, had a kind of electric charge to it – a faint hissing sound like that sometimes heard under pylons. There was a sense of pent-up energy just waiting to be released and when the bell rang, for five hectic minutes, chaos was come again.

Was I happy there? I don't remember, but I certainly wasn't miserable. I know I was always glad to get away, and first or second through the door when the bell rang. Often I would be jogging down Old Hall Lane before some of my classmates had finished packing their bags. But I did have a train to catch; but then, there was one half-an-hour later which still got me home with plenty of time before supper. In my later years, I would hang about and chat to avoid the crush at the bus stop, drift into town and look at the shops. When it was the Music Society meeting, two of us would linger even longer in our form room until the building seemed a vast, echoing shell, the quiet occasionally shattered by the bang of a desk lid or a keening cry made only for the effect it made in the empty corridors.

At the time, just being at MGS gave me a sense of belonging and bound me to an ethos of learning and endeavour. School was a kind of home: I knew the boundaries, I was surrounded by familiar faces and I was comfortable – not at ease in the physical sense of being warm and cushioned against the outside world – but sure that I knew where I was and that I fitted in. This sense developed as the years went by: nine of them, from the bewildered child in Prep 1 when the country was still at war and the school was buttressed with sandbags, to the rebellious adolescent of the second year Sixth, with a blasé sense of déjà vu – although I knew I hadn't. Then, quite suddenly, I felt: 'I've had enough of this. Life is elsewhere.' And the High Master agreed.